THE CITY OF NEW YORK

DEPARTMENT OF

Water Supply, Gas and Electricity

REPORT

OF

DELOS F. WILCOX, Deputy Commissioner,

in relation to the

Queens County Water Company

June 1, 1915

PRESS OF
CLARENCE S. NATHAN, INC.,
NEW YORK.

2142-15-2000 (N)

REPORT ON THE QUEENS COUNTY WATER COMPANY.

CONTENTS.

CONTENTS (Continued)

CONTENTS (Concluded)

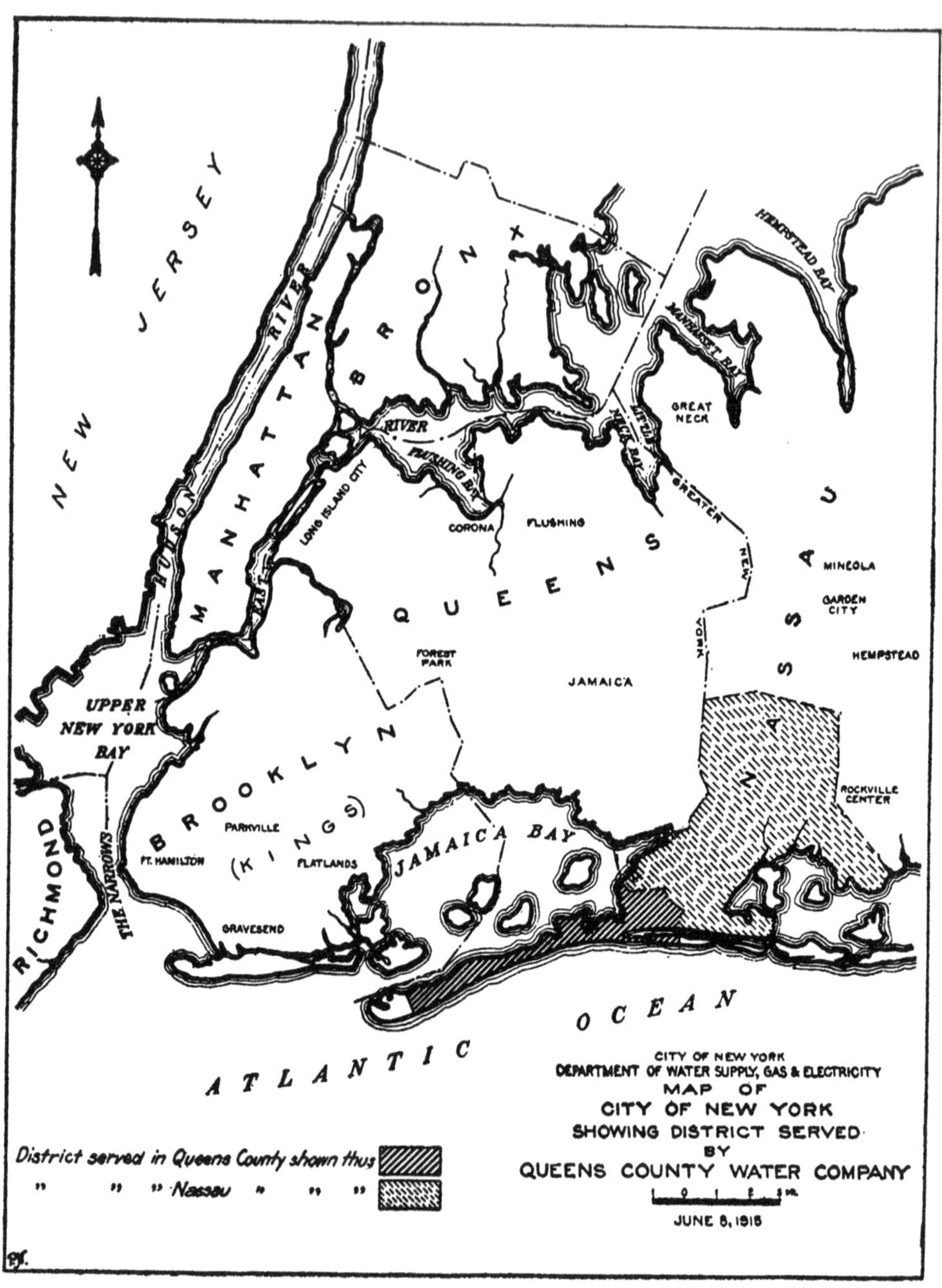
NEW JERSEY
HUDSON RIVER
MANHATTAN
BRONX
HEMPSTEAD BAY
MANHASSET BAY
GREAT NECK
LITTLE NECK BAY
EAST RIVER
FLUSHING BAY
LONG ISLAND CITY
CORONA
FLUSHING
QUEENS
GREATER NEW YORK
MINEOLA
GARDEN CITY
HEMPSTEAD
NASSAU
FOREST PARK
JAMAICA
UPPER NEW YORK BAY
BROOKLYN (KINGS)
PARKVILLE
FT. HAMILTON
FLATLANDS
JAMAICA BAY
ROCKVILLE CENTER
RICHMOND
THE NARROWS
GRAVESEND
ATLANTIC OCEAN
CITY OF NEW YORK
DEPARTMENT OF WATER SUPPLY, GAS & ELECTRICITY
MAP OF
CITY OF NEW YORK
SHOWING DISTRICT SERVED
BY
QUEENS COUNTY WATER COMPANY
JUNE 8, 1915
District served in Queens County shown thus
" " " Nassau " " "

REPORT ON QUEENS COUNTY WATER COMPANY

Hon. William Williams,
Commissioner of Water Supply, Gas and Electricity,
City of New York.

Dear Sir:—

Under date of May 1, 1914, Jacob Lauchheimer and others presented to you a complaint in relation to the rates charged by the Queens County Water Company for water, and petitioned that you investigate and thereafter reduce such rates to a proper basis. In order to assist you in arriving at a proper determination of this matter you directed me to undertake the investigation, on your behalf, and report to you my findings and recommendations. This work involved a careful inquiry into the value of the Company's property and this inquiry became gradually merged in negotiations with the company, instituted with the knowledge and approval of the Mayor, with a view to determining whether or not such of its property as might be useful to the City should be acquired on terms mutually equitable and advantageous.

I. GENERAL PLAN OF NEGOTIATIONS

To show more fully the purpose of these negotiations and the lines along which they were conducted I cite here the Department's letter addressed to the Queens County Water Company under date of February 18, 1915, as follows:

QUEENS COUNTY WATER CO.,
49 Wall Street, New York, N. Y.

Dear Sirs:

I herewith reduce to writing the outlines of a possible basis for negotiations between the City and the Company for the adjustment of the differences between them arising out of the water service in the Fifth Ward of the Borough of Queens. The Department believes that any such negotiations should be governed by the following considerations:

First: The City's municipal water service ought to be extended ultimately to all sections of Greater New York so that the City may supply water to all of its citizens at uniform rates.

Second: While the City has the right to enter your territory and parallel your mains in the public streets, yet it recognizes the disadvantages of active competition in water service, including the tearing up of the streets for the purpose of laying an additional set of mains, as well as the economic loss that would inevitably fall upon one or both of the competitors by such a process. The City does not desire you to lose any portion of your legitimate investment and will not resort to competition unless compelled to do so by an unreasonable attitude on your part.

Third: It is the duty of the Department to see that all sections of the city are given an adequate and suitable supply of water both for domestic purposes and for fire protection and that such water is supplied at reasonable rates. It will insist on these things being done in the Fifth Ward of Queens as well as elsewhere.

Fourth: Your rates to consumers are much higher than the City rates for similar service and are also higher than those of any of the other private water companies in the City. After making due allowance for the different conditions under which you operate, the Department is still of the opinion that your present rate schedule for metered water is unduly high and the subject of just complaint by residents of the Fifth Ward.

Fifth: The protection against fire in a portion of your territory is inadequate, and to render it adequate and also adequately to supply private consumers, improvements and extensions costing approximately $200,000 must be made to your distribution system in the Fifth Ward during the next two years.

Sixth: Fire hydrants, with their valves and connections, represent an investment made exclusively for fire protection. A certain proportion of your investment in distribution system, water-bearing lands, wells and pumping plant is attributable to the requirements of fire service. A water company's plant, in order to furnish sufficient water at proper pressure for fire service, has to be larger and more elaborate than would be necessary if it were devoted exclusively to domestic service.

Seventh: The City, by the expenditure of a very large amount of capital, has nearly completed the development of a great, new source of water supply from the Catskills. In the near future, when this water is available for distribution, the City will cease regularly to use its present sources of supply on the Long Island watershed with a developed capacity of approximately 150,000,000 gallons per day. The time when, if ever, the City will need additional sources on Long Island is remote. It is, therefore, unnecessary for the City to acquire your water supply sources, or with them your buildings, mechanical equipment, wells, suction lines, etc.

Eighth: Your business is transacted in part within and in part without the limits of Greater New York. The bulk of your water supply, lands, wells, and mechanical equipment, also a certain portion of your distribution system, lie within the County of Nassau. At the present time about 70 per cent. of your business is done in the Fifth Ward of Queens and 30 per cent. in Nassau County. It is estimated that the value of the portion of your property which the City might profitably acquire is approximately 40 per cent. of the value of your entire property now in use and necessary for your combined Queens and Nassau services.

Ninth: The Department has examined your distribution system in the Fifth Ward and is willing that, with the exception of the standpipes, it be acquired as a permanent part of the municipal water distribution system. It is willing also that your 24-inch trunk main, extending from the easterly city line to Fenhurst, and the small parcel of land on the north side of Crescent Street described as Lot 31 of Block 26, Volume 4, Fifth Ward, Borough of Queens, be acquired. Together with this portion of your property the City would naturally take your easements, maps and records pertaining to the distributing mains in Queens and the 24-inch main in Nassau. For the remainder of your property the City has no use.

Tenth: Your water supply lands, wells, pumping station and mechanical equipment located in Nassau County will remain useful and necessary to you in your Nassau County business, but for a number of years this portion of your plant will be considerably in excess of the requirements of the Nassau business, and your pumping plant will be somewhat ill-adapted to the limited Nassau County demands upon it.

Eleventh: The Department realizes that your business cannot be severed and disrupted at the present time without a loss for which you must be paid or compensated in some proper form.

Twelfth: Until the Catskill water is available the City could not supply the Fifth Ward of the Borough of Queens, even if it owned the distribution system, except through the purchase of water from your plant.

With the understanding that any agreement that may be reached between you and the Department is subject to ratification by the Mayor, the Comptroller and the Board of Estimate and Apportionment, the Department is willing to proceed to negotiate along the general lines hereinafter stated:

1. A definite valuation as of May 31, 1914, will be placed upon those portions of your property which the City desires to acquire, as follows:

    a. The distribution system in the Fifth Ward of the Borough of Queens, including mains, valves, hydrants, meters, corporation cocks in service, valve boxes and manholes, but excluding standpipes. (An estimate of the cost of replacing pavement over mains on the basis of the conditions prevailing at the time when the mains were laid and an allowance for the extra cost of railroad and trolley crossings, will be made.)

    b. The 24-inch trunk main extending from the city line to the pumping station at Fenhurst.

    c. The parcel of land on the north side of Crescent Avenue, described as Lot 31 of Block 26.

2. The amount of the future annual depreciation of the property above described will be fixed.

3. The Department is disposed to recommend that the City take over the property above described not later than May 31, 1924, with the right to take it over at any earlier time subsequent to the date when Catskill water becomes available for distribution by the City. The price to be paid when the property is taken will be the value of the property as now agreed upon, less depreciation at the rate agreed upon from May 31, 1914, till the date of acquisition by the City, plus an amount appropriate to indemnify the Company for the losses sustained by the severance of its plant and the disruption of its business, in case such severance and disruption take place prior to May 31, 1924. A maximum figure will be fixed for this indemnity, the same to diminish according to a definite schedule until it becomes nothing in case the City permits the Company to continue in operation in the Queens area until the expiration of the contract period, that is to say, May 31, 1924.

4. Mains in the Queens area shall be extended, the distribution system improved and strengthened, and hydrants installed as may be required from time to time by the Commissioner. Provision will be made for the construction prior to December 31, 1916, of certain specific extensions and improvements heretofore the subject of negotiation between the City and the Company, the cost of which is estimated to be approximately $200,000. The money for the extensions and improvements immediately necessary will be furnished by the Company and expended under the direction and with the approval of the Commissioner, who will so direct the work and expenditures as to meet the reasonable requirements of the City and the inhabitants of the Fifth Ward.

The rate of annual depreciation upon the extensions, additions and improvements to be made at the Company's expense will be determined by agreement, and the total cost of such improvements, less depreciation from the time the improvements are made to the time when the City acquires the property, will be added to the price which the City is to pay.

5. Any additions, extensions and improvements in excess of those immediately required and specifically described in the agreement are to be made from time to time, as deemed by the Department necessary, at the City's expense, all under proper safeguards, and so long as the Company shall continue to operate its system in the Fifth Ward it is to use and operate such extensions, additions and improvements as an integral part of its system and pay the City for the use thereof an annual rental. In case the additional revenues derived by the Company for the use of such additions, extensions and improvements shall be sufficient to pay the operating expenses properly chargeable thereto, such rental shall be the excess of such revenues over such operating expenses up to an amount equivalent to 7 per cent. per annum, cumulative, on the original cost to the City of such additions, extensions and improvements.

6. So long as the Company continues to operate in the Fifth Ward it will be required to render adequate service, both for private and public uses, and to maintain the portion of its property described in subdivision 1 hereof, together with all extensions, additions and improvements thereto described or referred to in subdivisions 4 and 5 hereof, in a condition satisfactory to the Commissioner.

7. When the City takes over the property described in subdivisions 1 and 4 hereof, the Company shall transfer to the City without additional cost its right, title and interest in contracts, rights of way and easements appurtenant to the portions of the distribution system acquired within the present city limits, and thereafter the Company shall not engage in the water supply business within the present city limits. The agreement shall provide for a valid right of way for the 24-inch main in Nassau County, and for its extension to a public high-

way north of the pumping station at Fenhurst. This may involve some additional payment.

8. The agreement will provide that the City shall assume outstanding accounts due the Company at the time the property is taken over by the City, or else provide some way for their collection. In this connection proper provision will be made for the disposition of the meter deposits in the custody of the Company.

When the City takes over the property referred to, the terms of all outstanding contracts under which money has been deposited with the Company by private consumers as a guaranty of revenue from extensions shall be deemed to have been complied with, and the Company shall as promptly as may be return all such deposits to the parties entitled thereto.

9. As a public service corporation the Company is entitled, so long as it renders adequate service, to earn a fair return upon the reasonable value of its investment used and useful in supplying water, provided that in order to earn such return it shall not be necessary to charge rates which, from the standpoint of the value of the service, are unreasonably high. For present purposes it will be necessary only that we be in general accord as to the fair present value of the investment attributable to the Queens service, as to the operating expenses and depreciation incident thereto and as to the rate of return to which the Company is entitled under the conditions established by the proposed contract. Thereupon, the net income which the Company ought to earn from the Queens business can readily be ascertained. A rate schedule will be fixed covering all uses of water, both private and public, and if this can be done consistently with the establishment of fair rates, this schedule will be such as to give the Company reasonable assurance of earning this income so long as it continues to operate in the Queens area.

10. In determining what is a fair payment for fire service the following principles will be followed:

(a) The investment in fire hydrants, with their valves and connections, is made exclusively for fire protection and the City should pay therefor in the form of a fixed rental per hydrant. The latter should take account of depreciation, special maintenance and what is a fair return on the investment.

(b) The difference between the total reproduction cost of the Company's system (exclusive of fire hydrants, hydrant valves, and connections) and the cost of a system adequate for supplying all of the demands of domestic consumers, represents the investment made by the Company for the purpose of rendering proper fire protection, and upon such difference, less accrued depreciation, the City ought to pay depreciation, taxes and return upon investment as a portion of the cost of fire service. For the purposes hereof a rough determination of the Company's total investment will be necessary, but inasmuch as the company has comparatively little interest in the source from which its revenues are derived, so long as they are adequate, it will be unnecessary for the Company to assent to the basis on which the Department distributes the investment between domestic service and fire protection.

11. If at any time during the continuance of the agreement to be entered into an emergency should arise wherein the City should require water for use outside of the Fifth Ward in excess of the supply available from its own system, the Company shall upon written demand from the Commissioner supply water to the City's system by pumping it directly at the Company's main pumping station at Fenhurst, Nassau County, through the City's 20-inch main heretofore laid to said pumping station into the City's gravity conduit up to the full capacity

of the Company's present well system and pumping plant in excess of the immediate needs of the Company's own consumers.

On the other hand, the City will, to the extent of its ability to do so, supply the Company with surplus water which the Company may require to carry its peak load or for emergencies in excess of the capacity of the Company's existing plant. This is for the purpose of relieving the Company from making additions to its investment which would become useless if the City were to take over the Company's business in Queens. The agreement will fix the price at which the Company is to supply water to the City and the price at which the City is to supply water to the Company, either under pressure or not under pressure, as the case may be.

12. Provision will be made for closer supervision of the Company's activities as a public service corporation by the Department of Water Supply, Gas and Electricity so as to protect the City's financial interest in the operations of the Company and so as to bring the Company's distribution system into effective co-ordination with that of the City.

In closing, the Department calls attention to the following as some of the advantages that will accrue to the Company through an agreement with the City along the lines above indicated:

(a) The Company will be protected from municipal competition.

(b) It will either be permitted to continue to transact business in the Fifth Ward until May 31, 1924, when it is estimated that the Nassau consumption will have grown up to what the total consumption now is, or it will be paid appropriate damages for its earlier withdrawal from such business.

(c) It will fix a limit to the amount of new capital required of the Company to take care of increase in its business in the Fifth Ward.

On the other hand, the Department feels that the City can afford to concede these advantages to the Company, both because it does not desire to destroy any legitimate investment and because it does desire to put an end to the friction and dissatisfaction which have characterized certain of the relations of the City, the Company and residents of the Fifth Ward during the past few years.

Respectfully,

William Williams,
Commissioner.

The negotiations, which had already been going on prior to the sending of this letter, were continued thereafter without interruption. For the purposes of the record, Mr. Henry de Forest Baldwin, president of the Company, by a letter dated March 13, 1915, made formal reply to your communication and stated that he was willing to negotiate with the Department along the lines indicated. The Company had already thrown open its books for examination by an accountant of this Department and had furnished, from time to time, all the material information asked for, and continued so to do as occasion arose thereafter. As a result, I am now prepared to submit to you this report, which deals with all the matters above referred to, including the value of the Company's property in detail; proper rates to be charged for water, both for domestic and fire purposes, and the possible acquisition of the portions of the Company's plant that would be useful to the City in case it should be determined to extend the municipal water service to the Fifth Ward, Borough of Queens.

II. AREA AND POPULATION SERVED.

The Queens County Water Company was organized in 1884 for the purpose of supplying water to portions of what was then the town of Hempstead, County of Queens. This was long prior to the annexation of the area included in the present County of Queens to the City of New York. The Company now supplies the Rockaway peninsula, constituting the Fifth Ward of the Borough of Queens, as well as a very considerable portion of the town of Hempstead, in Nassau County. The Company's location with reference to the City is shown on the map appearing on page 6 entitled: "Map of City of New York, showing district served by Queens County Water Company."

The Queens area includes the former incorporated villages of Far Rockaway, Arverne-by-the-Sea and Rockaway Beach, as well as the more recent community developments known as Belle Harbor, Neponsit and Edgemere. The western extremity of the Rockaway peninsula lying beyond the City's land known as Seaside Park is not as yet supplied by the Company.

The Queens district now served by the Company is about seven miles long east and west. If the service were extended to the western extremity, Rockaway Point, the district served would be about three miles longer. The entire area of the Rockaway peninsula within the limits of New York is about seven square miles.

At the last census the Fifth Ward of Queens had a permanent population of about 12,500. This population is very greatly increased in summer by the influx of people from other portions of the city, who occupy bungalows by the seashore for a few months during the hot season. There is also a great influx of temporary visitors, who throng the hotels and the beaches merely for a day, or for a few days at the most. This floating population increases the consumption of water, although not in proportion to its numbers. The peculiar conditions existing at the Rockaways tend to a very high peak load of water consumed during the summer months, especially on certain days in July and August.

The portion of the town of Hempstead, Nassau County, in which the Company now gives service or is expected to give service in the near future, comprises roughly an area of thirty square miles, with a population in 1910 of approximately 17,500. This includes the incorporated villages of Lawrence, Cedarhurst, Lynbrook, East Rockaway and Woodsburgh, besides much unincorporated territory, including Inwood, Valley Stream, Hewlett, Oceanside, etc. While there is a considerable influx of summer population into the Nassau County portion of the Company's area now supplied, this influx is relatively much less than in the Queens area. Accordingly, the peak load of summer consumption in Nassau County is less marked than the peak load in Queens.

The Nassau County area served is somewhat irregular in shape, but roughly described is about eight miles in length northeast and southwest, and from three to four miles wide northwest and southeast. As compared with the Rockaway peninsula it is a compact area, suitable for development by a population easily and readily served from a central source of supply.

Oversized Foldout

III. DESCRIPTION OF THE COMPANY'S FRANCHISES AND PROPERTY.

The Queens County Water Company was incorporated under the provisions of an act in relation to the location and formation of water works companies passed June 13, 1873, being chapter 737 of the laws of that year. Under this law the consent of the local authorities of the town or village in which service was to be rendered was required prior to the organization of a water company. On October 11, 1883, John Lockwood and six associates applied to the supervisor, justices of the peace, town clerk and commissioners of highways of the town of Hempstead for authority to organize a water works company with a capital stock of $50,000 to supply the town of Hempstead and its inhabitants with pure and wholesome water from wells sunk in the ground "in said township and vicinity." On October 22, 1883, the town authorities granted this application upon the following conditions: "Excepting the Village of Hempstead in said town, and Garden City or what is known as the Stewart Purchase, for the purpose of laying their water pipes and for repairing the same from time to time as may be necessary, providing always that the same is done with proper dispatch, so as not to impede travel through or over the same (sic) for a longer period than as is absolutely necessary for said works, and also that said streets or sidewalks or Public Grounds of the said town shall be put in as good condition, as near as may be, as they were before said excavations were made. Any accident to person or property that may occur during said excavation, the said Lockwood and associates or a company organized under the said laws shall be held liable. The work to be commenced on or before the first day of May, 1884, A. D., and the same to be completed on or before the first day of December, 1884, A. D."

The territory covered by the Company's franchise, the districts actually supplied by it and the general relations of its property are shown on the accompanying map entitled: "Map of Franchise Area of the Queens County Water Company, showing District Served and General Location of Lands, Pumping Station, Office, etc."

The corporation was organized March 20 and its certificate of incorporation filed March 27, 1884. It issued its capital stock in the amount of $40,000 May 1, 1884, to R. I. Mullins and others for the construction of works at Far Rockaway. On June 3, 1884, the directors of the Company authorized the issuance of $40,000 of 6 per cent. bonds to Mullins in part payment for building equipment and completing the works at Far Rockaway. A little later, the capital stock was increased from $40,000 to $50,000, and the additional $10,000 was subsequently, on

July 21, 1884, also issued to Mullins for construction and extension c works at Far Rockaway. The water works system constructed b Mullins was accepted by the Board of Directors on December 15, 1885. I appears that on July 31, 1886, the supervisor of the town of Hempstea entered into a contract with this Company, having previously bee authorized to do so by the Board of Supervisors of Queens County for the supply of a fire district comprising the unincorporated villag of Far Rockaway. This contract was for a term of five years. I November, 1887, the Company's capital stock was increased from $50,00 to $100,000, and the additional $50,000 was issued to Mullins in pa payment for sums expended by him as contractor for the constructio of the Rockaway Beach extension.

It appears that R. V. W. DuBois and others interested in th Company applied in June, 1887, to the local authorities of Hempstea for a renewal of the franchise granted in 1883. The renewal wa asked for in order to enable the Company to reorganize its financia affairs. DuBois stated that the business had extended beyond wha was contemplated at the time of the original organization and in par ticular that the continuation of the mains to Rockaway Beach re quired an enlargement of the Company's financial basis. On June 1 1887, a new franchise was granted, not directly to the Queens Count Water Company, but to DuBois and his associates, who proceede in October, 1887, to organize another corporation, the Queens Count Water Company of Long Island. The interrelations and subsequent com bination of the two companies are obscured by the mists that han over those early days of the Rockaway peninsula. It seems, how ever, that the original company had to issue scrip to pay the interes on its outstanding bonds. Between the new company and the old th mains got extended to Rockaway Beach. In 1890 a 25-year exclusiv contract was secured by the new company from the Rockaway Par Improvement Company, Limited, for supplying water to Rockawa Park, at that time a new development. This contract was afterwar transferred to the old company and was confirmed December 31, 189 by another contract with the improvement company. By these con tracts the Queens County Water Company appears to have acquire an inchoate water plant, including some real estate and pipes, fro the improvement company.

The water company's first pumping station and well system ha been constructed in Far Rockaway on a parcel of land bordering Car ton Avenue, just south of the Long Island Railroad right of way The water supply at this point proved to be insufficient and anothe station was established on Remsen Avenue north of the Long Islan Railroad right of way. This new source of supply also proved to b inadequate. The principal stockholders of the Company about 1890 o 1891 acquired a tract of land near Valley Stream and thereafter pu down wells and constructed a pumping station. This source of suppl proved to be satisfactory and the new plant was leased to the Company on February 1, 1893, the water supply and pumping stations in Far Rockaway being abandoned. Subsequently, on April 15, 1896, the Company purchased from the owners the Valley Stream water supply and pumping station.

During this early period the Company had been in financial straits. It had paid neither dividends nor interest, and, in fact, a foreclosure proceeding had been started under its original $40,000 mortgage. Dr. Abram DuBois had interested himself in the Company, and his sons as executors of his estate secured two judgments against the Company in 1893 in the amounts of $66,890.90 and $81,330.42, respectively. When the Valley Stream property was taken over in 1896 the accounts with the DuBois estate were settled by the issuance of $400,000 of stock and $200,000 of bonds to pay for the Valley Stream property, take up the original $40,000 mortgage, satisfy the judgments, and make good additional advances and interest thereon.

For the eighteen years subsequent to 1893 the Company secured its entire water supply from the Valley Stream plant, but by 1911 the increasing demand for water on the Rockaway peninsula during the summer months induced the Company to establish an auxiliary station at Rockaway Park for use for a few hours each day during the peak of the summer load.

On August 1, 1891, the Company secured a five-year contract for fire and street sprinkling purposes from the authorities of the village of Far Rockaway. This contract was renewed for a like period in 1896 and finally expired by limitation July 31, 1901. On November 27, 1897, the Company secured a hydrant rental contract from the village of Arverne-by-the-Sea. This contract ran to July 1, 1902. On December 28, 1897, the Company secured a hydrant rental contract from the village of Rockaway Beach. This contract also ran to July 1, 1902.

A supplementary contract was entered into on August 1, 1899, between the City and the Company, in accordance with a resolution of the Board of Public Improvements, adopted August 24, 1898, fixing the rental of all hydrants thereafter to be erected by private water companies at $20 per annum. This supplementary contract with the Queens County Water Company was made to expire on July 1, 1902, the date of the expiration of the contracts with the villages of Rockaway Beach and Arverne just referred to. Since 1902 there has been no contract in force between the City and the Company relative to fire service or water supply in the Fifth Ward, but the Company has continued to render service and has been paid therefor at the rates previously prevailing. The general $20 rate was fixed by the Board of Public Improvements without adequate investigation of the cost of fire service. Indeed, it must have been fixed arbitrarily, for the most cursory examination of the facts would have shown that a fire hydrant rental for one company operating in one part of the city might be quite unfair for other companies operating in other parts of the city under entirely different conditions. The City has continued to pay to the Queens company the rate fixed seventeen years ago, and has never, up to the present time, made any complete and conclusive inquiry as to what would be a just and adequate rate, although the records show that the engineers of this Department have long held the $20 rate to be insufficient so far as this Company is concerned.

The original law under which this Company was incorporated, as well as its original franchise from the local authorities of the town of Hempstead, gave the Company the right to lay mains in public streets. In the Rockaway district, however, the demand for water has in many cases preceded the legal opening of the streets, and to meet this demand the Company has been compelled to secure easements in private streets. Some of these easements are nominally exclusive. There is considerable uncertainty as to the present status of many of the streets in the Fifth Ward, some of them having recently been formally opened by the City subject to the public utility easements that were previously granted, while others are gradually being transformed into public streets by use, without formal proceedings.

Under the laws and decisions of this state it is clear that the Company's franchise in the public streets of the Fifth Ward is not exclusive, unless possibly in some of those streets in which the Company had mains under private easements before the streets were legally opened. The City unquestionably has the legal right either to extend its own mains and service through the public streets of the Fifth Ward, or to grant to some other company a franchise to do so. Except as to private streets or streets that were private when its mains were laid, the Queens County Water Company lays no claim to an exclusive franchise in this area.

It is to be noted from the records that the original consent of the town of Hempstead required the Company's water works to be completed by December 1, 1884, while as a matter of fact the works constructed under contract were not accepted by the Company until December 15, 1885, more than a year later. It is probable that the effect of this failure to comply strictly with the terms of the original consent has been cured, since for nearly thirty years the Company has been engaged in supplying water in this district without having its right to do so called in question.

At about the time of the expiration of the contracts as to fire service and the use of water for public purposes, a considerable rivalry between the City and the Company developed for the control of certain water-bearing lands in the watershed from which the Company derives its present supply at Valley Stream. It seems that the City on two occasions planned to extend an infiltration gallery along the line of the Brooklyn conduit across this watershed at a point somewhat to the north of the Company's line of wells. During a period of years extending from 1901 to 1909 the Company was engaged in buying up land for the purpose of controlling its watershed and preventing the City from acquiring any portion of it for municipal use. This rivalry was terminated in 1909 by a contract between the City and the Company under which the Company's watershed was defined and the City agreed not to sink any wells or construct any infiltration galleries in such watershed or draw any water therefrom, except to maintain its existing wells at Lynbrook, taking from them not more than 1,500,000 gallons in any one day, and to maintain its pumping station at Watts Pond, adjacent to this watershed, and take therefrom not more than 4,000,000 gallons in any one day. While this contract does not enlarge the Company's franchise rights for the distribution and supply of water, yet it does, if valid, fully protect the Company from any attempt of the City to invade the Valley Stream watershed and thus reduce the Company's source of water supply. As a result of this contract with the City, the Company felt justified in selling off most of the land which had been secured during the period from 1901 to 1909, such land being regarded as no longer necessary or useful for the Company's water supply.

The property and plant now held and maintained by the Company may be briefly described as follows:

(a) Land:

In Nassau County the company has a total of 285.22 acres of land. Of this total, 250.4 acres are in one large parcel at Fenhurst, about one mile south of Valley Stream. This parcel lies on the southwesterly side of Mill Road and includes about 80 acres of salt meadow lying on either side of Mott Creek, as well as upland on both sides of the two branches of this creek. The balance of the company's land in Nassau County, amounting to 34.82 acres, consists of certain irregular strips from 30 to 60 feet in width on either side of the two branches of Mott Creek northwesterly of Mill Road, a small triangular plot at Lynbrook, a small strip along the creek flowing out of Watts Pond, and a small strip on the northerly side of the Brooklyn conduit just east of Valley Stream. These outlying strips were retained by the company in part because of their supposed value for the protection of the brooks flowing into Mott Creek, and partly because of the supposed value of certain of these parcels as sites for future well development.

In the Fifth Ward of the Borough of Queens the company holds land at four locations, as follows:

(1) At Far Rockaway the Company owns a parcel of land on the northeasterly side of Carlton Avenue, between John Street and the right of way of the Long Island Railroad. This is the location of the Company's original pumping station, which was abandoned about twenty-four years ago. The frontage on Carlton Avenue is 264 feet and on John Street 243 feet. For assessment purposes the land is divided into three parcels described on the tax maps as lots 30, 36 and 37 of block 23, volume 4, Ward 5, Borough of Queens.

(2) The Company holds another small parcel in Far Rockaway with a frontage of 20 feet on the north side of Crescent Avenue and a depth of about 102 feet extending to the southerly side of the Long Island Railroad right of way. This parcel is used as a right of way for a 16-inch main. It is described on the tax map as lot 31 of block 26, volume 4, Ward 5, Borough of Queens.

(3) The Company also has a parcel of land at Arverne on the east side of another Carlton Avenue, south of the Long Island Railroad track. This parcel has a frontage of 100 feet on Carlton Avenue and a depth of 87 feet. The Company formerly maintained at this point a small booster station, the use of which has now been abandoned. This parcel is described on the tax maps as lot 12 of block 13, volume 3, Ward 5, Borough of Queens.

(4) Finally, the Company owns a parcel of land on the northerly side of Washington Avenue opposite Eastern Avenue. This parcel has a width of 188 feet on Washington Avenue and a depth of about 122 feet running northerly to the Long Island Railroad right of way. For assessment purposes this parcel is divided into three parts, described as lots 72, 75 and 76 of block 15, volume 1, Ward 5 of the Borough of Queens. At this point the Company maintains a standpipe, wells, and a temporary auxiliary pumping station.

(b) Well System, Suction Lines and Filters:

On the Company's Fenhurst property in the vicinity of its main pumping station there is a development which includes 75 shallow wells ranging from 22 to 32 feet in depth, and 52 deep wells ranging from 143 to 204 feet in depth. The deep wells are six inches in diameter and the shallow wells five inches, except one, which is ten. The shallow wells are driven through a bed of sand, while the deep wells pass through about 32 feet of sand, 7 feet of clay and 40 feet of hard blue clay into a stratum of sand and large gravel. The average age of all these wells is about ten years and their total present capacity is about 12,000,000 gallons of water per day. These wells are connected with the pumping station by cast-iron suction lines, no air lift system being in use by this Company.

In addition to the wells at Fenhurst the Company has one shallow well and three deep wells located near the Long Island Railroad, about one mile west of the Lynbrook station. These are 6-inch wells, 30, 110, 503 and 508 feet deep, respectively. The deep ones were constructed as experimental wells to be pumped by the air lift system. It was thought that they might be used in delivering water to Brooklyn. They are not available for use in connection with the Company's distribution plant and have been in the ground without use for a period of ten years. The Company also has three deep wells at Rockaway Beach which are used in connection with its auxiliary pumping station during the peak load of the summer months. Two of these, constructed prior to the 1914 inventory, are 6-inch wells, 760 and 780 feet deep, respectively. They are connected with the temporary pumping station by wrought iron suction mains.

The Company's water at Fenhurst in its raw state has too much iron in it to be suitable for domestic use, but otherwise is excellent. The water is, therefore, filtered before being pumped into the distribution system. For this purpose three slow sand filters have been erected. These filters have an area of about one and a half acres and an actual daily capacity of about 6,000,000 gallons, which can be increased somewhat in case of necessity. The raw water derived from the Rockaway Beach wells is most unsuitable for domestic use, but a small temporary filter has been installed to improve this supply until the reinforcement of the trunk mains shall make its further use unnecessary.

(c) Pumping Plant:

At the main pumping station the Company has nine pumps in all, with a rated capacity of about 42,000,000 gallons per day. There are three Tod pumps with capacities of 6,000,000, 7,500,000 and 8,000,000 gallons per day, respectively. There are five Worthington pumps with capacities ranging from 1,700,000 to 5,000,000 gallons daily. There is one Davidson pump with a capacity of 6,000,000 gallons. Because of the fact that the water has to be filtered, the Company has to provide for pumping the water twice: once from the suction mains into the filters, and once from the collecting well into the distribution system. When the double pumping is taken into consideration, as well as the necessity of keeping a proper reserve, the actual safe capacity of this pumping station for continuous service is about 16,000,000 gallons per day, or one-third in excess of the developed capacity of the well system tributary to it.

At the Rockaway Beach auxiliary station the Company has three Worthington pumps with an aggregate rated capacity of 3,500,000 gallons. The actual pumpage at this station is only about 150,000 gallons per day during the summer months.

In addition to the pump house at Fenhurst the Company has an office building, an abandoned pump house and several minor buildings at Far Rockaway. It has no pump house at Rockaway Beach.

(d) Distribution System:

The Company has about 179 miles of mains, of which approximately 84 miles are in Queens County and 95 miles in Nassau County. Of the Nassau County mileage, however, 12 miles are trunk mains leading from the Fenhurst pumping station down to the boundary line of the city, and used for the purpose of supplying both the Queens and the Nassau areas. The Company's mains range from 1¼ inches to 24 inches in diameter. About 43 miles of the mains are 4 inches or less in diameter, but two-thirds of these small mains are in the Nassau County area.

The contour of the land makes it impracticable for the Company to have any distributing reservoirs, but it does maintain two small standpipes, one at Far Rockaway and one at Rockaway Beach. The one at Far Rockaway is 20 feet in diameter and 140 feet high, and the one at Rockaway Beach 18 feet in diameter and 130 feet high. The two together have a capacity of 576,000 gallons.

The Company maintains about 630 fire hydrants in Queens and 387 in Nassau. All the Company's services are metered and the meters are furnished and maintained by the Company itself. The total number in use in the fiscal year ending May 31, 1914, was 8,389, of which 5,166 were in Queens and 3,223 in Nassau.

IV. RELATIONS OF THE COMPANY WITH THE CITY AND THE PUBLIC.

For many years the Company has been in a chronic state of litigation. Many of its lawsuits have been in connection with its special franchise taxes, but for a number of years it was engaged in active litigation with the City over the control of its watershed. Since the expiration of its hydrant contracts with the City in 1901 and 1902 it has been striving to secure a new contract for fire service, claiming that the compensation received at the old rate per hydrant was insufficient and inequitable. On the other hand, the City has maintained that the Company was not furnishing an adequate supply of water for proper fire protection in certain portions of the Rockaway peninsula, and that it should immediately enlarge and extend its mains in order to render this service. In spite of litigation and conflicting claims, however, the City for a number of years has purchased surplus water from the Company under the so-called "Brooklyn Contract." Under this contract the Company has delivered as high as 5,000,000 gallons a day at its Fenhurst station into a 20-inch main laid for the purpose to connect with the Brooklyn aqueduct. The City and the Company co-operated in laying this main, the City furnishing the pipe and the Company doing the work. The water furnished by the Company under this contract was delivered in its raw state, and not under pressure, at the price of $30 per 1,000,000 gallons. The purchase of this water by the City continued from 1904 to 1913, reaching a maximum in 1910 and 1911. In September, 1914, when the City experienced a shortage in its own Long Island supply, the purchase of water from this Company was temporarily resumed and continued until February 3, 1915.

The Company's consumers appear to have been very generally pleased with the quality of water supplied, except during the summer months for the last three or four years, when the Company has been pumping raw water into its mains at Rockaway Beach from its deep wells located there. This water contains so much iron that it has caused great discontent among the Company's consumers on the western portion of the Rockaway peninsula. The consumers have also been full of complaints on account of the high rates charged by the Company. A rate case was brought before the Commissioner of Water Supply, Gas and Electricity in 1910, but the consumers were given no relief.

During the 1914 session of the legislature the representatives of the Company supported the proposed legislation known as the "Maier Bill," which would have deprived the City of New York of the right to parallel the mains of a private water company without the consent of the State Conservation Commission, and would have transferred to that commission the control over the charges of such companies. The Department deemed this legislation inimical to the City's interests and induced the Governor to veto it.

To summarize, the Company and the City were for many years competing for the water supply now under the Company's control. This competition caused the Company to invest large sums of money in the purchase of land, which later was deemed to be unnecessary for water purposes. For many years the Company has been persistently fighting its franchise tax assessments and delaying the payment of its taxes. For many years the Company has had no hydrant rental contract with the City, and has been claiming that the annual rentals paid were far below the cost of the service. The Company has also claimed that the City was threatening to parallel its mains and destroy its business. The City, on the other hand, has stoutly maintained that the fire service supplied by the Company was totally inadequate, and has complained of the danger of conflagration in the Fifth Ward of the Borough of Queens and of the high fire insurance rates resulting therefrom. The consumers have been vigorously protesting against the high rates charged by the Company, and during the summer season in recent years they have loudly complained about the quality of the water supplied in the Rockaway Beach section.

The acute issues are, therefore, first, the improvement of the quality of the water supplied during the summer months; second, the establishment of rates fair to private consumers; third, adequte fire service; fourth, the payment by the City of the fair cost of such service; fifth, the protection of the Company's investment from the danger of municipal competition; and sixth, the ultimate acquisition of the distribution system in Queens by the City to enable it to extend the municipal service at uniform rates to all sections within the city limits.

V. EXISTING RATES AND REGULATIONS.

The company's rate schedule is made up of a combination of minimum rates and meter rates. The minimum rates are due on the first of June and are collected annually in advance. These rates are based upon the size of the meter. For a ½-inch or a ⅝-inch meter the minimum rate is $10; for a ¾-inch meter, $15; for a 1-inch meter, $20; for a 1½-inch meter, $30; for a 2-inch meter, $40; and for a 3-inch meter, $80. The water actually consumed is charged for on the basis of 40 cents per 1,000 gallons for the first 50,000 gallons; 30 cents per 1,000 for the next 200,000 gallons, and 20 cents per 1,000 for all over 450,000 gallons used during the year. In general the meters are read monthly, and bills for water used are rendered monthly after the amount consumed at the meter rate exceeds the minimum charge paid by the consumer in advance.

Of the Queens consumers, about 20% pay only the minimum rates, while of the Nassau consumers about 45% pay only the minimum rates. For the $10 minimum charge on an ordinary ⅝-inch meter 25,000 gallons of water may be used. In order to keep within the minimum rate, a family of five, using water throughout the year, would have to use less than 14 gallons per capita daily. If such a family used 25 gallons per capita per day it would consume a total of 45,625 gallons during the year, and would have to pay $8.15 for this water in addition to the minimum charge of $10. If such a family used 40 gallons per capita per day it would use a total of 73,000 gallons during the year, for which it would have to pay $16.90 in addition to the minimum charge of $10, making a total of $26.90. This would include $20 for 50,000 gallons at the maximum rate of 40 cents per 1,000, and $6.90 for 23,000 gallons at the rate of 30 cents per 1,000. In order to get the benefit of a meter rate less than 30 cents per 1,000 gallons a family of five would have to use more than 137 gallons per capita per day for the entire year and pay in excess of $80 for water. Even then the lower rate would apply only to the excess use.

It is to be noted that a consumer applying for water at any time during the month of May pays the minimum charge for the twelve months commencing the first of June, so that in reality his minimum covers a period of thirteen months. If a consumer applies for water in August the minimum charge for a ⅝-inch meter for the balance of the fiscal year is $9. This charge is reduced $1 per month, so that a consumer applying for water in April will pay only $1 to cover the minimum charge for the balance of the year ending May 31. When minimum charges have once been paid, however, there is no rebate if consumption is stopped prior to the end of the fiscal year. During the year ending May 31, 1914, out of 671 consumers in the Queens area who paid only the $10 minimum charge, 184 used the service less than seven months. In the Nassau area, out of 1,274 who paid only the $10 minimum rate, only 39 used the service less than seven months.

The Queens company's rates may be compared with the city rates and with the rates charged by the Citizens' Water Supply Company of Newtown. Actual illustrations will be illuminating. In my own case I pay the Citizens' company in Elmhurst frontage rates for a two-story house with 20-foot front, without extra bath, water closet or outside hose connection. The frontage rate is $3.50 for six months or $7 per annum. The Citizens' company charges 30 cents per 100 cubic feet, which is approximately equivalent to 40 cents per 1,000 gallons, for the first 1,000 cubic feet consumed during the half year; 20 cents per 100 cubic feet for the second 1,000, and 10 cents per 100 cubic feet, or the city meter rate, for the next 98,000 cubic feet. This schedule is modified, however, so that ordinary consumers pay only the 10 cent rate upon water consumed in excess of the allowance under the frontage rate. With a family of six persons and an average consumption of 20 gallons per capita per day, my water bills for the year ending October 31, 1914, were $10.40. At the city frontage rates I would have paid $7.00, unless the inspector had counted the third floor with its two furnished rooms as an extra story and had objected to the use of hose without a $5.00 permit, in which case I should have been charged $13.00, or $1.60 more than I paid the Citizens' company. At the Queens County rates I would have paid $17.70. This comparison shows that in a case like this the Queens County rates are 70 per cent. in excess of those of the Citizens' company. A neighbor of mine with a house frontage of 29 feet pays the Citizens' company $8.00 every six months and never runs over the minimum. Her bills do not show the amount of water consumed, but as the family is small and careful, it is quite probable that under the Queens County rates her bills would not exceed the minimum charge of $10.00 a year. Under the city, she would probably have to pay for a third story and a hose, which would make $22.00 in all as against the $16.00 she now pays. On the other hand, Mr. Paul Stier, an extensive builder in the Ridgewood section, was charged by the Citizens' company a total of $1,936.70 for water consumed during the year ending November 1, 1914, in 69 two and three-family attached houses. The "City rates" as scheduled by the Company amounted to only $1,113.00 and the balance, $823.70, was paid for water used in excess of the minimum allowance. For the same consumption the Queens company would have charged $3,741.95. The following comparison of what Mr. Stier actually paid with what he might have paid under other circumstances is very interesting:—

One year at City frontage rates	$1,113.00
One year at City meter rates	1,522.70
One year at Citizens' Water Supply Company's rates	1,936.70
One year at Queens County Water Company's rates	3,741.95

These comparisons do not take into account the fact that the Queens company furnishes and maintains the meters, while both the City and the Citizens' Company compel the property owners to bear this expense.

The commencement of the Queens County company's fiscal year has been fixed at June 1 in order to enable the Company to collect the minimum rates in advance from the more or less transient population taking water during the summer months. In order to insure complete collections the Company has to follow up pretty closely its bills for metered water. As a further precaution against loss the Company's rules provide that applications for a water supply other than by the owner of the premises must be accompanied by a deposit of not less than $10.00. This deposit is returned to the consumer upon proof that he has settled his account in full, and either that his meter has been removed and the water shut off or that application by a new owner or lessee for a continued supply has been accepted by the company. Legal interest is payable on meter deposits and is actually paid if demanded by the consumer. The consumer agrees to notify the Company of any change of ownership or tenancy of the premises supplied. Under this rule the amount of the meter deposits held by the Company on May 31, 1914, was $28,485, of which $23,570 represented deposits by consumers in the Queens area.

The consumer pays the Company $2.50 for a ½-inch corporation cock and tapping, and $3 for a ⅝-inch corporation cock and tapping. The consumer pays the cost of the service pipes from the house to the point of connection with the main in the street, and agrees not to permit any work to be done in connection with the water pipes except by a plumber licensed by the Company. All services are metered and the company loans and keeps in ordinary repair one meter for each tap. In case the meter is found to be defective the Company agrees to replace it by another meter immediately. From the time when the meter ceases to register until a new meter is installed the amount of water consumed is estimated on the basis of the average amount consumed for a future period, as shown by the new meter, or by the average amount of the charge made by the Company during a previous corresponding period. The determination as to which of these two methods of estimating the charge shall be used is left to the Company. Whenever a consumer disputes the accuracy of a meter the Company will, upon application, test the meter, and if it is found accurate within two per cent. the consumer is required to pay a testing fee of $2. All expenses of repair to a meter occasioned by fire, frost, accidents or the act of any person on the premises are to be borne by the consumer.

The Company reserves the right to discontinue service upon twenty-four hours' notice if any bill for water is not paid within five days after it is due, or if plumbing work upon the water pipes connected with the premises is disapproved by the Company's engineer, or if water is wilfully wasted on the premises. The consumer is not entitled to a supply of water until he has paid all sums due from him to the Company, including a reasonable charge for turning the water off and on, and for replacing the pavement in cases where the service has been discontinued. The Company reserves the right to shut off the water in any of its mains without notice in case of conflagration or in order to make repairs and extensions or for other reasonable and proper purposes. The Company reserves the right to decrease or temporarily discontinue the water for business purposes or for hose use whenever in time of drouth the entire supply is needed for domestic use or to meet the conditions of its contracts with municipal authorities. The Company assumes no liability to any consumer for damages resulting from the public enemy, the elements, or any accident, misfortune, failure or break in machinery, reservoirs or pipes of the Company. The Company reserves the right to add to or modify its rules at any time. Furthermore, the consumer agrees to sell to the Company at any time at its fair market value the consumer's interest in the service pipe extending from the main to the point where the pipe enters the premises, together with any right of way possessed by the consumer enabling him to lay and maintain such pipe.

The printed rules of the Company do not cover extensions of mains. It is the practice of the Company, however, to require new consumers to advance the capital necessary for extending mains until such time as the extensions shall earn what the Company considers a fair return upon the investment. Formerly this was fixed at 10 cents per linear foot but later was fixed at 14 cents. The moneys so deposited are returned to the consumers without interest in four equal instalments, as follows: First instalment when the gross earnings reach 25% of the standard requirement; second instalment when the earnings reach 50%; third, when the earnings reach 75%; and final instalment when the earnings reach the full estimated amount required to carry the investment. On May 31, 1914, the Company held in trust extension guarantee funds of $38,215.65, of which approximately two-thirds, or $25,678.90, was for extensions of mains in the Queens area.

VI. AUTHORITY OF THE COMMISSIONER OF WATER SUPPLY, GAS AND ELECTRICITY.

While the State Conservation Commission has been given jurisdiction to control the development of water supplies so far as there is a likelihood of one company or municipality encroaching upon the watershed of another, the control of rates, service and competition in distribution has not been vested in any state commission, public body or official other than the Commissioner of Water Supply, Gas and Electricity, who, by section 472 of the Charter, is authorized "to examine into the sources of water supply of any private company supplying the City of New York or any portion thereof or its inhabitants with water, to see that the same is wholesome and the supply is adequate, and to establish such rules and regulations in respect thereof as are reasonable and necessary for the convenience of the public and the citizens." Also the Commissioner "may exercise superintendence, regulation and control in respect of the supply of water by such water companies, including rates, fares and charges to be made therefor, except that such rates, fares and charges shall not, without the consent of the grantee, be reduced by the said Commissioner beyond what is just and reasonable; and in case of a controversy, the question of what is just and reasonable shall be finally determined as a judicial question on its merits by a court of competent jurisdiction."

The Commissioner's authority to fix rates has never been effectively exercised. Rate cases were started in 1910 against the Queens County Water Company and the Citizens' Water Supply Company of Newtown, but the Commissioner then in office decided that the evidence presented to him did not warrant him in reducing the rates of either company. In the case of the Citizens' company, he ordered certain modifications in its rules and regulations, but his order has not been obeyed and no action has been taken by the City to enforce it.

The initiative in fixing such rates must, unless exercised by the legislature itself, be exercised by the Commissioner. The section of the Charter under which he must act is quite different from the public service law. Unless the rates established by him are acceptable to the company to which they apply, his action will be of no effect except as a basis for a court proceeding. Apparently if a company were to refuse to put the rates prescribed into effect the City could bring a proceeding to compel it to do so, or, on the other hand, the company might bring a proceeding to prevent the Commissioner from enforcing such rates. In either case the controversy would apparently be opened up to the very bottom and the City and the company might be entitled to put in all relevant evidence, irrespective of whether or not it had been placed before the Commissioner.

It will be observed that the law lacks specific and detailed provisions as to how the Commissioner shall ascertain the facts necessary to be considered in the proper determination of rates. He is not given authority to subpoena witnesses, to compel the production of books or to take evidence under oath, nor are private water companies specifically required to make reports to the City. The law of rate regulation has advanced to a point where it is not considered proper for a commission or public officer, acting under delegated power, to attempt to fix the rates of a public service corporation without investigating the value of the Company's property, its earnings and operating expenses, its capitalization and, as far as possible, its original investment.

Doubtless, however, the Commissioner's powers under section 472 of the Greater New York Charter should be read in connection with section 854 of the code of civil procedure, which is as follows:

> "When a judge or an arbitrator, referee or other person * * * has been heretofore or is hereafter expressly authorized by law to hear, try or determine a matter, or to do any other act in an official capacity, in relation to which proof may be taken, or the attendance of a person as a witness may be required; or to require a person to attend, either before him or it, or before another judge, or officer, or a person designated in a commission issued by a court of another state or country, to give testimony, or to have his deposition taken, or to be examined, a subpoena may be issued, by and under the hand of the judge, arbitrator, referee or other person * * * requiring the person to attend, and also, in a proper case, to bring with him a book or a paper. * * *"

Fortunately, in the case of the Queens County Water Company the Commissioner was not embarrassed by the refusal of the Company to furnish the data which it alone possesses. This Company has taken the position that the Commissioner is entitled to know all about its business and to examine its books and vouchers to whatever extent he deems desirable. He has thus been able to obtain all the evidence necessary for a proper determination of rates without resort to litigation.

VII. APPORTIONMENT BETWEEN QUEENS AND NASSAU DISTRICTS.

One of the most difficult elements in the problem of rates, so far as it affects the Commissioner's jurisdiction over the Queens County Water Company, is the proper allocation of the investment as between the Fifth Ward of the Borough of Queens and the portion of Nassau County served by this company. The Commissioner's jurisdiction as to rates extends only to the portion of the company's territory lying within the city limits. Therefore it is necessary to determine the relation between the company's earnings in the Fifth Ward and the portion of its investment properly chargeable to service in that district. The only part of the investment that could be attributed to service in either locality without the necessity of applying some relative percentage rule for splitting it up, is that portion invested in the local distribution systems, exclusive of the Far Rockaway standpipe, the latter being considered of approximately equal service to the two districts. For the trunk mains leading from the source of supply to the Queens County line, for the buildings, mechanical equipment, wells, suction lines, filters, land, tools and miscellaneous supplies, it is necessary to find some basis for a fair distribution of the capital as between the two areas. For the purpose of arriving at the proper percentages the following comparisons were made:

TABLE I—COMPARISONS OF QUEENS AND NASSAU DISTRICTS

BASIS OF COMPARISON	Percentage of total in Queens	Percentage of total in Nassau
Length of mains in local distribution system	50.9	49.1
Present value of local distribution system	61.4	38.6
Taps in use year ending May 31, 1914	60.3	39.7
Meters in use year ending May 31, 1914	61.6	38.4
Fire hydrants for which rental was received, year ending May 31, 1914	67.2	32.8
Gross earnings from sale of water (excluding water pumped to Brooklyn) year ending May 31, 1914	69.8	30.2
Gross earnings from sale of water (excluding water pumped to Brooklyn) four years ending May 31, 1914	69.9	30.1
Total consumption of water as shown by meter readings, year ending May 31, 1914	72.1	27.9
Total consumption of water as shown by meter readings, 9 months—September, 1913, to May, 1914	66.8	33.2
Total consumption of water as shown by meter readings, 3 months—June to August, 1913	77.5	22.5
Average daily rate of pumpage during summer months, plus reserve for fire protection	72.4	27.6
Average maximum hourly rate of pumpage during summer months, plus reserve for fire protection	73.4	26.6

After due consideration it seemed clear that the relative mileage of mains in the two areas was not a proper basis for the allocation of capital invested in other portions of the plant. It further became clear that the present value of the local distribution systems in the two areas was not a proper basis for this allocation. Some argument could be presented for using the relative number of taps, the relative number of meters in service, or the relative number of fire hydrants in service, but these tests also seemed to be of little value, as they gave no accurate measure of the amount of service which the Company in actual fact had to be prepared to render in the two areas. Fortunately, all domestic services are metered, and it was therefore possible to ascertain with comparative accuracy the actual quantity of water consumed during a given year in Queens and in Nassau. On its face, actual consumption would seem to furnish the best basis for an allocation of capital. It was urged, however, that if the relative consumption in the two districts for a full year were taken the result would be too favorable to Queens, for the reason that the peak load during the summer months is relatively higher in Queens than in Nassau. This claim was based upon the argument that there is relatively a much greater influx of summer population to the Rockaways than to the villages served by the Company outside of the City. During the first three months of the fiscal year—June, July and August—when the minimum rates are likely to cover the amount of water consumed, the Company does not read all the meters regularly once a month. Therefore, it was impossible to get the amount of actual consumption for a shorter summer period than the entire three months. A comparison of the actual consumption in the two areas in the summer months of 1913, as shown above, indicates a considerably larger percentage of demand in Queens during the summer season than during the entire year. A comparison of the three summer months of 1914 showed that Queens consumed 80 per cent. of the water used during that period. Because of the heavy rainfall during the greater portion of the summer of 1914, which naturally resulted in a decreased consumption of water for lawns in the Nassau County area, the figures of relative consumption for the summer season of 1914 were not believed to be typical, and for that reason the relative consumption during the summer of 1913 was thought to be more nearly normal.

In order to get a closer approximation to the relative demand of the two areas upon the capacity of the system it was necessary to take into consideration not merely the actual consumption of water during the summer season, but the consumption based upon the hourly peak load, plus leakage, plus the reserve capacity necessary for fire protection. The actual metered consumption for the summer months was 77.3 per cent. of the total pumpage, the remaining 22.7 per cent. being attributable to unmetered uses and leakage. This 22.7 per cent. was assumed to be distributed between the two districts in the same proportion as the use of metered water, thus giving 77.5 per cent. of the total pumpage to Queens and 22.5 per cent. to Nassau. An examination of the pumping profiles showed that the highest rate of pumpage for any one hour in the day, averaged for all the days of the summer season, gave a rate 75 per cent. greater than the actual average 24-hour rate during the same period. Accordingly, the total average daily pumpage for the two areas, respectively, was increased by 75 per cent. to get an approximate average peak load of pumpage during the hours of maximum use. This gave a peak rate of 6,253,000 gallons for Queens and 1,816,000 gallons for Nassau.

It was estimated that the possible demands on the fire service required a reserve of 7,000,000 gallons daily capacity for the Queens area, and of 3,000,000 gallons daily capacity for the Nassau area in addition to the actual peak load carried for domestic and ordinary public uses. Adding this assumed reserve for fire protection, we found a total capacity of 13,263,000 gallons chargeable to Queens and 4,816,000 gallons chargeable to Nassau, which established a ratio of 73.4 per cent. for Queens and 26.6 per cent. for Nassau.

While the ratio arrived at in this manner might be considered as the normal ratio for the distribution of the portions of the investment not localized, a little further examination made clear that this ratio could be applied properly only to the pumping plant, buildings and general equipment. So far as the trunk mains serving both Queens and Nassau were concerned, it was necessary to make a further adjustment on account of the fact that all of the Queens supply had to pass through these mains, while a portion of the Nassau supply, namely, the supply for the Valley Stream area, was delivered directly from the pumping station through a separate main. Furthermore, the remainder of the Nassau supply was taken off from the trunk mains all the way down to the city line. Giving the proper weight to these considerations, it was found that as to the trunk mains the proportion of the entire capacity properly attributable to the Queens service was approximately 76.8 per cent., leaving 23.2 per cent. for Nassau.

As to the well system, suction lines, filters and lands, it seemed improper to take into consideration the hourly peak, as the extraordinary demands made upon the system during the short time of maximum use each day could be carried by the normal reserve in the filter beds and standpipes. Accordingly, for these portions of the investment a ratio was established on the basis of the total summer pumpage plus fire reserve. This gave 72.4 per cent. attributable to the Queens service, and 27.6 per cent. to the Nassau service.

Combining the localized investment in distribution systems with the distributed investments in other portions of the plant according to the ratios arrived at on the basis already described, it appears that the total investment attribuable to the Queens service is about 67 per cent. of the total for both counties. The gross earnings from hydrant rentals and the sale of water in Queens for the year ending May 31, 1914, amounted to 69.8 per cent. of the total earnings in both areas, miscellaneous revenues and receipts from the Brooklyn Contract being disregarded. The difference in these percentages tends to show that the rates in Queens should be slightly lower than the rates in Nassau, or else that the Company should be content for the present with a somewhat lower rate of return from its more recently developed Nassau business than from its better established Queens business. However, the difference in the relation of gross earnings to investment as between the two areas is so small as to be nearly negligible. A schedule of rates fixed for Queens which would give the Company a fair return upon 67 per cent. of its total investment would not inflict a serious hardship upon the Company if also applied to the Nassau area, especially as the Nassau earnings are increasing more rapidly than the Queens earnings.

The following table shows the subdivision of revenue derived from hydrant rentals, water rates and measured water (exclusive of the Brooklyn Contract) for the fifteen years from June 1, 1899, to May 31, 1914:

TABLE 2—DISTRIBUTION OF REVENUES

YEAR	QUEENS COUNTY		NASSAU COUNTY	
	Amount	Per cent.	Amount	Per cent.
1899–1900	$44,188.21	87.2	$6,491.72	12.8
1900–1901	48,442.03	85.1	7,932.49	14.9
1901–1902	56,301.98	85.6	9,504.90	14.4
1902–1903	64,543.57	84.2	12,155.29	15.8
1903–1904	68,189.39	82.1	14,825.73	17.9
1904–1905	75,318.26	82.0	16,535.05	18.0
1905–1906	81,317.66	80.5	19,685.21	19.5
1906–1907	92,082.64	78.2	25,621.77	21.8
1907–1908	101,694.93	77.1	30,145.56	22.9
1908–1909	110,968.14	75.3	36,471.64	24.7
1909–1910	125,679.15	73.4	45,521.27	26.6
1910–1911	132,654.61	69.4	58,410.55	30.6
1911–1912	144,828.48	69.8	62,588.05	30.2
1912–1913	153,075.14	70.5	64,062.34	29.5
1913–1914	172,367.11	69.8	74,570.19	30.2
Last 4 years	602,925.34	69.9	259,631.13	30.1

VIII. DOMESTIC SERVICE AND FIRE PROTECTION.

A public service corporation is primarily interested in results. If it secures a fair return upon its investment in the business it is not greatly concerned as to the distribution of the charges among its various classes of consumers, except in so far as obvious discrimination and injustice in this distribution would tend to create ill feeling and thereby deprive the Company of the good will which is always advantageous to it. But if the distribution of the costs of service is made by the public authorities in accordance with some established public policy, the Company is thereby relieved from the odium which may attach to this policy, even if such policy is not entirely just. A water company, for example, is entitled to a revenue that will take care of operating expenses, including taxes and depreciation, and leave a net income sufficient to afford a fair return upon the legitimate investment, provided that this result can be obtained without the imposition of excessive rates upon the consumers. If the rate fixing authority determines that fire service and other general services shall be rendered free or for less than cost, and that the deficiency so caused shall be added to the rates chargeable to private consumers, the Company has no particular reason to complain.

As between the general public and the individual consumers of a public utility service, however, it is important that an equitable distribution of costs of service should be made. In the case of the municipal water supply, the City of New York has always pursued the policy of furnishing fire service and water for all public uses free of charge, except as interest charges on water bonds may have been paid from time to time out of taxes when necessary. No allowance is made in the annual budget for the payment of hydrant rentals to the Water Department, and, in fact, all water furnished to public buildings, including schools, hospitals and all sorts of public institutions, and even including private charitable institutions, is supplied free of charge and no account is made of the value of these services. On the other hand, the property of the Water Department within the city limits is not subject to taxation, and it might be urged that this exemption from taxation is, in a rough way, an offset for the free public services supplied by the Department.

In the case of the private water companies operating within the City limits, it has been the policy of the City to pay hydrant rentals in the shape of a fixed amount per annum per hydrant except in the case of the Flatbush Water Works Company, where the City has paid a lump sum per annum for fire service and most other public uses. As to the public services which could properly be metered, there has been no uniform rule. In some cases these services have been thrown in in consideration of the hydrant rentals paid, and in other cases the City has paid for water used at meter rates.

In a case like that of the Queens County Water Company, where domestic rates are greatly in excess of those charged by the City and also by other companies within the city limits, it is a matter of high importance to investigate and determine whether a reason for such excessive rates is failure on the part of the City to pay its fair proportion of the cost of service chargeable to public uses and particularly to fire protection, and if so, to rectify this condition. Whatever policy the City may be justified in pursuing with reference to the municipal rates, it would be difficult to justify its refusal to pay to the Queens County Water Company the fair cost of the public service rendered, if by so doing it compelled the Company, in order to earn a fair return upon its investment, to maintain domestic rates greatly in excess of the rates charged to residents in other sections of the city not supplied by this company. Therefore, it became necessary as a part of this investigation to endeavor to determine the cost of the fire service rendered by the Queens County Water Company in the Fifth Ward of the Borough of Queens.

A proper allocation of costs as between public and domestic water services is a problem of considerable difficulty. A water supply system is usually installed for the twofold purpose of supplying water (a) for domestic use and (b) for fire protection, which latter carries with it the necessity of adequate pressure and abundant quantity. It is often difficult in a given case to determine which is the primary and which the incidental or additional purpose.

The policy heretofore followed by the City of New York has been to impose the entire burden of carrying the municipal water plant (except the taxes) upon the domestic consumers. In fixing the rates of a private company this policy cannot be followed. In this investigation it has been assumed that the water plant established by this company was primarily for the purpose of supplying water to domestic consumers, and that the rendering of fire service was additional and to a certain extent incidental. This assumption is the most favorable one to the City that could be made. We have proceeded as follows: An estimate was made of the investment in the various portions of the plant necessary to make them fully adequate for domestic service without reference to fire protection. The investment in various portions of the plant as actually constructed for both domestic service and fire protection was then ascertained. The difference between the cost of a system that would have been adequate for domestic service and the actual cost of the existing system was regarded as the portion of the investment chargeable to fire service. This proportion was then applied to the total investment chargeable to the Queens service, and the cost of fire service properly chargeable to the City for the Queens area was estimated upon the basis of a fair return upon the extra capital invested in this service, together with a proper allowance for depreciation, taxes, maintenance and operation. In view of the fact that the major portion of the investment chargeable to fire service would remain the same without reference to the number of fire hydrants in use, the cost of fire service should be divided into two parts: First, the cost attributable to the general fixed investment, which would be measured as a lump sum per annum, and second, the cost attributable to the particular investment in and maintenance of fire hydrants, which would be measured in the form of a fixed sum per hydrant per annum. Obviously this method of distributing the cost would be more equitable to both parties than either a flat lump sum or a flat annual rental per hydrant. Under this plan the City could require the Company to put in a large number of additional hydrants, paying therefor the additional cost attributable to the additional investment and maintenance expenses required, which would be much less than the cost of additional hydrants if the entire cost of the fire service was to be borne in the form of hydrant rental. On the other hand, a lump sum representing the total cost of the fire service at any particular date would subsequently become inadequate from the Company's standpoint if a large number of additional hydrants was required by the City. Either the lump sum payment or the straight hydrant rental payment would be unscientific and in most cases unjust to one party or the other.

The net result of this method applied to conditions existing on May 31, 1914, was a finding (see Table 29) that 23 per cent. of the total Queens investment and 15 per cent. of operating expenses and taxes were attributable to fire protection. When allowance was made for depreciation and interest on investment, the cost of fire protection was found to be approximately 21 per cent. of the total.

Up to this time the Queens County Water Company has received from fire service in its entire area of supply only a very small proportion of its total earnings. From January 1, 1892, to May 31, 1914, a period of 22 years and 5 months, the Company's gross earnings from fire service and the sale of water, excluding water pumped to Brooklyn, amounted to $2,212,782.62. Of this total only $164,101.47 was received on account of fire service and other public uses paid for in hydrant rentals. This was 7.4 per cent. of the total. The amounts of revenue derived from hydrant rentals in the Queens and Nassau areas, respectively, during the past fifteen years, and the percentages which these amounts bear to the total revenues, excluding receipts from the Brooklyn Contract and from tapping and miscellaneous items not separated between the two districts, are shown by the following table:

Table 3—HYDRANT RENTALS

Year	Queens Amount	Queens Percentage of total Revenue	Nassau Amount	Nassau Percentage of total Revenue
1899–1900	$4,380.00	9.9	$400.00	6.1
1900–1901	4,680.00	9.7	400.00	5.0
1901–1902	4,720.00	8.4	450.00	4.7
1902–1903	5,070.78	7.9	480.00	3.9
1903–1904	4,883.70	7.2	520.00	3.5
1904–1905	5,683.75	7.5	493.30	3.0
1905–1906	6,204.25	7.6	912.10	4.6
1906–1907	6,584.76	7.2	1,050.30	4.1
1907–1908	7,315.73	7.2	1,925.61	6.4
1908–1909	7,344.42	6.6	2,138.15	5.9
1909–1910	8,040.36	6.4	2,497.13	5.5
1910–1911	8,195.47	6.2	4,045.87	6.9
1911–1912	8,727.11	6.0	4,579.11	7.3
1912–1913	9,225.09	6.0	3,838.41	6.0
1913–1914	11,008.34	6.4	5,562.31	7.5

Assuming that the cost of the fire protection furnished by the Company in both areas since 1902, when the Company's old hydrant rental contracts for the Queens area expired, has been 21 per cent. of the total cost of the service rendered, and assuming that up to May 31, 1914, the Company did not receive more revenues in the aggregate from domestic service and miscellaneous services (other than the Brooklyn Contract) than the fair cost of these services, the Company should have received for fire service during these twelve years approximately $456,633 instead of the $116,326 actually received. Of the deficiency, amounting to $340,307, about 76 per cent. should be charged to Queens. Thus the payments of the City for fire service during this twelve-year period were about $258,633 less than the cost to the Company of the service rendered.

It should be noted, however, as an offset to this deficiency, that during this period the City paid the Company $273,041 under a contract for water for use in Brooklyn, and that the cost to the Company of delivering this water was estimated to be only $47,701.72. It might be considered, therefore, that the City had in effect paid nearly the full cost of fire protection, and had received the water delivered under the Brooklyn Contract as an incidental benefit. In this view of the case the Nassau area would still be indebted to the Company some $82,000 for fire service rendered during the past twelve years in order to make the amount paid for such service relative to cost the same as the amount paid for domestic service relative to cost. In case it be found that the Company has not received in the aggregate a fair return upon its investment, this amount due from the Nassau communities should go to reduce the amount of the deficiency to be distributed over the entire service in future rates.

That the 7.4 per cent. of total revenues actually received by the Company from hydrant rentals is greatly below the cost of the service rendered and that the 21 per cent. herein estimated as the proper charge is very conservative, may be seen by some comparisons with the findings of rate fixing authorities elsewhere.

In Wisconsin, where the Railroad Commission has had jurisdiction over the rates of water companies for seven or eight years, a considerable number of cases have arisen in which the Commission was called upon to determine the proper distribution of the investment as between the requirements of fire service and the requirments of domestic use, and also to make a similar distribution of operating expenses. The Wisconsin Commission has followed a plan quite different from the one pursued in this investigation. The Wisconsin Commission assumes that fire protection and domestic use are to be treated as equally important and essential elements of an ordinary water supply. Accordingly, it has adopted the plan of estimating the cost of a plant that would be adequate to furnish domestic service without regard to fire protection, and also the cost of a plant that would be adequate to furnish fire protection without regard to domestic service. The investment in the existing plant is then assigned to fire service and domestic use in proportion to the relative costs of the two assumed independent plants. The result of this method has been the assignment in several cases of more than 50 per cent. of the investment to fire service. For example, in the case of the **City of Janesville v. Janesville Water Co.,** decided August 17, 1911, and reported in volume 7 of the Wisconsin Railroad Commission's Reports, at page 628, out of a total investment of $226,913, the sum of $122,183, or 54 per cent., was assigned to fire service. In the case of the **City of Ashland v. Ashland Water Co.,** 4 Wisconsin Railroad Commission Reports, 273, the proportion of the investment attributed to fire service was 55.2 per cent. In the case of the **City of Ripon v. Ripon Light and Water Co.,** 5 Wisconsin Railroad Reports, 1, the proportion attributed to fire service was 65.2 per cent. In the case of the **City of Washburn v. Washburn Water Works Co.,** 6 Wisconsin Railroad Commission Reports, 74, this proportion was 56.7 per cent. In the case of **Dick et al. v. Madison Water Commissioners,** 5 Wisconsin Railroad Commission Reports, 731, the proportion was 49.6 per cent., and in the case of the **City of Green Bay v. Green Bay Water Co.,** 11 Wisconsin Railroad Commission Reports, 236, the proportion was 48.7 per cent. The Wisconsin Commission recognizes, however, that the proportion of operating expenses chargeable to fire protection is much smaller than the proportion of the investment so chargeable. As a rule the Commission divides the operating expenses into "capacity" and "output" expenses, and more recently it has still further differentiated by adding the "direct" or individual consumer's expenses. Taking into consideration the cost attributable to the investment as such and the various elements of the cost comprising operating expenses, the Commission arrives at a proportion of the gross earnings which should be supplied by the City on account of fire service. In the Green Bay case this proportion was 30 per cent. of the total; in the Ashland case, 27.5 per cent.; in the Ripon case, 47 per cent.; in the Madison case, 46.5 per cent., and in the Janesville case, 40.8 per cent. Under these decisions all public services, other than fire protection and possibly sewer flushing, are metered and paid for by the City in accordance with the amount of water used.

It is obvious that the plan followed by the Wisconsin Commission throws upon the community at large a much greater proportion of the total cost of water service than the plan followed in this investigaion. While the Wisconsin Commission has acquired great prestige in rate cases, and some argument might be made in favor of its method of distributing the costs of water service, especially in the case of municipal plants, it does not seem that this method would be equitable if applied to an enterprise like that of the Queens County Water Company. In the great majority of cases private water plants are established primarily for the purpose of selling water to private consumers at a profit. This seems to have been the fact in the case of the Queens County Water Company, and the adaptation of its water plant to the demands of the general public for fire protection has been rather incidental to the main purpose of the enterprise. This view tends to justify the conservative basis adopted in this report for estimating the proportion of the cost of the service chargeable to fire protection in the present case. It is noteworthy, however, that even on this basis the amount paid for fire service should be greatly increased. It is obviously unjust that private consumers in the Fifth Ward of the Borough of Queens should be compelled to pay rates two or three times as high as the rates charged by the City, while at the same time the City itself is paying only a fraction of the cost of fire service estimated on the most conservative basis.

IX. MINIMUM AND METER RATES.

As already explained, the Company charges a flat minimum rate in proportion to the size of the meter. It has been the purpose of the Company to fix this rate high enough to cover the "capacity" or "ready-to-serve" costs of the service. The conditions, in the Queens area especially, are peculiar. In order that the Company may receive a return upon its necessary investment it is compelled to derive a disproportionate amount of revenue from its service during the summer months. Obviously, it costs the Company very little more to supply water to any particular individual through the entire year than it does to supply him during a period of ninety days. About the only saving is in the amount of coal used for the pumps and the expense of meter readings. It seems reasonable, therefore, under the conditions prevailing in this Company's area of service, to make a minimum charge almost as high as the cost to an ordinary consumer for an entire year's water service. Combined with this minimum rate is the meter rate, which begins to be effective as soon as the amount of water consumed is equal to the amount allowed under the minimum charge at meter rates.

During the year ending May 31, 1914, a total of 5,152 meters were in service in Queens County and 3,237 in Nassau County. These meters, with relation to the revenues derived from them, may be distributed as follows:

TABLE 4—CLASSIFICATION OF CONSUMERS ACCORDING TO SIZE OF WATER BILLS

CLASS	Number in Queens County	Number in Nassau County
Consumers at the $10 minimum rate who used no excess water	993	1,449
Consumers at other minimum rates who used no excess water	62	19
Consumers using excess water whose bills were from $1 to $10 (See full explanation of minimum rates under subdivision V, *ante*)	56	24
Consumers using excess water whose bills were from $10 to $20	1,169	890
Consumers using excess water whose bills were from $20 to $30	1,132	314
Consumers using excess water whose bills were from $30 to $50	994	284
Consumers using excess water whose bills were from $50 to $100	551	181
Consumers using excess water whose bills were from $100 to $200	127	60
Consumers using excess water whose bills were from $200 to $500	36	11
Consumers using excess water whose bills were over $500	5	1
City meters, free taps, etc	27	4
Average revenue per meter	$31.37	$21.27

It is noteworthy that only a very few consumers get the benefit of any rate lower than 30 cents per 1,000 gallons. Only 102 taps in Queens County and 31 in Nassau received the benefit of the 20-cent rate, which is the rate charged for water used in excess of 450,000 gallons per annum. Only 244 taps in Queens and 104 in Nassau received the benefit of the 25-cent rate, which is the rate charged for water used in excess of 250,000 gallons and less than 450,000 per annum. The total amount of water for which the Company received pay at the different rates in the two areas is shown by the following table, made up from the "consumers' register" for the year ending May 31, 1914:

Table 5—SUMMARY OF CONSUMERS' REGISTER, 1913-14

	Queens County	Nassau County
Gallons used at 40c. rate	205,940,000	95,501,100
Gallons used at 30c. rate	188,315,900	64,210,500
Gallons used at 25c. rate	36,024,700	12,230,900
Gallons used at 20c. rate	49,124,300	13,414,800
Total gallons passing through meters	479,404,900	185,357,300
Net revenue from 40c. rate	$87,026.12	$44,030.70
Net revenue from 30c. rate	56,158.83	19,236.63
Net revenue from 25c. rate	8,445.39	3,057.48
Net revenue from 20c. rate	9,728.43	2,683.07
Total net revenue from metered water, excluding "Brooklyn contract"	$162,270.35	$69,235.44

The character of the establishments which received the benefit of the 20-cent rate is shown by the following table:

TABLE 6—CLASSIFICATION OF 20-CENT RATE CONSUMERS

CLASS	Number in Queens County	Number in Nassau County
Bathing pavilions	2	...
Boarding houses	8	...
Livery stables	1	...
Bottling establishment	1	...
Bungalows (5 to 100)	9	1
Tents (10-30)	3	...
Private schools	3	...
Clubhouses	2	3
Hotels	29	1
Dredges	1	...
Flats and stores	18	1
Hospitals	3	...
Golf Links	...	1
Homes for children, reduced rate	3	...
Laundries	2	...
Lumber mill	1	...
Ice factory	2	...
Milk depot	1	...
Railroad stations	1	1
Residences and large grounds	3	21
Public schools	2	1
Refrigerating plants	1	1
Total	96	31

X. ELEMENTS OF A FAIR RETURN AND LIMITS OF A FAIR RATE.

A public service corporation is entitled to earn a fair return upon the fair present value of its property, used and useful for the public service, provided that such a return can be secured without charging rates that are unreasonable to its consumers. Before any return whatever upon the investment can be paid the gross earnings must be sufficient to pay the necessary operating expenses and taxes. Maintenance, repairs, and depreciation reserve adequate to provide for the ultimate replacement of the depreciable property, are to be treatd as a part of operating expenses. It is clearly settled as a matter of law and public policy that a corporation is entitled to an allowance in its rates for actual measurable depreciation, and much can be said in favor of making an additional allowance for prospective or contingent depreciation, which usually accrues as functional depreciation in the form of inadequacy or obsolescence.

After all the running costs of operation have been taken care of and provision has been made for keeping the property intact, the annual rate of return upon its investment to which the corporation is entitled, in addition to these costs, depends upon various factors of time, place, the character of the business and the ultimate security of the investment. If it is possible to give the investor absolute assurance (1) that the tangible property which represents his investment will be maintained in a state of undiminished usefulness; (2) that the annual return upon the investment will be steady and certain; (3) that ultimately the investment itself will be returned to him in case the physical property goes out of actual use or is transferred to another, then the annual rate of return demanded by the investor will approximate the rate of interest on long term municipal bonds or other iron-clad securities. The elimination of the risk to the capital itself and to the annual return upon it would naturally reduce the rate of profit necessary to induce the investment of capital in public utilities. On the other hand, if a public utility corporation is operating under a short-term franchise, with no guaranty that it will be permitted to continue in business after the expiration of the grant, or if it is threatened by or subject to destructive competition, either by rival corporations or by the municipality, or if the utility is such or the community is such that the demand for the service is likely to diminish or cease entirely within a comparatively few years, or if the particular conditions surrounding the plant are such that the Company's present sources of supply are likely to fail or its plant be destroyed or become obsolete, then naturally the risk involved calls for a higher rate of return upon the investment. Otherwise, capital could not be induced to lend itself to the enterprise and the public utility service could not be rendered.

A distinction should also be made between a rate of return that is fair and a rate of return that barely escapes being confiscatory under the provisions of the United States Constitution. It has been held by the United States Supreme Court that under conditions prevailing in the gas business on Manhattan Island an exercise of the rate regulating power in such a manner as not clearly to reduce the Company's net return below 6 per cent. upon its investment is not in conflict with the provisions of the Constitution guaranteeing private property against attack. It was assumed by the court that the manufacture and supply of gas in the crowded portions of New York City under conditions that gave a practical monopoly was a very safe business. It has been generally assumed, therefore, that a clear return of 6 per cent. upon the full fair present value of the investment used and useful in the public service is approximately the minimum rate toward which regulation may gravitate.

In its reports to the State Board of Tax Commissioners the Queens County Water Company sets up the claim that if the Consolidated Gas Company is entitled to earn 6 per cent. upon its investment, the Queens County Company should be entitled to earn at least 10 per cent. on account of the exceptional conditions under which it operates. The Company states that on former occasions the City of New York has attempted to invade its watershed and has thus threatened the very foundation of its business; that more recently responsible city officials have advocated the policy of acquiring the distribution system only, leaving the Company with the major portion of its investment and only a small portion of its business, and if this project cannot be carried through on terms satisfactory to the City, then of paralleling the Company's mains; that the City has persistently refused to enter into a contract with the Company to pay the adequate cost of the fire protection service rendered by the Company, and, finally, that the peculiarities of the Fifth Ward of the Borough of Queens, where the demand for water during the summer months is very greatly in excess of the demand during the balance of the year, are such as to make it difficult, if not impossible, to collect from domestic consumers an amount sufficient to provide an adequate return upon the investment.

The Company does not call attention, however, to certain important considerations in its favor. In the first place, the Company enjoys a perpetual franchise, and furthermore, while this franchise for the use of public streets is not exclusive, yet a large portion of the Company's system has been constructed on private streets under easements acquired by the Company, many of which are alleged to be exclusive. This condition would put the City or another corporation at a considerable disadvantage in establishing a competitive plant. Moreover, in order to bring a municipal water supply into the Rockaways the

City would have to construct at great expense submarine trunk mains across Jamaica Bay, or else lay mains around the easterly end of the bay through a portion of Nassau County. The large investment thus required in addition to the increased difficulty and cost of duplicating the distribution system itself would put the city at great disadvantage, which would certainly in part overcome the advantage of being able to make use of a gravity supply for this district after the Catskill water is available. Certainly no private competition could secure an adequate supply for the Rockaway peninsula as advantageously located as the existing supply of the Queens County Water Company. Accordingly, in spite of the fact that the Company's public franchise is not exclusive. it has certain very decided advantages which are likely to deter others from actually entering upon the policy of competition for domestic consumers unless under extreme provocation. Even the establishment of a separate salt-water system for fire protection would be expensive and undesirable as an exclusive substitute for the fire service now rendered by the Company. If the City determined to install a separate fire protection system it would probably still wish to make use of the Company's fresh water system in so far as it is at present available and except in great emergencies. Accordingly, even the establishment of this duplicate fire system would not be likely to deprive the Company of its present revenues from hydrant rentals, although it might prevent a further development of the Company's system which would otherwise be necessary to meet the increasing fire hazard. Indeed, this result might be of considerable advantage to the Company, as it would relieve it of the necessity of investing large amounts of additional capital in a service for which, in the Company's estimation, it has heretofore been inadequately paid. A still further advantage enjoyed by this Company arises from the nature of the utility supplied by it and the stage of development at which the Company's business has now arrived. The demand for water is not a temporary demand, but, on the contrary, the demand will constantly increase. The future of this utility is more certain than that of any other. The Company has passed through a long period of development and has now reached a period of comparative prosperity where its earnings for the future under normal conditions seem to be well assured.

All these considerations tend to offset the risks to which the Company calls attention, and to reduce the rate of return to which the Company is justly entitled. Nevertheless, it is obvious that if the City of New York pursues a policy of hostility to the Company, refuses to pay the fair cost of fire protection rendered, threatens to enter into active competition in the supply of water to the Rockaways, or otherwise renders the Company's investment hazardous and its continued profits uncertain, this fact would constitute an element of risk which in law and equity would entitle the Company, while it could, to earn a higher rate of return than would be necessary or fair in the case of a protected investment. It is also obvious that unless the City is in a position actually to enter into competition with the Company and supply the consumers of the Fifth Ward of the Borough of Queens with municipal water, and unless in good faith it intends to pursue this policy, it will be advantageous both to the City and to the consumers for the City to adopt a policy of protecting the Company's legitimate investment, making reasonably sure the Company's possession of a fair earning power so long as it continues to serve a portion of the city with water, and of guaranteeing it against substantial loss of capital when it is superseded by the City in the business of supplying the Fifth Ward. If the City pursues this policy and is willing to give this guaranty so long as the Company yields to reasonable regulation and adequately performs its functions as a public service corporation, then it would seem reasonable to limit the Company's rate of net profit to the 6 per cent. minimum which the courts are inclined to consider as not being confiscatory.

The discussion thus far has not taken into consideration the question of the Company's being entitled to make up in its future profits for lack of adequate profits during past years. This question involves a consideration of the problem of "going value" or "development costs." The correct policy to be pursued in this matter has not yet been fully established in the practice of public service commissions or in the rules laid down by the courts. The Court of Appeals in the Kings County Lighting case decided specifically that going value should be taken into consideration in the fixing of rates. The court did not lay down a specific or iron-clad rule as to the manner in which going value should be treated. It suggested three possible ways: First, by adding early deficits in the form of developmental expenses to the permanent capital investment; second, by temporarily capitalizing such expenses and subsequently amortizing them out of earnings as rapidly as possible; and third, by treating them as deficits in the rate of return to be subsequently made up when the earnings permit by the allowance of a higher rate of return than would otherwise be fair and reasonable. It would appear that in this state in any particular case the rate fixing authority would be permitted to determine under all the circumstances of the case which one of these three methods should be followed. If development expenses and possible losses not due to unreasonable negligence or lack of foresight on the part of the Company are added to the investment in arriving at the fair present value of the property upon which the Company is now entitled to earn a fair return, and if these expenses and losses as a recognized part of the investment share the protection of the physical property so far as the future is concerned, then it will be unnecessary to make any additional allowance in the rate of return on account of them. If, on the other hand, these early losses and expenses are not capitalized and are treated as a deficit in net earnings to be made up later on, it becomes necessary to ascertain whether or not in the history of a particular company they have already been made up by earnings in subsequent years in excess of the minimum fair rate of current profit. If it can be shown that the Company has earned the interest necessarily paid on borrowed money and not less than an average of 6 per cent. on the additional capital furnished by the stockholders from the inception of the enterprise, it may be fairly assumed for the future that, under the guaranties of safety already outlined, a return of 6 per cent. upon the present value of the physical property will be sufficient.

At this point, however, it is necessary to consider the other side of the question, namely, what is the limit of rates that will be fair to the consumers, including both the City itself as a user of fire protection and other public services, and the private individuals who are patrons of the Company. The absolute value of water, for either domestic or public uses, is almost unlimited. Water is a prime necessity for sanitation and safety from fire. It is also a prime necessity of domestic life. It is not to be assumed, however, that a public service corporation supplying water will be entitled to charge its monopoly value even though such a change would be necessary to enable the Company to earn a fair return upon its investment. What is the upper limit of a reasonable rate to the public should be determined partly by the prices generally charged for similar services in communities of similar size and similarly situated with reference to water supply, and partly by the estimated cost of furnishing the same service by means of a new plant constructed by the City or by another corporation. In other words, even for the purpose of earning a fair return upon its investment, a Company is not entitled to charge a monopoly rate, or a rate greatly in excess of what would be the cost of the service from other sources, if the same governmental privileges were granted on the same terms to others who might engage in the business. This limitation of the rate may be based upon the assumption that the community served by the Company is not yet fully developed and, therefore, that the business has not yet reached a profitable stage, or upon the assumption that the Company in making its investments did not exercise sufficient care and foresight and therefore must be prepared to bear a partial loss rather than charge an unreasonable rate for public service. The very fact that a public water supply is a fundamental necessity of urban life, and that water in extremity is of almost unlimited value, tends to make the charging of unreasonable rates peculiarly abhorrent. Every consideration of human necessity, social equity and sound public policy requires that water rates should be kept reasonably low and as near the actual and necessary cost of the service as possible.

XI. DETERMINATION OF LAND AND OTHER PROPERTY HELD BY THE COMPANY NOT NECESSARY OR USEFUL FOR THE PUBLIC SERVICE.

The first step in the consideration of the value of the Company's land for the purpose of fixing rates is to determine whether all or only a portion of it is used and useful for the public service. In the case of the Queens County Water Company this is a particularly difficult problem. As already stated in a preceding section of this report, the Company acquired a large tract of land at Fenhurst, near Valley Stream, with the pumping station and system of wells already constructed in 1896, and subsequently for the purpose of heading off the efforts of the City to take water from the same watershed, it acquired between 1901 and 1909 a great many additional parcels which, together with the original tract, made a total of about 840 acres in Nassau County. In a proceeding for the review of the special franchise assessment of the Company for the year 1905 Justice Kellogg, in the Appellate Division, Third Department (157 App. Div., 165) held that under the cricumstances the Company was entitled to earn upon the value of these lands acquired for the purposes stated. In 1909 the Company effected a settlement with the City and secured a contract protecting its watershed from future encroachment. Subsequent to the execution of this contract it determined to sell off a portion of the lands it had acquired as being no longer necessary in its business as a water supply corporation. The Company claims that prior to the disposal of these lands it engaged the services of Nicholas S. Hill, Jr., a well-known engineer, who advised it that a portion of its lands could be properly disposed of if sold under restrictions to prevent any possible encroachment upon its water supply or any possible contamination of it. Accordingly, the water company organized a new corporation, namely, the Norumbega Company, to take over these surplus lands. The Norumbega Company was incorporated with a capital stock of $700,000 par value. On May 21, 1910, the board of directors of the water company received from the Norumbega Company an offer to take over certain of the water company's lands for the sum of $200,000 in cash and the entire authorized capital stock of the land company, the shares of which were to be issued directly to the stockholders of the water company. This proposition was accepted, and by deed dated May 31, 1910, approximately 555.46 acres of the water company's Nassau County lands were transferred to the Norumbega Company. Subsequently the water company issued a new general mortgage in which is described in detail the portion of the lands which it retained.

The water company claims that the Department of Water Supply, Gas and Electricity, in a rate proceeding instituted in 1910 and determined by former Commissioner Henry S. Thompson on May 12, 1911, recognized all of the land retained by the Company as necessary and useful for its business as a public service corporation. The opinion of Commissioner Thompson, coupled with the valuation of the Company's property made at this time by Mr. Edward Wegmann, Consulting Engineer of the Department, with the assistance, so far as land was concerned, of Mr. George S. Skilton, Assistant Engineer, seems to indicate that the Commissioner accepted as being necessary and useful for water purposes tracts of land which roughly correspond with the tracts still held by the Company in Nassau County. In that proceeding the Commissioner held that the Company was not earning more than a fair return upon the value of its property under the conditions then prevailing. So far as the record goes, it does not appear that the lands valued by the Department and recognized as useful for water purposes were exactly the same as the lands which the Company determined to retain. Assistant Engineer Skilton's map and measurements showed 391.5 acres, while the figures furnished by the Company at that time showed 449 acres. The figures given by the Company to the so-called Gaynor Commission in 1913 for the lands actually retained by the Company in Nassau County showed a total of 288.7 acres. The figures now given by the Company covering the same lands show a total of 285.2 acres. So far as I can see, there is nothing in the determinations of the Department heretofore made or in the judicial determinations that have been called to my attention to prevent the present Commissioner, in the exercise of the authority conferred by section 472 of the Greater New York Charter, from making a new determination of the amount of land actually used and necessary for the public service in connection with this Company's water supply under the circumstances now prevailing.

I have therefore made an investigation of this matter, and with the advice of Deputy Chief Engineer William W. Brush and Assistant Engineer William F. Laase, have arrived at the conclusion that only about one-fifth of the Company's land in Nassau County is necessary for the purposes of its water supply system. Following the established practice of the City with reference to its own supplies on the Long Island watershed, we have fixed as a maximum width necessary for the full development of the Company's well system and the protection of the wells from contamination a strip of land 500 feet wide, extending 250 feet on either side of this line of wells. At the pumping station an additional width is allowed for the present filters and any additional filters which may be required in the future. We have also allowed a strip 50 feet in width for the maintenance of the Company's embankment across the salt meadows at the westerly end of its property. We have also allowed a roadway for entrance to the pumping station, and a right of

Oversized Foldout

way for the company's tracks for the delivery of coal, supplies, filter sand, etc. These allowances we believe to be ample. They require approximately 60 acres instead of the total amount of 285.2 acres in Nassau County now claimed by the Company. These 60 acres are shown on the accompanying map, entitled: "Map of Nassau County lands of Queens County Water Company showing portion deemed necessary for water supply purposes."

In the determination of this question certain matters of special importance have been taken into consideration.

(a) The Company has retained certain strips of land extending along one or both banks of both branches of Motts Creek from the Mill Road northerly to points adjacent to the City's right of way for its 72-inch steel pressure main. The Company maintains that these narrow strips are useful in preventing the contamination of its water supply. As a matter of fact, in the case of both branches of the brook there are long stretches where the land held by the Company is along one side only of the stream. If the retention of a strip of land for the protection of the brook were conceded to be necessary, it is clear that the provision made by the Company is wholly inadequate so long as one side of the stream remains unprotected. Furthermore, at points where the highways cross the brooks the drainage from the roadways is turned directly into the brooks. These brooks are dry during a considerable portion of the season. The water table is drawn down by the Company's wells during the dry season, with the result that there is no water flowing in the creek beds.

(b) All of the Company's wells are driven through a bed of sand and gravel which appears to be of sufficient depth to remove any contamination which might affect the water on the surface of the soil. If the Company properly protects its wells from the immediate inflow of water about the pipes so that the entire supply is filtered through a bed of sand and gravel which has a minimum thickness of 20 feet, it is believed that all danger of contamination under conditions now existing or that are likely to exist within a reasonable time in the future will be avoided. Certainly this natural infiltration is the only adequate protection which the Company now gives to its water supply as taken from the wells.

(c) The Company has to maintain a filter plant for the removal of the iron from the water. If it could be shown that in spite of the natural infiltration through the earth the water reached the wells in a dangerously impure condition, the Company could equip and operate its filter plant for bacterial purification at a much less expense than it could carry the large tracts of land that would be necessary to insure the safety of a surface water supply. As a matter of fact, the Company has not for many years used surface water as a part of its supply, and all its arrangements for doing so are now considered obsolete. The use of surface water is wholly unnecessary and would become increasingly dangerous as the watershed comes to be studded more and more thickly with human habitations.

(d) The Company holds about 80 acres of salt meadow south of the Fenhurst pumping station on either side of Motts Creek. This meadow land, with the embankment separating it from the land of F. B. Lord, constitutes the so-called "Meadow Reservoir." The Company has gone on the theory that the embankment referred to serves two useful purposes: first, to shut out the salt water at high tide from the meadow to the north, and, second, to hold the fresh water in the meadow and thus prevent it from running into the sea and being lost. The embankment is not now being well maintained. As to the alleged advantage of holding back the spring floods of fresh water in the meadows for the purpose of furnishing a "head" for the wells, we can see nothing at all in it. On the other hand, the embankment tends to make the salt meadow north of it more valuable for other purposes than a water supply, if the gates are shut to the incoming tide and open to the outgoing flood, and at the same time it assists in getting the chlorine washed out of the meadow and away from the zone of attraction of the Company's wells. The salt meadows are not necessary for water supply purposes, and the embankment would tend to help rather than to hinder their being disposed of for other uses.

In Queens County the parcel of land held by the Company at Rockaway Beach is considered necessary and useful for its present purposes, although it will cease to be useful except for storage when the Company's distribution system has been reinforced so as to make the use of the Rockaway Beach auxiliary wells and pumping station no longer necessary. The parcel of land at Arverne formerly used as a site for a booster station is no longer necessary to the Company, though it is being used to a slight extent for storage purposes. The parcel of land at Far Rockaway where the Company's office is located is in part necessary and useful. A portion of this parcel located on the north side of John Street is occupied by dwelling houses and was purchased some years ago by the Company because at that time the overflow from its standpipe was an annoyance to the people living in these houses. The Company thought that by purchasing this property it could rent the houses to its own employees, whose opinions on the subject of an overflowing standpipe would not have to be considered. Since then the standpipe has been rebuilt, made much higher and provided with a check drain, so that the former conditions have been corrected and there is no longer any reason from any standpoint why these dwelling houses and the land which they occupy should be considered necessary or useful to the Company in its water business. Accordingly, this portion of the Far Rockaway land has been excluded from consideration. The small parcel on the north side of Crescent Street extending to the Long Island Railroad right of way is useful as a right of way for an important

16-inch trunk main, and, incidentally, for an outdoor storage place, and therefore has been allowed.

In the development of a water supply plant covering a period of thirty years, various units of the property will naturally go out of use or become obsolete. The "Meadow Reservoir," the infiltration gallery, the experimental wells at Lynbrook and the dismantled booster stations are no longer of any use. The auxiliary wells and station at Rockaway Beach, though useful now as a means of maintaining pressure in that section during the summer peak load, will be practically discarded within a year or two when the Company's distribution system has been properly reinforced. If the City acquired the Queens distribution system, the Company's lands, standpipes and buildings in Queens would become practically useless for water purposes. These various items, except the land listed above, may properly be included in the inventory and valued according to their present uses and non-uses.

The Company has a considerable outfit of farm machinery, tools and horses, which is housed on the Norumbega property, but operated by the water company. At first blush, it would seem that this property should be excluded from the inventory and appraisal, but upon further inquiry it appears that the "farming" operations consist largely in hauling pipe and taking care of the water company's grounds, and that when work is done on the Norumbega Company's farm the water Company derives a revenue from it. The services are disposed of as a sort of by-product. I have therefore decided to include the farm equipment in the appraisal and include the net revenue from "farming" operations in the Company's earnings.

At first blush, also, it would seem as if the pumping plant were overdeveloped, considering the relatively small total pumpage. But consideration of the peak load in the summer time and the proper reserve for fire emergencies has led me to the conclusion that I could not properly exclude any substantial part of the Company's mechanical equipment as unnecessary or useless. In such matters the Company has to be given a certain leeway for the exercise of judgment.

XII. PRESENT VALUE OF THE PROPERTY BASED ON REPRODUCTION COST NEW LESS DEPRECIATION.

For the appraisal of the physical property Mr. William F. Laase, Mr. Thomas J. Gannon, Mr. Joseph Goodman and Mr. Joseph Ryan, engineers of the Bureau of Water Supply, were assigned to work under my supervision. They were instructed to follow the reproduction cost new less depreciation method. In the application of this method they were instructed to assume fair average unit prices prevailing over an immediately preceding period of from three to five years; to assume that the plant was to be reconstructed as a whole and not built up "piecemeal," and that it was to be built under physical conditions similar to those actually existing when it was built, particularly with reference to pavements; to include contractor's profit in the unit prices; to determine the amount of accrued depreciation and annual depreciation by the straight line method, using an estimated life for each unit of the property based upon actual observation of the plant under the conditions peculiar to it, supplemented by the best data available as to the life of similar plant units elsewhere; to estimate the proportion of the investment in each class of property rightly attributable to the Queens and Nassau services, respectively; and to determine the proportion of the investment in each class of property rightly attributable to domestic service and to fire service, respectively. The valuation of the water supply sources and works was assigned to Mr. Laase; that of the buildings and mechanical equipment to Mr. Gannon; that of the distribution system to Mr. Goodman; and that of the supplies, tools and miscellaneous items to Mr. Ryan. Naturally, the instructions given had no particular application to the valuation of the land itself or to the determination of going value, both of which I reserved for my own personal consideration.

(a) Land:

The difficulty of arriving at the fair value of the land used and useful for water purposes has been considerable. So far as the land in Queens County is concerned the problem is comparatively simple, as all of this land is city real estate and its value is easily comparable with that of other similar lands in the immediate vicinity. Indeed, so far as the lands in Queens County are concerned, the assessed valuation is of great assistance, for within the city limits the assessment rolls show the value of the land separated from the value of the improvements, and the great advance made in recent years in the application of scientific principles to the assessment of land values by the Department of Taxes and Assessments makes the tax valuations placed upon the parcels of land held by this Company in the Fifth Ward of the Borough of Queens a very important criterion of value.

In Nassau County the situation is very different, not only because the values of the land and of the improvements upon it are not fixed separately by the assessors, but also because the lands of the water company and the lands of the Norumbega Company have not yet been separately assessed by the town authorities, with the result that more than fifty different parcels, ranging from a fraction of an acre up to 292 acres, irregular in shape and more or less uncertain in location, are assessed upon the tax books as the property of the water company. Moreover, upon inquiry it was found that the assessors of the town of Hempstead, in fixing the value of various properties for tax purposes, have merely exercised their personal judgment after a cursory examination, and have never applied scientific principles or taken any effective steps to systematize their valuations or establish with any degree of nicety uniform standards of value.

It is said that about five years ago the assessors increased the assessments in the town of Hempstead by a flat addition of 150 per cent. No substantial change has been made in the assessments of the water company's property in Nassau County since 1910. In spite of the great increase in assessments in that year, the town authorities and Mr. Franklin B. Lord, one of the principal stockholders of this Company, and himself a large owner of real estate in the vicinity, felt that an injustice had been done to the town of Hempstead by the board of equalization in not adjusting the assessments of the town in comparison with those of North Hempstead and Oyster Bay. It was believed that the assessments in the two latter towns, which, with the town of Hempstead, constitute Nassau County, were at a very much lower rate as compared with their true value than the assessments in the town of Hempstead. An appeal was taken on the State Board of Tax Commissioners without result, and then suit was brought in the Appellate Division, Third Department, to review by **certiorari** the determination of the state board. The Appellate Division, for the purpose of equalization, held a few months ago that the assessments in the town of Hempstead were on the basis of 50 per cent. of full value, while those in the towns of North Hempstead and Oyster Bay were only 25 per cent. of full value. (See **State, ex rel. Town of Hempstead v. State Board of Tax Commissioners,** 163 App. Div. 803.) This decision was recently set aside by the Court of Appeals, and the matter was referred back to the State Tax Commission for further hearing on the merits. The Queens County Water Company does not admit that the assessors of the town of Hempstead have discriminated in its favor in making their assessments upon real estate. Mr. Lord maintains, however, that the actual basis of assessments in the town of Hempstead is only about one-third of full value, alleging that the determination of the Appellate Division was only approximate and for the purpose of equalization with the other towns, where, as a matter of fact, the assessments are actually much less than 25 per cent. of full value. So far as the town of North Hempstead is concerned, some facts have come to my attention in connection with the lands of another water company which seem to bear out Mr. Lord's contention that the 25 per cent. basis found by the court is in excess of the actual basis of the assessors' valuation.

In arriving at a conclusion as to the value of the water company's Nassau County lands I have had assistance from four different sources as follows: (1) the water department appraisal made in 1910; (2) the terms of the sale to the Norumbega Company; (3) the finance department's appraisal furnished to the Gaynor Commission in 1914; (4) the assessed valuation.

(1) Early in 1910 several complaints were presented to the Commissioner of Water Supply, Gas and Electricity against the rates of the Queens County Water Company in the Fifth Ward of the Borough of Queens, by the Progress Society and several other citizens' organizations, all represented by David May, Esq., as counsel. An investigation was made by the Department, and subsequently formal hearings were held and a determination reached by Commissioner Thompson on May 12, 1911, denying the applications of the complainants for a reduction of rates. As an incident to this inquiry Assistant Engineer George S. Skilton, then of the real estate division of the Department, made a valuation of the company's lands in Nassau County, which was transmitted to Deputy Commissioner Bemis by Chief Engineer de Varona on July 25, 1910. This valuation was used by the Commissioner in arriving at his determination as to the reasonableness of the Company's rates. The Skilton appraisal included 391.5 acres of land, to which he gave a total value of $254,225. In his report Mr. Skilton said: "In arriving at the following estimates of values of certain lands belonging to the Queens County Water Company in Nassau County, included on the Company's map, I have taken off the areas by a planimeter and have consulted six persons of the neighborhood who are handling real estate. Note has also been taken of the town assessments for taxes for six years on about 70 parcels as assessed to the company. Note has also been taken by consultation with Assistant Corporation Counsel Wilson, of probable awards by the Commission for the 72-inch pipe line for lands in the vicinity. For the purpose of this estimate the property considered is divided into parcels indicated here and on the map by the same letters. Pumping station and piping are excluded. An effort has also been made to eliminate any augmentation of values because of any supposed and specific use for which the lands can be utilized."

As previously stated, the lands appraised by Mr. Skilton, while they correspond in a general way with the lands now held by the Company, are far from being precisely the same. The principal difference is in the reduced area now held. The Company's figures show only 285.2 acres as against 391.5 acres appraised by Mr. Skilton. The Skilton appraisal averaged approximately $649 per acre. At this average rate the smaller area now held by the company would be valued at approximately $185,000. It is to be noted, however, that Mr. Skilton found in the large parcel where the Company's pumping station is located some 300 acres which he divided into two parts for purposes of the appraisal. He found 73 acres of land "said to be five feet above mean high tide," and 227 acres of "low land and salt meadow." Upon the high land he placed a valuation of $1,200 per acre, and upon the low land a valuation of $500 per acre. The separate strips of land along the brooks were valued by Mr. Skilton at rates ranging from $150 an acre along the south branch just north of Mill Road, and $200 an acre along the north branch just north of Mill Road, to $1,000 or $1,200 an acre along the south branch at Lynbrook, and $750 an acre along the north branch north of Rockaway Avenue.

(2) In 1910 the Water Company sold to the Norumbega Company, already referred to, some 555.46 acres of land for $200,000 in cash plus the entire capital stock of the land company. In its tax reports the water company states that the $200,000 cash was in excess of the original cost of this land, but intimates that it was much less than the present value of the land. In fact, the Company's estimate of $1,500,000 for the value of its lands in Nassau County prior to the sale to the Norumbega Company was reduced subsequent to the sale to "upwards of $800,000." The Company does not contend, however, that these estimates are to be taken seriously as applied to the value of the land as real estate. The Company, in its tax report, referring to the Norumbega sale and its effect upon the value of the Company's stock, suggests $400,000 as the possible value of the land disposed of to the Norumbega Company. The water company's records show that the Norumbega Company offered to pay an additional sum of $127,000 in cash for the land, making a total cash offer of $327,000. The stock of the land company, which was issued as full paid to the stockholders of the water company might be considered as not representing any actual present value, but rather as representing the "water" in the transaction. But the Norumbega land, without any large improvements, is assessed at $248,937, according to the water company's own distribution of the assessments. On the basis of a 33 1/3 per cent. assessment, this would indicate a full value of $746,811 for the Norumbega land. Even on the basis of a 50 per cent. assessment in 1910, this value would be for that year nearly $500,000. The land transferred to the Norumbega Company contains no salt marsh and generally is of an elevation satisfactory either for farming or for development purposes. Moreover, the Norumbega land has the advantage of better access to established highways and a large portion of the lands are on either side of the Long

Island Railroad. It should also be noted that perhaps 30 acres of it lie within the village of Lynbrook and other large tracts are near Valley Stream. If we count the cash value of this property as $747,000 we get an average value of approximately $1,346 per acre. If this is a correct value for the Norumbega land there can be no doubt that the average value per acre of the land still held by the water company, viewed from the standpoint of its usefulness for general purposes, would be much less, probably no more than half as much per acre, or, say $673. The location of the Norumbega land in relation to the land retained by the water company is shown on the accompanying map entitled: "Map of lands of Queens County Water Company and Norumbega Company in Nassau County."

(3) The large parcel of land at Fenhurst upon which the Company's pumping station, well system and filters are located, was appraised in 1914 by Mr. Charles A. O'Malley, real estate expert of the Finance Department of the City of New York, at $600 per acre, giving a total of $150,240. The strip lying along the brooks, a triangular piece at Lynbrook, and certain other isolated parcels still held by the Water Company and amounting to 38.334 acres, were appraised at $1,500 an acre, except one plot of two acres north of the Merrick Road, which was appraised at $2,500 an acre. The total of Mr. O'Malley's valuations for the Nassau County lands was $209,741, giving an average for the entire area of $762 per acre. It should be noted that Mr. O'Malley's appraisal was based upon the price which, in his judgment, a willing buyer would pay a willing seller for this land for general real estate purposes. It did not take into consideration any special value for water purposes.

(4) The assessed valuations of the Company's real estate in Nassau County for each year from 1910 to 1914 inclusive are the same. Inasmuch as these assessments include the Norumbega land, the water company is compelled to make an adjustment every year as between its own holdings and the holdings of the land company in order to determine what portion of the taxes levied against the water company are properly chargeable to the Norumbega Company. This is a problem of extreme complexity. The following tabulation, giving lot numbers, acreage, assessment, assessment per acre and division of each lot as to acreage and assessment as between the water company and the land company, has been prepared from data furnished by the water company.

Oversized Foldout

TABLE 7—ADJUSTMENT OF REAL ESTATE ASSESSMENTS IN NASSAU COUNTY BETWEEN QUEENS COUNTY WATER COMPANY AND NORUMBEGA COMPANY

Lot No.	Total			Water Company		Norumbega Company	
	Acres	Assessment	Assessment per acre	Acres	Assessment	Acres	Assessment
1	3.0	$200.00	$66.67	3.0	$200.00	....	....
5	2.0	125.00	62.50	0.7	43.75	1.3	$81.25
7	5.0	350.00	70.00	4.3	301.00	0.7	49.00
8	10.0	2,800.00	280.00	....	......	10.0	2,800.00
9	24.0	22,000.00	916.67	....	......	24.0	22,000.00
11	8.0	4,100.00	512.50	....	......	8.0	4,100.00
28, 26	14.0	8,000.00	571.43	....	......	14.0	8,000.00
35, 36	6.0	1,600.00	266.67	0.2	53.33	5.8	1,546.67
38, 39, 40	40.0	18,000.00	450.00	3.0	1,350.00	37.0	16,650.00
41	9.0	3,800.00	422.22	0.3	126.67	8.7	3,673.33
42, 43, 44	46.0	14,500.00	315.22	2.3	725.01	43.7	13,774.99
45, 46	22.0	6,000.00	272.72	....	......	22.0	6,000.00
47	3.0	800.00	266.67	....	......	3.0	800.00
48	*	2,510.00	....	....	......	*	2,510.00
49, 50, 61	33.0	8,500.00	257.58	2.5	643.95	30.5	7,856.05
51, 52	47.0	13,000.00	276.60	1.0	276.60	46.0	12,723.40
Carried forward,	272.0	$106,285.00	......	17.3	$3,720.31	254.7	$102,564.69

* 33 lots.

TABLE 7—ADJUSTMENT OF REAL ESTATE ASSESSMENTS IN NASSAU COUNTY BETWEEN QUEENS COUNTY WATER COMPANY AND NORUMBEGA COMPANY—Continued

Lot No.	Total			Water Company		Norumbega Company	
	Acres	Assessment	Assessment per acre	Acres	Assessment	Acres	Assessment
Brought forward,	272.0	$106,285.00	......	17.3	$3,720.31	254.7	$102,564.69
52, 53	21.0	4,500.00	$214.29	....	......	21.0	4,500.00
53	2.0	800.00	400.00	....	......	2.0	800.00
54	4.0	250.00	62.50	....	......	4.0	250.00
55, 56	7.0	2,700.00	385.91	....	......	7.0	2,700.00
57	20.0	4,000.00	200.00	2.0	400.00	18.0	3,600.00
58	40.0	11,000.00	275.00	....	......	40.0	11,000.00
59	0.25	800.00	3,200.00	....	......	0.25	800.00
60	17.0	5,000.00	294.12	1.6	470.59	15.4	4,529.41
62	*	275.00	....	....	......	*	275.00
63	5.0	2,000.00	400.00	1.25	500.00	3.75	1,500.00
65	0.3	200.00	666.67	0.3	200.00	....	....
66, 67, 68	2.5	700.00	280.00	0.5	140.00	2.0	560.00
69	0.5	200.00	400.00	....	......	0.5	200.00
70	0.625	150.00	240.00	0.3125	75.00	0.3125	75.00
71	2.0	700.00	350.00	2.0	700.00	....	....
72, 73, 74	4.5	1,600.00	355.56	....	......	4.5	1,600.00
75	10.0	5,500.00	550.00	1.7	935.00	8.3	4,565.00
76	3.0	900.00	300.00	....	....	3.0	900.00
78	8.0	2,000.00	250.00	7.0	1,750.00	1.0	250.00
Carried forward,	419.675	$149,560.00	......	33.9625	$8,890.90	385.7125	$140,669.10

* 5 lots.

TABLE 7—ADJUSTMENT OF REAL ESTATE ASSESSMENTS IN NASSAU COUNTY BETWEEN QUEENS COUNTY WATER COMPANY AND NORUMBEGA COMPANY—Concluded

Lot No.	Total			Water Company		Norumbega Company	
	Acres	Assessment	Assessment per acre	Acres	Assessment	Acres	Assessment
Brought forward,	419.675	$149,560.00	......	33.9625	$8,890.90	385.7125	$140,669.10
79, 77	4.0	1,600.00	$400.00	1.0	400.00	3.0	1,200.00
81	6.0	1,600.00	266.67	....	....	6.0	1,600.00
82	6.0	3,500.00	583.33	....	....	6.0	3,500.00
84, 85, 86, 87, 88	20.0	15,343.00	767.15	....	....	20.0	15,343.00
89	34.0	20,000.00	588.24	4.1	2,411.78	29.9	17,588.22
90	7.0	5,500.00	785.71	0.3	235.71	6.7	5,264.29
91, 92	2.0	500.00	250.00	0.2	50.00	1.8	450.00
93	9.0	5,000.00	555.56	....	....	9.0	5,000.00
94	6.0	3,500.00	583.33	1.0	583.33	5.0	2,916.67
95	8.0	6,500.00	812.50	1.0	812.50	7.0	5,687.50
96	4.0	2,500.00	625.00	0.5	312.50	3.5	2,187.50
97	7.0	4,000.00	571.43	1.0	571.43	6.0	3,428.57
98	4.0	3,000.00	750.00	1.5	1,125.00	2.5	1,875.00
99	.5	900.00	1,800.00	....	....	0.5	900.00
100	4.0	3,500.00	875.00	0.3	262.50	3.7	3,237.50
101	.5	800.00	1,600.00	0.25	400.00	0.25	400.00
102	3.0	800.00	266.67	0.1	26.67	2.9	773.33
106	4.0	1,300.00	325.00	....	....	4.0	1,300.00
A	292.0	200,000.00	684.93	240.0	164,383.64	52.0	35,616.36
Total,	840.675	$429,403.00	*$507.48	285.2125	$180,465.96	555.4625	$248,937.04

* Not including lots Nos. 48 and 62 which are not assessed on an acreage basis.

This tabulation shows a total assessment of $180,465.96 against the real estate, including both land and improvements, held by the water company in Nassau County, excluding, of course, the franchise and mains in the public streets, which are separately assessed by the State Board of Tax Commissioners. The State Board in 1914 equalized this Company's special franchise assessments in Nassau County on the basis of 65% average valuation of other real estate in the vicinity for tax purposes as fixed by the local assessors. Taking this basis, the full value of the water company's lands, including pumping station and other improvements, would be approximately $276,000. On the basis of a 50% average assessment, as held by the Appellate Division in the equalization case, the value of this property would be approximately $361,000. On the basis of a 33 1/3% assessment, which Mr. Lord claims to be about the actual basis, the full value of this property would be approximately $541,000. It is to be noted that in fixing the value of this property for tax purposes the assessors are entitled to take into consideration all of the elements of value which the Company may claim. Certainly any special value which the land might have for the purposes of the water company which could legitimately be taken into consideration in fixing rates could also with propriety be considered by the assessors in fixing the value of the land for tax purposes. As already noted, the assessments in Nassau County are not made separately for the bare land and the improvements thereon. If we assume, therefore, that the assessed valuation is one-third of the full valuation, the full value would be $541,000. It is necessary to subtract from this figure the full value of the wells, filters, pumping station and its contents, suction and delivery pipes and other improvements, which are taken into consideration separately in our appraisal for rate fixing purposes. The full present value of these improvements, as determined by the engineers of the Department assigned to do this work under my supervision, is approximately $330,000. Subtracting this amount from the $541,000, we should have left about $211,000 as the value of the land alone.

Comparing the results of these four methods of arriving at the true value of the water company's present holdings in Nassau County we have the following:

On the basis of the Skilton valuation	$185,000.00
On the basis of the Norumbega transaction, with the adjustments above described	191,805.00
On the basis of the O'Malley appraisal	209,741.00
On the basis of the assessments corrected as above described	211,000.00
Average	$199,386.50

I shall assume $200,000 as the present value of the water company's Nassau County lands for general purposes.

It is to be noted that all valuations mentioned above refer to the entire amount of land held by the water company in Nassau County, not to the much restricted portion of this land which, in our judgment, is necessary and useful for the Company's business as a water supply corporation and which therefore must be taken into consideration in fixing rates. Moreover, none of these estimates is based in any degree upon the actual cost of these lands to the Company. They are all estimates of the present value in connection with a general appraisal of the Company's property on the basis of reproduction cost new less depreciation of those portions of the property which are depreciable. What the Company actually has invested in this land will be taken into consideration under a separate heading in our discussion of original cost.

It should also be noted that these estimates, with the possible exception of the one based upon assessments, do not take into consideration any special value of the land for water purposes over and above its general value as real estate. It does not appear that in a rate case the Company is entitled to an augmented value of its land on account of its special availability for the particular function to which it is devoted. Neither is it entitled to a valuation of its land based upon the theory that lands furnishing a substitute source of supply equally good could not be obtained except at an increased cost. The question of whether or not the Company should be allowed a separate value for its water rights so called, based upon the cost of litigation, negotiation and protection secured by contract will be considered separately later on. Here we have only to determine as to the fair present value of the portion of the Company's lands which, in our judgment, is useful and necessary for water purposes. The amount of land required we have determined to be approximately 60 acres. Its location has already been described. The elevation in the immediate vicinity of the pumping station and filters is about seven feet above high tide, but along the line of wells in either direction this elevation decreases to about two and a half feet. The average value per acre of the several estimates given above of all the Company's Nassau lands is $700. In my opinion, an estimate of $1,000 per acre for the 60 acres necessary for the Company's purposes would be liberal. I have, therefore, found the fair present value of the Company's Nassau County land, used and useful for the purposes of water supply, to be $60,000. This includes all special consideration of location and shape, but allows no added value on account of water. It assumes that the owner, having no other probable purchaser in sight who could use the land for water purposes, would be willing to sell it at the figure mentioned.

In regard to the value of the Company's land in Queens County we have the double check of the assessed valuations and the Finance Department's appraisal. The assessed valuations for the year 1914 for land alone aggregate $42,500. The Finance Department's appraisal of the same property, with the exception of the small lot on the north side of Crescent Avenue, was $55,750. Eliminating the single lot referred to from the comparison, we have an assessed value of $41,800 as compared with an appraisal of $55,750. On the basis of the appraisal the assessed value is approximately 75% of full value. In the equalization of special franchise assessments in Queens County for the year 1914 the State Board of Tax Commissioners assumed that local assessments of real estate generally in Queens County were 89% of full value. Under all the circumstances, including facts learned in connection with valuations in other portions of Queens, I am of the opinion that a valuation based upon the assumption of a 75% ratio in the assessments would certainly be fair to the Company, and in view of the elimination of portions of the property from consideration, also fair to the public. Taking the assessed valuation as a basis, therefore, and eliminating those portions of the Company's land not properly useful in connection with its water business, we get an assessed valuation of approximately $30,000. This calculation leaves out entirely lot 12 of block 13, the site of the former booster station, and a strip 100 feet wide along the southerly side of the Far Rockaway property, including lot 30, lot 37, and a projection between these two lots from lot 36. This 100-foot strip, with a frontage of about 244 feet on John Street, is occupied by four dwelling houses, to which reference has already been made. On the basis of an assessed valuation of approximately $30,000 I find, therefore, that the fair value of the water company's land in Queens County, used and useful for the purpose of its business, is $40,000. This is the estimated price the Company would have to pay to the owner in case of purchase, or the price that the Company could get for the land in case of sale for general purposes.

In the case of land acquired for a water plant, the reproduction cost theory, strictly applied, would take account of something more than the price paid to the former owner. Land-looking, surveys, experimentation, etc., preliminary to actual purchase, cost something. For these items I think that 10% additional on the assumed purchase price would not be excessive. It has been assumed that it would require two years for the reproduction of the pumping plant and buildings. It certainly would not be safe to go ahead with the construction of a pumping plant until all the lands necessary for the water supply and filters had been acquired. Portions of the Queens lands might not have to be acquired quite so long in advance, but it is fair to assume that all the land on the average would have to be held two years before the commencement of operation. Therefore, an additional allowance of 12% on the assumed purchase price might properly be allowed on account of interest during construction. Some question of the propriety of allowing these percentages on land might be raised by a reference to the opinion of Justice Hughes in the Minnesota Rate cases. There the value of railroad rights of way and terminal property had been estimated on the basis of the present value of the land for railroad purposes, and certain percentages had been added for engineering and interest during construction. Justice Hughes ruled out the special value on account of the purposes to which the land was put and also the percentages. These were rate cases pure and simple, and involved the appraisal of land devoted to a public use which tends to increase enormously the value of lands adjacent to the lands so used. This is not quite on all fours with the Queens County Water Company case where, in my opinion, the percentages should be allowed. No special value has been attributed to the land on account of the use to which it is put.

With the percentages added, the reproduction cost of the useful land in Nassau will be $73,200 and of that in Queens $48,800, making a total of $122,000.

The Company claims that all its present holdings in Nassau County are useful and necessary for its water supply business, but that even if only 60 acres were necessary at the present time, it would be entitled to an allowance for interest on the cost of its total holdings during the period when it would be experimenting for the proper location of its line of wells. It may be that in reproducing such a plant it would be found more economical to pick up a large tract quietly and then dispose of so much as was not needed after the wells were located. But if the land were acquired in this way it would probably cost less per acre than I have allowed, and the interest during the holding period would probably be made up in the profits at the time of sale. I am not satisfied that any additional allowance should be made on this account.

For the purpose of proving the Company's balance sheet it is necessary to ascribe values to the land excluded from the inventory of useful property. I estimate this portion of the Nassau lands at $140,000, and this portion of the Queens lands, including the dwelling houses, at $17,700. As to the Queens property, this is substantially the assessed valuation.

(b) **Well system and filters:**

The appraisal of the Company's well system, suction lines, infiltration gallery, "Meadow Reservoir," so called, etc., constituting the portion of the plant designed to preserve and develop the water supply in the ground and make it suitable for domestic consumption, was made under my supervision by William F. Laase, Assistant Engineer in charge of the Brooklyn Watershed, and Assistant Engineer John T. Metcalf. The methods pursued in arriving at their estimates are described in the report of the engineers, as follows:

"ESTIMATE OF DEEP AND SHALLOW WELLS.

"The estimated labor cost for driving deep wells was based upon the work of our well gangs and compared with contract prices for work under similar conditions of stratification and depth of well, and this cost for the shallow wells was based on our observation of actual work done by the maintenance gang in replacing a shallow well at the Fenhurst plant.

"To determine the depth of the wells, 22 were opened and examined and comparisons made with information secured from the Company; for the estimate the Company's information was used.

"Material cost was based on prices for delivery of similar material to our driven well section at Clear Stream, Long Island.

"For the life of the wells, the conditions as to the contents of iron and chlorine were compared with similar conditions at our line pumping stations.

"It was estimated that the life of a well was the life of the wrought iron pipe, or 25 years, but from experience in our well work it was apparent that the life of the wrought iron pipe (that is, 25 years) would be materially shortened by the presence of the iron and chlorine in the water, together with the combination of iron pipe and brass gauze of which the strainer in the shallow wells is made; this causes a galvanic action, which results in pitting the pipe and in breaking down the iron in the water to a suspended form which lodges in the strainer. Under these conditions the strainer would be so completely corroded in fifteen (15) years as to be of little or no use. This condition is modified by the system employed for cleaning by the maintenance gang. This is done by removing the well from the ground, remodeling and replacing it, which work, due to the excessive clogging of the strainer, has to be done at intervals of about three years. By replacing the affected parts when the well is cleaned, it is assumed that the life of these wells would be extended to twenty-five (25) years.

"The strainers in the deep wells are not covered with brass gauze.

"INFILTRATION GALLERY.

"This gallery consists of 1,600 feet of open trench with a concrete and brick receiving bay centrally located. The bay is connected to the station by means of a 20-inch steel riveted suction main. The estimate is made from the plan received from the Company the sections of the ditches being checked by means of cross sections of the existing conditions.

"For depreciation it was assumed that there would be no deterioration of the ditches, that the pipes could be replaced under a maintenance charge, and 100 years (the life of the masonry work) was therefore fixed as the life of the gallery. This, however, is modified by the effect of the operation of the driven wells, which causes the elevation of the ground water table to fall below the bottom of the ditches, so that no water could be obtained therefrom. The present value of nothing is therefore assigned.

"COLLECTING (MEADOW) RESERVOIR AND EMBANKMENT.

"This reservoir consists of an earthen embankment of about 1,000 feet in length constructed across the valley for the purpose of impounding fresh water, and is intended to prevent the influx of salt water to the driven wells at the station. Above the dam the stream beds were widened and deepened to remove the mud and silt from the sand, and it was proposed to maintain the fresh water in the reservoir at an elevation as high or higher than tide water, and thus shut off the influx of salt water by delivering fresh water through the sand in the stream beds.

"The reservoir would be called upon to perform this function, only at times when the operation of the wells had lowered the ground water for some distance from the station. Under these conditions, the flow of fresh water to the reservoir is intercepted by the wells, and if the ditches were free from silt the water would be lowered and the reservoir would cease to perform its function. If the ditches were allowed to silt up no fresh water would pass out of the reservoir to prevent the influx of salt water.

"In view of the foregoing it was decided that the reservoir was of little use and the only office performed would be by means of the dam to retard the flow of tide water over the marsh lands above the dam. A depreciation of 100 per cent. was therefore assigned to the reservoir and the dam or embankment retained as a separate item.

"SUCTION MAINS.

"The quantities used are the result of a survey of the entire system made to determine the lengths of the various sizes of pipes, thickness of castings, number of gates, special castings, etc.

"The unit prices for furnishing and laying the main were determined from the records of constructing our Gravesend, Canarsie and New Lots driven well stations.

"The depreciation applied is based on the life of the cast iron suction main, it being assumed that anything of a shorter life could be replaced on a maintenance charge. The mains installed are sufficiently large adequately to handle the available water, and no functional depreciation was assigned.

"PUMP WELL AND FILTERS.

"The quantities for this estimate were determined from plans and information furnished by the Company. The original plant, which consisted of Filters Nos. 1 and 2, pump well, drainage wells, etc., was constructed with masonry walls, floors, etc., of brick laid in Rosendale cement with a finishing coat of Portland cement mortar.

"Filter No. 3 is of later construction and the masonry work throughout is of Portland cement concrete.

"For depreciation a life of 100 years was assigned to the masonry work. It was assumed that this was the controlling feature as the depreciation of pipes, loss of sand, etc., could be replaced on a maintenance charge.

"No functional depreciation was applied because the work required of the filters in removing iron from the water does not exact such rigid conditions as are necessary for bacteriological work; a depreciation such as a loss of sand in cleaning, etc., would not materially affect the quantity or quality of the work performed."

The engineers estimated that a fair allowance for engineering and inspection would be 10% of the actual cost of the physical property itself. They estimated that the construction of the system would take about a year and a half, and accordingly interest at the rate of 6% for one-half that period was allowed. This would amount to 4½%, making a total of 14½% on physical cost for engineering, inspection and interest during construction.

In accordance with the methods above described, the present value, on June 30, 1914, of the "water supply sources and works," other than land, based on an estimate of reproduction cost new less depreciation, was found to be as follows:

Table 8—VALUE OF WATER SUPPLY SOURCES AND WORKS

Shallow wells at Fenhurst	$3,937.55	
Deep wells at Fenhurst	14,723.97	
Deep wells at Lynbrook	....	
Deep wells at Rockaway Park	5,821.20	
Infiltration gallery at Fenhurst	....	
Collection reservoir at Fenhurst	....	
Embankment for collection reservoir at Fenhurst	750.00	
Suction mains at Fenhurst	33,114.14	
Suction mains at Rockaway Park	261.71	
Pump well at Fenhurst	961.12	
Filters at Fenhurst	48,847.16	
Total		$108,416.85
Add 10 per cent. for engineering and inspection		10,841.68
Add also 4½ per cent. for interest during construction		4,878.76
Total present value		$124,137.29

I believe that the engineers' estimate of present value of the water supply sources and works is substantially correct, and therefore I find that the cost of reproduction new less depreciation of the wells, suction lines, filters and embankment is $124,137.

(c) **Buildings and mechanical equipment:**

The inventory and valuation of the buildings and mechanical equipment have been made by Assistant Engineer Thomas J. Gannon, who gave long and careful study to the problems involved in the valuation of these portions of the Company's plant, based upon his experience in charge of the mechanical division in the Department. His inventory was divided into thirteen sections, as follows: (1) boilers with foundations; (2) flues; (3) pumping units with foundations; (4) compressors; (5) water piping; (6) steam and auxiliary piping; (7) reciprocating steam auxiliaries; (8) electrical equipment; (9) coal storage; (10) standard railroad tracks, ties, rails, fastenings, etc.; (11) miscellaneous mechanical equipment; (12) buildings complete; (13) chimneys complete.

In each of these classes Mr. Gannon ascertained for each unit the following items: (1) life in years; (2) age; (3) estimated weight, where applicable; (4) cost to reproduce new; (5) estimated scrap value; (6) total use value, being the difference between cost to reproduce new and scrap value; (7) accrued physical depreciation in percentage of use value; (8) additional accrued depreciation due to obsolescence in percentage of use value; (9) total accrued depreciation in percentage of use value; (10) total accrued depreciation, amount; (11) present value, being the difference between cost new and total accrued depreciation; (12) amount of annual depreciation.

Mr. Gannon's apraisal was based upon a careful study of the actual condition of the plant and the circumstances of its operation. For example, although the life of a pumping unit under conditions of constant use to full capacity might not be more than fifteen years, Mr. Gannon estimated that under the special conditions prevailing in connection with this Company's plant, due in part to the extraordinary peak load carried during the summer months, and partly due to the fact that this Company's pumping plant has been developed considerably beyond the capacity immediately required for domestic service, even at the peak load, a fair estimate of life for the pumping units would be forty years. He estimated that the cost of engineering and inspection in connection with the installation of a plant such as this would be about 12% of the actual physical costs, and that a period of two years would be required to construct the buildings and install the machinery of such a plant, making necessary a total allowance of 6% for interest during construction. Accordingly, a sum equal to 18% of the physical costs was added for these overhead charges.

The present value, as of June 30, 1914, of the various classes of property included in Mr. Gannon's appraisal was found to be as shown in Table 9.

TABLE 9—VALUE OF BUILDINGS AND MECHANICAL EQUIPMENT

At Fenhurst:		
Boilers with foundations	$6,024.20	
Flues	327.00	
Pumping units	96,549.00	
Air compressors	300.00	
Water piping	2,992.00	
Steam and auxiliary piping, etc.	2,500.00	
Reciprocating steam auxiliaries	375.00	
Electrical equipment	244.00	
Coal storage	2,800.00	
Standard railroad tracks	3,340.00	
Miscellaneous mechanical equipment	876.00	
Buildings	39,065.00	
Chimneys	3,280.00	
Total		$158,672.20
At Rockaway Park:		
Boilers	$913.00	
Pumping units	2,106.00	
Steam and auxiliary piping	345.00	
Reciprocating steam auxiliaries	42.00	
Buildings	660.00	
Total		4,066.00
At Far Rockaway:		
Buildings	$15,922.00	
Chimneys	240.00	
Total		$16,162.00
At Arverne (abandoned booster station):		
Steam and auxiliary piping	$110.00	
Miscellaneous mechanical equipment	1,789.00	
Buildings	1,230.00	
Total		3,129.00
Grand total physical costs		$182,029.20
Add interest during construction at 6 per cent		10,921.75
Add engineering and inspection at 12 per cent		21,843.50
Total present value		$214,794.45

I believe that Mr. Gannon's methods in making this appraisal were sound and that his conclusion as to the present value of the property is correct. Accordingly, I find that the reproduction cost new less depreciation of the Company's buildings, chimneys, boilers, pumps and other mechanical equipment on June 30, 1914, was $214,794.

(d) **Distribution system:**

The inventory of the distribution system was taken and the appraisal made by Assistant Engineer Joseph Goodman. Inasmuch as the portion of the distribution system local to Nassau County would not in a strict sense enter into our calculations, either for the purpose of fixing rates in the Queens area or for the purpose of ascertaining the price which the City ought to pay if it acquired the portion of the distribution system in Queens, it was thought unnecessary to make a detailed appraisal of the local Nassau County mains and their appurtenances. The local mains, valves, valve boxes, hydrants, standpipes, meters and corporation cocks in Queens were separately inventoried and appraised. So also were the trunk mains through which water is delivered from the pumping station at Fenhurst into the local Queens distribution system at the City line. These trunk mains, being used for both the Queens and the Nassau services, had to be treated separately.

The methods pursued in making the appraisal are stated as follows in Mr. Goodman's report:

"ESTIMATED COST PER FOOT OF VARIOUS SIZES OF MAINS.

"The estimated cost per foot of the various sizes of mains was based upon average contract prices in the past five years. The cost of laying was based upon actual force accounts kept by the Department upon several contracts, with 20 per cent. added for superintendence and profit. The weight of pipe was checked at the time that cuts were made for examination of tuberculation.

"From the various contracts for laying mains and appurtenances in Brooklyn and Queens, entered into by the Department during the past five years, eight were selected at random, representing conditions as similar to those existing in the Fifth Ward of Queens as possible. The contract prices paid by the City upon these eight contracts varied from $2,818.87 to $153,482.35 and totaled $444,726.03. By applying the valuation figures to the contract quantities, the cost of all of the contracts would have exceeded the amount the City paid, the average excess of valuation figures over actual contract prices on all eight contracts being approximately 6.2 per cent.

"WATER MAINS, VALVES, HYDRANTS, METERS, ETC.

"The lengths, sizes and kinds of pipe, number and sizes of valves, valve boxes, hydrants, meters and corporation cocks, together with the dates of installation, were obtained from the records kept by the Company. These records are complete in every way back to the year 1905, are fairly good as far back as 1896, but prior to 1896 the compilation made by the Company in 1912 had to be relied upon.

"The number and location of hydrants were checked by an inspector of the Department. The lengths of the various sizes of mains were scaled from the distribution map furnished by the Company and tabulated street by street. The pipe as copied from the records and the pipe as scaled from the map compare as follows:

Size	Queens County		Nassau County	
	Scaled lengths	Company's records	Scaled lengths	Company's records
2 inches............	29,370 feet	42,831 feet	....	....
3 inches............	5,230 feet	5,530 feet	....	....
4 inches............	16,390 feet	29,054 feet	....	....
6 inches............	259,440 feet	259,001 feet	....	....
8 inches............	50,960 feet	51,688 feet	....	....
10 inches............	500 feet	501 feet	....	....
12 inches............	26,550 feet	26,801 feet	....	....
14 inches............	1,850 feet	1,856 feet	....	....
16 inches............	29,170 feet	30,513 feet	38,800 feet	38,804 feet
20 inches............	....	....	3,600 feet	3,718 feet
24 inches............	2,500 feet	2,249 feet	20,600 feet	20,646 fee

"There is a very close agreement between the two sets of figures except as to the 2-inch and 4-inch pipe. Since the discrepancy in the 4-inch pipe could not be accounted for by the Company, the scaled length for that particular size was used in the valuation figures. It is very likely that the hydrant connections were included by the Company in the linear feet of 4 inch pipe laid, and this would account for about 5,000 feet. These connections are included with the hydrants. All other figures of the Company were accepted as correct.

"All mains of the Company in Queens County 12 inches in diameter and larger, as well as the trunk mains in Nassau County which supply both Queens and Nassau Counties, were measured in the field to check the scaled distances.

"Valve boxes were opened at random throughout the system and the cover over the mains was found to average slightly over 3½ feet—ranging from 2 feet to 4 feet, with over 4 feet in few instances, and with the exception of about a mile of the 24-inch main in Nassau County over which the average cover is but one foot.

"The records as to dates when the pavements were laid are incomplete in the Bureau of Highways; nor did the Company have any data bearing upon that question. Taking into consideration the fact that streets which are now paved with brick, asphalt or asphaltic concrete were originally macadam, and that the Company endeavors to lay mains where possible in anticipation of paving, the assumption that streets equivalent to one-half of the mileage of mains were paved with macadam prior to laying of same, is certainly fair to the Company, if the value of pavements laid after the mains were installed is to be excluded. * * * * * *

"DEPRECIATION.

"The life of the various parts of the distribution system was assumed to be as recommended by the most recent authorities. In order to determine the reasonableness of these assumptions, an examination was made of the pipe in the ground.

"The pipe at half a dozen different places, in both wet and dry soil, laid 10, 20 and 27 years ago was uncovered, sections about three feet long cut out, the exterior and interior examined, size of tubercles was noted, the reduction in area caused by tubercles determined by actually measuring the volume of water displaced by the tubercles scraped from measured lengths of pipe, and depth of pitting obtained. The examination proved the water to be what might be termed tuberculating, due to its softness combined with the presence of free CO_2.

"The Queens County Water Company has cleaned a comparatively large amount of mains in recent years. An 8-inch main on the Boulevard near Beach 47th Street, laid in 1887 and cleaned in 1906, showed the exterior coating intact, the lower half of the interior entirely tuberculated and approximately three-quarters of the upper half covered with tubercles, the maximum height of tubercles being three-fourths inch. The soft metal beneath the tubercles from which the iron had been eaten away could be easily detected by cutting with a knife and extended to a depth of 0.06 of an inch. The tubercles took up 2.8 per cent. of the volume of the pipe, more than a pipe of the same age, subjected to similar conditions which had never been cleaned. It proved the experience of others that scraping will temporarily restore the carrying capacity of pipe, but must be repeated at frequent intervals. The process removes the coating, leaving the iron exposed to the action of the water, and cannot be considered as a means of prolonging the life of the pipe indefinitely.

"While the reduction in area of cross-section of the pipe by tuberculation does not indicate the large decrease in carrying capacity due to the rough surface of the tubercles, it may be compared with other specimens cleaned. An 8-inch main in the Borough of Brooklyn, cleaned in 1909, had its carrying capacity reduced 40 per cent. four years after cleaning (coefficient of discharge before cleaning, 18.8; immediately after cleaning, 63; four years subsequently, 38); this pipe was cut five years after cleaning and found to be tuberculated over the entire interior area to a maximum height of 1 inch, reducing the area of the pipe by 5.4 per cent. A 12-inch pipe cleaned at the same time had its carrying capacity reduced 38 per cent. four years after cleaning (coefficient of discharge before cleaning, 15; immediately after cleaning, 78; four years subsequently, 48); five years after cleaning it was cut and upon examination the same condition was revealed as in the 8-inch pipe; the tubercles reduced the area of cross-section by 4.4 per cent. Pitting in both pipes extended in spots to a depth of 7/16 inch after 67 years of service, out of a total thickness of ½ inch and 9/16 inch respectively for the two pipes.

"ENGINEERING AND INSPECTION.

"The average amount of work done, including materials furnished, on the distribution system of the Queens County Water Company, in both Queens and Nassau Counties, amounted to approximately $70,000 per year during the past two years; the average amount charged on the books of the Company for superintendence of construction during the same period was $3,666 per year, or 5.2 per cent. of the estimated cost; this included office work, since salaries of draughtsmen are charged to it.

"The average cost to this department for the preparation of plans, specifications and contracts for laying mains, including extended studies of the distribution system in all boroughs, during 1911, 1912 and 1913 was 1.8 per cent. of the total cost of the work actually placed under contract; the cost of the engineering and inspection on the work, approximately 7 per cent. of the contract price, and the cost of inspection of the materials at the shop a shade less than 1 per cent.; the total cost of engineering not exceeding 10 per cent.

"As the Company does not inspect material at the foundry, nor does it keep inspectors on the work, as it need not prepare plans with such elaborate detail as the City, its engineering and inspection should cost less than the City's.

"The inventory is practically complete and the unit prices cover all omissions; no expert engineering is required and litigation is charged elsewhere, hence 7½ per cent. would certainly be a fair allowance to the Company under the usual term of 'Engineering and Contingencies' for this part of its property, whatever method of valuation is adopted."

Mr. Goodman estimated that about two years should be allowed for the construction of the distribution system in Queens other than meters, and about eight months for the construction of the trunk mains in Nassau County. Assuming that the two-year period could be reduced by four months, or the equivalent of one winter season, it appeared to be proper to allow interest during construction at the rate of 6% for ten months, or a total of 5% so far as the Queens distribution system other than meters was concerned. For the trunk mains an allowance at the rate of 6% per annum for a period of four months, or a total of 2% was deemed proper. It was estimated that the installation of the meters could be accomplished within a period of one year and therefore only 3% was allowed for interest during construction as applied to meters.

One of the most interesting and important parts of Mr. Goodman's work was the determination of the unit costs per foot for laying the various sizes and types of pipe. When the Progress Society and other civic organizations of the Rockaways made a complaint against the Company's rates five years ago and a year later were denied relief by the then Commissioner, the attorney for these societies took exception to the valuation placed upon the water company's pipes, because it was far in excess of the valuation which the Company's own engineer had placed upon these pipes in connection with a tax proceeding. The Company's record on this point is still embarrassing in making a just appraisal. The Company claims that the figures presented in the tax case are not to be taken seriously as applicable to another purpose, namely, the fixing of rates or the determining of value for purchase purposes. While not fully appreciating these nice distinctions, upon investigation I was fully convinced that the unit prices used by the Company's engineer from 1900 to 1909 in the valuations submitted to the State Board of Tax Commissioners were altogether too low, certainly as compared with costs at the present time. Mr. Goodman, as stated in his report, based his valuation upon the actual observed costs on a considerable number of typical City contracts for laying water mains on the City's system under conditions as nearly like the conditions existing in the Rockaways as could be found. It is believed that these prices are fair and even liberal to the Company. At the same time a comparison with figures used in the Staten Island appraisals, in a recent Denver appraisal, and in reports of actual costs in St. Louis and Seattle, would seem to indicate that Mr. Goodman's prices are not excessive. The following table gives the unit prices, exclusive of pavement, of the different sizes and character of pipe used by Mr. Goodman; the unit prices used by the commission of engineers that valued the Staten Island water plants for municipal purchase in 1906; those reported by the Company in its tax reports; those used by Mr. Wegmann in his 1910 appraisal for the Department, based upon an estimate of original cost; those used by Mr. Wegmann in his 1913 appraisal for the Gaynor Commission, based on reproduction cost less depreciation; those used by the Fellows Committee of engineers in the appraisal of the Denver water works in 1914; and those shown by the record of cost of the St. Louis municipal water works.

TABLE 10—COMPARATIVE UNIT PRICES—WATER WORKS CONSTRUCTION—MAINS.

("C.I." means cast iron; "W.I." wrought iron, and "S.R." spiral riveted.)

Diameter and character of pipe	Goodman, Queens County Water Company 1914	Burr Commission, Staten Island Water Companies 1906	Queens County Water Company, Tax Reports 1899 to 1909	Queens County Water Company, Tax Reports 1910 to 1912	Queens County Water Company, Tax Reports 1913 and 1914	Wegmann, Original Cost Appraisal, Queens County Water Company 1910	Wegmann, Reproduction Cost Appraisal, Queens County Water Company 1913	Fellows Appraisal, Denver Water Company 1914	Allison Report, City of St. Louis, Actual Cost 1888-1912
1" W.I.	$0.21	$0.35	$0.14	$0.18	$0.20	$0.38	$0.20	....	....
1¼" W.I.	.24	....	.15	.18	.20	.41	.20	....	....
1½" W.I.	.26	.35	.20	.20	.22	.43	.22	....	....
2" W.I.	.32	.35	.24	.25	.28	.49	.28	....	....
2½" W.I.	.37	....	.30	.30	.35	.54	.35	....	....
4" W.I.	.52	.60	.40	.40	.50	....	.50	....	....
4" S.R.	.50	....	....	....	.50	....	.50	....	....
6" S.R.	.64	.55	....	....	.70	....	.70	....	....
3" C.I.	.47	....	.35	.38	.50	.63	.50	$0.51	$0.39
4" C.I.	.57	.60	.38	.40	.60	.69	.60	.66	.48
6" C.I.	.79	.80	.50	.60	.82	.90	.82	.90	.65
8" C.I.	1.07	1.10	.70	.95	1.07	1.31	1.07	1.27	.89
10" C.I.	1.40	1.50	.85	1.10	1.30	1.51	1.30	1.69	1.13
12" C.I.	1.68	1.80	1.00	1.20	1.60	2.16	1.60	2.00	1.41
14" C.I.	2.11	2.20	1.40	1.80	1.90	2.25	1.90	2.59	*2.03
16" C.I.	2.44	2.60	1.55	2.00	2.30	2.61	2.30	3.06	*2.03
20" C.I.	3.36	3.50	2.50	2.80	3.10	3.67	3.10	4.29	3.03
24" C.I.	4.37	5.00	....	4.10	4.40	4.70	4.40	5.64	....

* 15-inch; no 14-inch or 16-inch pipe in St. Louis.

The unit prices of valves and hydrants show a much smaller variation in the various estimates. I omit the figures of the Commission of Engineers that valued the Staten Island water plants, for the reason that their unit prices give "net value" at the time of the appraisal,—not reproduction cost new. The St. Louis and Denver figures on these items also are not available in comparable form. The following table, therefore, gives the unit prices on valves and hydrants used by Mr. Goodman, compared with the Company's unit prices in its tax reports and the unit prices used by Mr. Wegmann in his two appraisals.

Table 11—COMPARATIVE UNIT PRICES—WATER WORKS CONSTRUCTION —VALVES AND HYDRANTS.

Unit	Goodman Queens County Water Co. 1914	Queens County Water Co. Tax Reports 1899 to 1914	Wegmann Original Cost Appraisal Queens County Water Co. 1910	Wegmann Reproduction Cost Appraisal Queens County Water Co. 1913
1½" valve	$3.00	$5.00	.....	$4.00
2" valve	5.00	6.00	$4.00	5.00
3" valve	8.00	10.00	7.50	7.50
4" valve	12.00	11.50	10.00	10.00
6" valve	16.00	16.30	17.00	16.00
8" valve	23.00	23.00	26.00	23.00
10" valve	30.00	30.00	.....	32.00
12" valve	42.00	38.00	43.00	40.00
14" valve	65.00	60.30	64.00	66.00
16" valve	110.00	110.00	88.00	104.00
20" valve	150.00	170.00	135.00	168.00
24" valve	200.00	220.00	223.00	219.00
4" hydrant	40.00	35.00	30.00	36.00
4" hydrant cut in	55.00	.....	.....	47.00

Mr. Goodman assumed a life of 75 years for cast iron pipe from 24 in. down to 12 in. in diameter; a life of 60 years for 10 in. and 8 in. cast iron pipe; a life of 50 years for 6 in. and 4 in. cast iron pipe; a life of 33 1/3 years for 3 in. cast iron pipe; a life of 33 1/3 years for 6 in. spiral riveted pipe; a life of about 28 years for 4 in. spiral riveted pipe; and a life of 25 years for wrought iron pipe from 4 in. down to 1 in. in diameter. The shorter life assumed for the smaller sizes of pipe was based upon the fact that under many conditions the smaller pipes have to be replaced on account of inadequacy before they are worn out, and also on the fact that the smaller pipes are sooner clogged up on account of corrosion. Mr. Goodman assumed a useful life of 50 years for gate valves from 24 in. down to 10 in.; a life of 40 years for 8 in. and 6 in. gate valves, hydrants and standpipes; a life of 33 1/3 years for 4 in. and 3 in. gate valves and all meters; and a life of 25 years for 2 in. and 1½ in. gate valves.

The present value, as of June 30, 1914, of the local distribution system in the Queens area, as appraised by Mr. Goodman, was as shown in Table 12.

TABLE 12—VALUE OF DISTRIBUTION SYSTEM IN QUEENS.

Water mains	$326,644.00	
Valves, exclusive of hydrant valves	11,655.00	
Valve boxes and manholes, exclusive of hydrant valve boxes	2,674.00	
Corporation cocks	2,653.00	
Pavements replaced in laying mains	29,535.00	
Railroad crossings	840.00	
Standpipes	23,400.00	
Total		$397,401.00
Add 7½ per cent. for engineering and contingencies		29,805.00
Add also 5 per cent. for interest during construction		19,870.00
Total present value of distribution system other than hydrants and appurtenances, and meters		$447,076.00
Hydrants and connections	$20,132.00	
Hydrant valves	4,685.00	
Hydrant valve boxes	1,783.00	
	$26,600.00	
Add 7½ per cent. for engineering and contingencies	1,995.00	
Add also 5 per cent. for interest during construction	1,330.00	
Total for hydrants, hydrant valves, boxes and connections		29,925.00
Meters	$45,077.00	
Add 7½ per cent. for engineering and contingencies	3,381.00	
Add also 3 per cent. for interest during construction	1,352.00	
Total for meters		49,810.00
Grand total for local distribution system in Queens		$526,811.00

In connection with the appraisal of the distribution system in Queens two points require special attention. One is the matter of pavement over mains, and the other the assessment of the mains and their appurtenances for tax purposes.

The decision of the Court of Appeals in the Kings County Lighting case settles once for all in this state the rule as to pavement over mains in a rate case. A company is entitled to consideration for the cost of cutting through and replacing pavement that was in place when the mains were originally laid, but is not entitled to an allowance for pavement laid subsequent to the installation of the mains. The records of the Bureau of Highways with reference to the improvement of the streets in the Fifth Ward of the Borough of Queens are very imperfect, partly because many of these streets are still technically private streets or were improved by the land companies before being ceded to the City, and partly because incomplete records were turned over to the City by the incorporated villages that occupied the Rockaway peninsula prior to consolidation seventeen years ago. The water company has pursued the policy of laying its mains in advance of the paving of the streets as far as possible, and Mr. Goodman has assumed from the best data available that the macadam pavement was in existence when the mains were laid along one-half of the mileage. Upon this assumption, allowing for the disturbance of the street three feet in width, and estimating the cost of cutting through and replacing the macadam at 50 cents per square yard, we have allowed $36,919 for the cost new of pavement over mains laid before the mains were laid. It is estimated that this pavement is subject to a depreciation of 20%, which is about the average rate of depreciation for the mains themselves. This brings the paving allowance down to $29,535, which with the percentages added for engineering and contingencies and interest during construction, makes a total of $33,227. This is believed to be liberal to the Company on the basis of the rule laid down by the Court of Appeals. Note should be made of the fact that in Mr. Wegmann's appraisal for the Gaynor Commission as of January 1, 1913, he allowed, including overhead charges, the sum of $145,569.30 on account of repaving over mains of the Company's entire system. Mr. Goodman found that the amount of paving in place prior to the laying of mains in Nassau County was so small as to negligible.

In regard to the assessments, it is to be noted that in Queens since 1905 the mains laid in private streets have been assessed by the City Department of Taxes and Assessments as "real estate of corporations." The mains in public streets have been assessed as a part of the "special franchise" by the State Board of Tax Commissioners. The special franchise assessments include all permanent fixtures in the streets as well as the intangible right to occupy the streets. A combination of the special franchise assessment and of the local assessment for "real estate of corporations" ought to cover all portions of the distribution system in Queens except standpipes and meters. The mains, valves, valve boxes, hydrants and corporation cocks are fixtures in the streets. The following table shows these assessments from 1905 to 1914, inclusive:

TABLE 13—SPECIAL FRANCHISE ASSESSMENTS.

YEAR	Special Franchise Assessment	Real Estate of Corporations Assessment	Total Assessment of Tangible and Intangible Values in Public and Private Streets
1905	$190,000	$6,000	$196,000
1906	216,000	6,500	222,500
1907	240,000	6,750	246,750
1908	300,000	5,750	305,750
1909	275,000	7,750	282,750
1910	250,000	7,750	257,750
1911	250,000	7,750	257,750
1912	222,500	30,000	252,500
1913	222,500	35,000	257,500
1914	231,400	35,000	266,400

The present value of the local distribution system in Queens, less meters and standpipes, was found by Mr. Goodman to be $450,676, while the combined assessments for the year 1914, including franchise value, amount to only $266,400. For many years the Company persistently fought its special franchise tax assessments, and evidently it succeeded in getting these assessments reduced far below the actual value of the physical property alone. The Company has constantly maintained that the intangible portion of its "special franchise," as defined in the law, has no value whatever. The total assessment being only 59.2% of the present value of the physical property as found by our appraisal, we are in a position to give enthusiastic support to the Company's claim that its intangible franchise has no value.

A separate valuation of the three trunk mains leading from the Company's main pumping station in a southwesterly direction to the City line and thence into the Queens area was necessary for the reason that these trunk mains are used to supply most of the water delivered into the Queens distribution system. They are also used for the transportation of most of the water delivered into the local distribution system in Nassau County. It was necessary, therefore, to make as careful an examination and appraisal of these mains as of the mains in Queens in order to arrive at a value to be apportioned between the services in the two districts. The reproduction cost new, less depreciation, of these mains and their appurtenances, as found by Mr. Goodman, was made up as follows:

TABLE 14—VALUE OF TRUNK MAINS IN NASSAU COUNTY.

24-inch main, with valves, gear cases, air valves, valve boxes and railroad crossings, including an extra allowance for wet excavation	$89,661.00	
Add 7½ per cent. for engineering and contingencies	6,725.00	
Add 2 per cent. for interest during construction	1,793.00	
Total for 24-inch main		$98,179.00
20-inch and 16-inch mains, with valves, etc	$87,793.00	
Add 7½ per cent. for engineering and contingencies	6,584.00	
Add 2 per cent. for interest during construction	1,756.00	
Total		96,133.00
Grand total for all trunk mains in Nassau County		$194,312.00

In the appraisal of the local distribution system in the Nassau County area it was not necessary to make the same minute examination as in the case of the Queens mains. The mileage of mains was scaled from the maps, and was found to correspond so nearly with the figures furnished by the Company that the latter were taken. The same unit prices used in the valuation of the Queens distribution system were applied and an average depreciation of 20% was deducted. While the mains in Nassau County are not on the average as old as the mains in Queens County, yet the small sized mains, which have a shorter life, constitute a much greater proportion of the local Nassau system than of the local Queens system. It appeared to be sufficiently accurate, therefore, to apply the same general percentage of accrued depreciation to the Nassau mains as had been applied in the case of the Queens mains. Upon this basis the present value of the local distribution system in Nassau County was made up as follows:

TABLE 15—VALUE OF LOCAL DISTRIBUTION SYSTEM IN NASSAU COUNTY.

Mains, valves, hydrants, etc., cost new	$333,893.00	
Less 20 per cent. for depreciation	66,779.00	
	$267,114.00	
Add 12½ per cent. for engineering, contingencies and interest during construction	33,389.00	
		$300,503.00
Corporation cocks (no depreciation)	$1,667.00	
Add 12½ per cent. for engineering, contingencies and interest during construction	208.00	
		1,875.00
Meters, cost new	$31,640.00	
Less 18 per cent. for depreciation	5,695.00	
	$25,945.00	
Add 10½ per cent. for engineering, contingencies and interest during construction	2,724.00	
		28,669.00
Grand total present value of local distribution system in Nassau County		$331,047.00

Combining the values of the local distribution systems in Queens and Nassau and the trunk mains, with their appurtenances, I find the total present value of the entire distribution system as of June 30, 1914, on the basis of reproduction cost new less depreciation, to be as follows:

Queens local distribution system	$526,811.00
Nassau County trunk mains	194,312.00
Nassau local distribution system	331,047.00
Total present value of distribution system in both counties	$1,052,170.00

(e) **Supplies, tools and miscellaneous equipment:**

Under this heading Assistant Engineer Joseph Ryan, with the assistance, on certain items, of appraisers from the Comptroller's office, made an inventory and appraisal of all the items of the Company's property necessary and useful in its business, but not incorporated into its physical
sary and useful in its business, but not incorporated into its physical
plant. The inventory includes pipe supplies, hydrants and meters in

stock, machinery, tools, office furniture and fixtures, automobiles, horses, etc. Mr. Ryan's appraisal of the items above described is summarized as follows:

TABLE 16—VALUE OF SUPPLIES, TOOLS AND MISCELLANEOUS EQUIPMENT.

ITEM	Reproduction cost new	Amount of accrued depreciation	Present value
Stock and equipment—stable and office yard	$5,318.45	$3,544.70	$1,773.75
Cast iron pipe, B. & S.	9,301.05	....	9,301.05
Cast iron specials, B. & S.	2,767.66	....	2,767.66
Universal pipe and fittings	106.03	....	106.03
Flexible joint pipe	480.00	240.00	240.00
Cast iron pipe flanged	2,389.94	....	2,389.94
Cast iron pipe flanged specials	1,607.29	....	1,607.29
Wrought iron pipe and fittings	2,773.18	277.32	2,495.86
Wet connections specials	879.90	....	879.90
Steel riveted flanged pipe	4,318.00	4,318.00	....
Globe specials	1,536.87	....	1,536.87
Gates, manhole heads and covers and hydrant gate boxes	1,385.90	138.59	1,247.31
Hydrants and hydrant repairs	931.50	....	931.50
Meters and meter repairs	6,484.61	....	6,484.61
Machinery	4,606.15	921.23	3,684.92
Tools	1,949.41	292.41	1,657.00
Supplies	2,765.53	....	2,765.53
Brass goods	2,514.49	....	2,514.49
Furniture and office fixtures	8,332.93	1,835.58	6,497.35
Farm stock and equipment	4,242.00	2,725.00	1,517.00
Total	$64,690.89	$14,292.83	$50,398.06

Stores and miscellaneous equipment fluctuate a good deal from month to month, and the difficulties in the way of an accurate inventory and appraisal are very considerable. But for the purposes of this case, I find their present value as of June 30, 1914, to be $50,398, which is believed to be a fair figure for average conditions.

(f) **Franchise value:**

The discussion of the question of franchise value was greatly simplified in this case by the fact that the Company laid no claim for it as a separate element of value. In fact, the Company has consistently maintained that its intangible franchise is of no special value. As already stated in a previous section of this report, the Company has succeeded in persuading the State Board of Tax Commissioners to assess its "special franchise" at less than the actual present value of the physical property in the streets. The Company's renunciation of an intangible franchise value is based in part upon its claim that it has never earned a fair return upon its investment, and in part upon the theory that, being subject to public regulation of rates, it will never be permitted to earn more than a fair return.

The Company's franchise is not exclusive. The City need not buy it in order to get the right to go into the water business in the Fifth Ward of Queens. On the other hand, from the standpoint of rate fixing there appears to be nothing in the history of this Company that would bring it within the rule laid down by the United States Supreme Court in the Consolidated Gas case, as this Company has never been consolidated and has never issued securities against a valuation of its franchises specifically authorized by law, as the Consolidated Gas Company did.

If the Company's property were to be taken over by the City in condemnation proceedings or in any other manner involving a forced sale on the part of the Company, then doubtless some consideration might be given to the value of the franchise even under the peculiar conditions affecting this Company. A strict working out of the theory of reproduction cost would also call for some allowance for the franchise. It is well known that under the procedure now required by the Greater New York Charter and the rules of the Board of Estimate and Apportionment, the cost of acquiring a new franchise is considerable. Indeed, it is extremely doubtful whether a new water franchise could be obtained from the City of New York at the present time under any conditions or for any price.

But the reproduction cost theory has to be modified and limited in various ways, and in view of the fact that the Company lays no claim to special franchise value, it seemed unnecessary to give it further consideration in this appraisal.

(g) **Going value:**

The matter of going value presented considerable difficulty, both because the method of estimating going value for any purpose is not very well established, and because in this particular case both rate-fixing and possible purchase are involved.

The theory that going value is to be included in the valuation of a public utility for purchase, unless it is excluded by contract or ignored in the voluntary negotiations, is well established. In the case of the **National Water Works Company v. Kansas City,** 62 Fed. 863, Mr. Justice Brewer defined going value as the difference between the actual reproduction cost of the physical plant and the value of the plant with its connections established and actually doing business. This is a leading case where the question of municipal purchase under contract is concerned. The actual allowance for going value appears to have been about 10% on the reproduction cost less depreciation of the physical property. The definition laid down by Justice Brewer has been applied with more or less consistency in numerous purchase cases during the last twenty years, but since the establishment of public service commissions for the regulation of rates, the definition of going value and the method of estimating it for a rate case have been thrown into great confusion. This has resulted from the tendency of the commissions and courts in later years to revert wherever possible to actual cost, or original investment, as the basis for determining the rates which a public service corporation shall be entitled to charge. In many jurisdictions decisions have been rendered to the effect that going concern value is not a proper element to be given separate consideration in a rate case, and this issue has not yet been clearly determined by the United States Supreme Court. In the State of New York, however, since the decision of the Court of Appeals in the Kings County Lighting case, 210 N. Y. 479, the recognition of going value in a rate case has been fully established. Though there was some doubt in the Court's mind as to the method by which going value should be measured, yet the Court's inclination was to define it according to the general principle followed by the Wisconsin Railroad Commission and the New Jersey Board of Public Utilities by which "going value" is practically an interchangeable term for "development expenses." Under the New York decision it would appear that in cases where the Company has earned a fair return upon its legitimate investment from the beginning of the business, or where early losses have been fully recouped by excessive earnings in later years, no going value should be allowed. This New York decision applies to a rate case, and we have no clear guidance as to how the New York courts would have going value estimated in a purchase case. As a result of this confusion, coupled with the fact that the valuation of a portion of the Queens County Water Company's property is for the purpose of fixing a price at which the City may take over the Queens distribution system and business, while the valuation of the remainder of the property is merely for the purpose of determining the investment upon which the Company is entitled to earn a fair rate of return pending the purchase by the City of the distribution system within the City limits, it has seemed best to make an estimate of the going value of the entire property in its present condition on the general basis approved by Justice Brewer in connection with a purchase case. In a later section the matter of development expenses or cost of establishing the business will be considered separately as a part of the estimate of the Company's actual investment, which for the purpose of this report, will be used to check the present values arrived at on the basis of reproduction cost new less depreciation.

In my conferences with the Company the latter maintained that it was entitled to a separate allowance of value for

(1) Promotion and organization;
(2) Financial arrangements;
(3) Water in the ground and watershed rights;
(4) "Happy outcome";

(5) Pavement over mains;

(6) Working capital.

After very extended consideration it seemed best to treat all of these elements so far as they are allowable at all as combined in the single item of going value, broadly defined. It will be necessary, however, to discuss the separate items in order to determine in what way they entered into the final conclusion.

(1) Promotion and organization:

The Company maintained that a separate allowance should be made for promotion and organization as a necessary cost in the establishment of a public utility business. In fact, in the readjustment of some of the items going to make up the balance sheet where the cost of the original plant on the Rockaway peninsula was given at a figure higher than the estimated cost of the assets traceable to this cost, the Company had arbitrarily charged the sum of $5,000 to organization and promotion. In addition to this, the Company called attention to the fact that the DuBoises, who were the controlling stockholders for many years and who secured the services of the late Franklin B. Lord for the purchase of the Valley Stream lands and the promotion of the Company's interests through a period of years, had paid Mr. Lord about the year 1901 or 1902 by the sale to him of 1,000 shares of stock at 25 and 50 shares at 20, making a total discount of $79,000 from the par value of the shares sold. This amount the Company claimed as an actual element of cost to the stockholders in the promotion and organization of their present successful business. This transaction was entirely between the DuBois family as the owners of the Company's stock and Mr. Lord and does not appear in any way upon the Company's books. The Company suggested to me that about $40,000 would be a proper allowance for promotion and organization on the basis of cost of reproduction. After full consideration I determined not to make a separate allowance, deeming that it was in part covered by the allowance already made for engineering and contingencies, and for the rest would be taken care of in connection with the valuation of the Company's financial arrangements, which will next be considered.

(2) Financial arrangements:

The Company called attention to the fact that the $667,000 of bonds now outstanding issued at par a few years ago could not have been issued at par except as a part of a special financial arrangement which the peculiar circumstances of the Company enabled Mr. Baldwin to make. The $500,000 of first mortgage bonds previously outstanding were subject to call at 110, and when it became necessary to refund the Company's obligations Mr. Baldwin found that the DuBoises were anxious to sell their stock, and that by finding them a purchaser for the stock at a good figure he could induce them to take the new bonds at par. The cost of the shift from first mortgage to general bonds as carried on the books is therefore limited to the $50,000 premium paid for the retirement of the first mortgage bonds, and an item of $14,847 attributed to "bond expense." The Company maintained that its present financial arrangements were particularly advantageous and that their present value was at least what it cost. This would have meant an allowance of $64,847 for bond discount and expenses, without taking into consideration various items charged under this heading in connection with earlier bond issues no longer outstanding. The real issue seemed to be whether or not, in a new enterprise reconstructed under present conditions so far as the development of the area of supply, the earnings and the rates are concerned, with all of the elements of safety and of danger entering into the Company's present situation, it would be necessary to allow bond discounts as a separate item of expense in securing the money required to reproduce the property and business. It is to be noted that the Company's outstanding bond issue of $667,000 bears interest at 5%. These bonds represent a trifle less than 40% of the value of the physical property as found in this appraisal. It was alleged that in the existing condition of the bond market such bonds would have to be sold at a discount of eight or ten points. On the other hand, it appears that since June, 1911, the Company has been paying annual dividends of 8% upon all of the shares of its capital stock outstanding aggregating a par value of $1,050,000. Prior to 1911 6% dividends were paid for 2½ years and prior to that 5% dividends for two years. At the last known sale of any considerable number of shares of the Company's stock, the price realized was 127. This sale is said to have taken place prior to the transfer of a large portion of the Company's land to the Norumbega Company at a substantial reduction from its true value. The amount of the loss in that transaction of which we can be certain from the Company's records is $127,000. Applied to the par value of the stock outstanding this would mean a loss of about twelve points, which, on the basis of the 127 price, would bring the value down to 115. The price of 127 was realized just at the time when the Company was beginning to pay 8% dividends. True, this was also at the time when the Company was selling to the City a large amount of water under the Brooklyn Contract, so called, and thereby adding to its earnings, but the loss of the Brooklyn Contract has already been made up by the increase of domestic consumption. The Company has continued to pay 8% dividends and it is unlikely that its stock, in case its present financial arrangements and earnings were reproduced in connection with the reproduction of its physical property, would sell for less than 115. At that rate the premium realized on the sale of its stock would be over $150,000 to offset a possible discount of $60,000 or $70,000 in the sale of its bonds. This margin seems to be ample to cover whatever element of promotion and organization cost might otherwise be claimed, not already included in engineering and contingencies, and to completely eliminate from further consideration any possible value to the property resulting from the Company's present financial arrangements. After full consideration, the Company conceded this point, admitting that whatever value these arrangements may have is a value going to the stockholders and not to the enterprise as such.

(3) Water in the ground and watershed rights:

The Company was disposed to claim a separate large but unmeasured value for water in the ground. Mr. Baldwin cited the precedent of the purchase of the private water companies on Staten Island effectuated by the City a few years ago and suggested that an estimate be made of the value of the Queens County Water Company's water in the ground on the same basis. I maintained, however, that the Staten Island precedent was not at all in point inasmuch as the committee of engineers in that case found a limited supply which the City was to purchase and which the City could not secure from other sources except on the basis of a monopoly value of $70 per million gallons delivered in the mains. I pointed out that the advent of Catskill water will remove the only possible purchaser of the Company's water other than the Company's own consumers. The City is not asking to purchase this water and nobody else is at all likely to want it. Accordingly, it would have been futile to attempt to make an estimate of its value upon the precedents of the Staten Island purchases. Moreover, I maintained that from the standpoint of rate fixing it would be wholly inadmissable to require the consumer who is buying the water to pay a price for it in excess of the cost of delivering it plus a fair profit to the Company on such cost.

The Company suggested that a comparison of the cost of development of the City's Brooklyn watershed property in relation to the amount of the daily supply available, with the cost of the Company's watershed on the same basis, would throw an interesting side light upon the real value of the Company's water supply. Accordingly, an inquiry was made as to the cost of the development of the Brooklyn watershed outside of Brooklyn itself and not including the aqueduct, the 72-inch pipe line, filters, storage reservoirs or pumping plants designed to lift the water a second time. On this basis the cost was estimated by the engineers of the Department as follows:

	Portion in use Jan. 1, 1915	Total including abandoned portion
Cost of lands	$774,800.00	$829,600.00
Cost of development	4,941,400.00	6,337,200.00
Total	$5,716,200.00	$7,166,800.00

The safe yield of the Brooklyn watershed is about 135 million gallons daily. Therefore, on the basis of the foregoing estimate, the cost of developing this watershed was $42,280 per million gallons daily capacity, if we count the cost of only that portion of the water supply still in use in 1914, and $53,010 per million gallons daily, if we take the cost of the entire development including the portion now abandoned. On this basis, the reproduction cost value of the Queens County Water Company's development, with a safe daily capacity of twelve million gallons, would be $507,360. This would include water bearing lands necessary for the Company's supply and the wells and suction lines now in use. If we turn now to our appraisal, we find that these elements of the Company's property could be reproduced now for about $180,000. If to this were added the value of the land held by the Company in Nassau County on the claim that it is necessary for the protection of its water supply, we should get a total of approximately $320,000, or a rate of $26,667 per million gallons of the Company's development as opposed to the rate of $42,280 in the case of the Brooklyn supply. These figures would tend to show that as compared with the Brooklyn watershed the Company's watershed is an economical development, and this fact might possibly lead to a valid claim for some allowance on this score if the City were seeking to purchase the Company's supply, which it is not. In fact the twelve million gallons per day corresponds to an actual annual consumption of less than three million gallons per day and an actual maximum load, aside from the peak reached for a very short time during a few days of the summer, of not more than six million gallons. Under these circumstances, while the comparison is interesting, it does not have any direct bearing upon the Company's claim for an allowance of value on account of the water in the ground. Accordingly, it seemed unnecessary from any point of view to make an allowance in this appraisal for the alleged value of the Company's water in the ground, which, as is well known, goes to waste when it is not used and is replenished from time to time by the operation of natural forces.

The Company maintained, however, that aside from the value of the water as such, it was entitled to consideration of the value of its watershed rights which it had acquired by means of expensive litigation and negotiations. It claimed that the purchase of the land subsequently sold to the Norumbega Company was made necessary by the City's threatened attack upon its water supply, and that the interest and taxes on this investment up to the time when the land was sold, as well as the entire expense of litigation and negotiations in connection with the whole proceeding, constituted an element of cost properly attributable to watershed rights and reflected in their present value. Generally speaking, the watershed protection which the Company has secured consists of the contract with the City under which the City has agreed not to invade its watershed except for the pumpage of a definitely limited amount; restrictions imposed by contract on the purchasers of the Norumbega property, and the enactment a few years ago of the law requiring the consent of the State Conservation Commission before one company or municipality can invade a watershed against the protest of another company or municipality already using it for a public supply.

It was comparatively easy for the Company to show an expense of $150,000 or more, figured on the basis referred to above, as the cost of its present watershed rights. It was pointed out, however, that in estimating the cost legitimately chargeable under this heading, consideration must be given to the Norumbega transaction in which the Company underwent a voluntary loss. I maintained that if the Company was justified in acquiring this land for the protection of its consumers, then when other provision had been made for the protection of these rights the Company was bound to dispose of the property upon the best basis possible and give the water enterprise and its consumers the benefit of any advance in the value of the land over its original cost. Moreover, the deciding factor in the appraisal of the Company's existing watershed rights is not their original cost but their present value. Upon this basis it appears that the advent of Catskill water, the removal of the City as a possible competitor for the Company's supply, and other conditions that have arisen since the cost was incurred have greatly depreciated the value of the protection secured. Fortifications are unnecessary unless there is some possibility of attack. Accordingly, it seemed proper, even giving full consideration to the recent decision of the United States Supreme Court in the California case, **San Joaquin and Kings River Canal & Irrigation Company v. Stanislaus County, et al.,** 233 U. S. 454, not to accord to the Company's watershed rights anything more than a nominal value. This will contribute to the general item of going value, on the assumption that the water lands and wells have been tested and the water supply has passed the experimental stage.

(4) "Happy outcome":

The Company made a claim that some allowance should be made for its successful experimentation in the selection of a site for its pumping station, in the location of wells and in the testing of its pumps and boilers. This allowance was vaguely described as "happy outcome." No definite figures were put forward and it seemed useless to attempt to separate this item, even if we conceded that it was to be taken into consideration. It is admitted by the City's engineers that the Company's location is a good one and that its station is fairly well adapted to the demands upon it. If the station were to be located over again, with the Company's present experience it would not be put in exactly the place where it is now, and it may be said of the pumps that they are adapted to a full load rather than to the light load for which they are now being used. If the City had continued to take water under the Brooklyn Contract well up to the limit of the Company's available supply in excess of the demands of domestic consumption and fire protection, the station would have been much better adapted to the conditions confronting it than it now is. Accordingly, while the claim for "happy outcome" is not altogether unreasonable, there is no adequate basis for making any other allowance on this score than the general allowance contained in the broad term "going value." This item has been treated accordingly.

(5) Connections, easements and pavement over mains:

The Company stoutly maintained that in a condemnation case the cost of relaying pavements laid since the water mains were put down would be allowed by the court on the theory that in constructing a competing plant the City would now be put to the cost of cutting through the existing pavements. This principle cannot be put forward as having been completely adjudicated, yet it seems that the reasoning of the New York Court of Appeals in the Kings County Lighting case would naturally be extended, in this State at least, to a condemnation case. On this theory the City would not be compelled to pay for the pavement laid at its own cost or at the cost of the abutting owners and without any expense to the Company. The Company suggested, however, that irrespective of the justice of its claim in regard to pavements, the existence of the pavements in their present condition was a valuable protection against competition. It also pointed out that many of the "streets" of the Rockaway peninsula are not yet public streets in the full sense of the word, and that the Company has secured private easements in many cases exclusive in form under which it maintains its distribution system. This state of facts would also tend to increase the cost to the City or any other Company of laying a competing system. Furthermore, the connections with this Company's mains are all made and practically all the houses in the district are supplied with plumbing fixtures and depend upon water under pressure. It was estimated that the cost of making these connections, to say nothing of the interior plumbing, had been about $350,000 to the property owners, and that this investment having been made in conjunction with the Company's own investment added a certain amount of protection and consequently of value to the Company's own plant. There can be no question that these conditions are a great protection to the Company against any competitor who might otherwise desire to enter its territory. It is to be noted, however, that this very protection which the Company claims as an added element of value gives stability to its investment and materially diminishes the perils and alarms to which it has so frequently and so eloquently called attention in the last ten or fifteen years. In other words, the added value resulting from the pavements, the easements and the connections largely goes to reduce the rate of return to which the Company can justly lay claim upon its investment. Moreover, in a rate case it is not permissible to capitalize the artificial monopoly value which the Company may enjoy by reason of such advantages. Certainly the private consumer ought not to be penalized because he has gone to the expense of putting the plumbing in his house and making connection with the Company's mains by which the Company is enabled to do a profitable business.

When it comes to a question of purchase by the City, it also seems inadmissible for an allowance to be made for this monopoly value, especially in a case like the present one where the City is endeavoring to give the Company all possible security and thereby get for the consumers a reduction in rates to approximate in some degree the rates at which the City furnishes water to its citizens in other places. As already stated, there is considerable precedent for the allowance in a purchase case of an intangible value based upon the fact that the distribution system is a going concern. This rule does not seem to be exactly applicable to the present case so far as the fixing of the price at which the City might purchase the physical property is concerned. As a matter of fact, if the City acquired the Queens portion of the distribution system with connections, the revenues from minimum rates and metered water, which in 1914 amounted to $161,358, would immediately fall at City rates to about $63,000, unless the City scrapped the meters which it had purchased. In fact, the extension of City water to the Rockaways under the existing City rates, with the meters retained, would be very unprofitable for the reason that the City is not now entitled to charge a minimum rate and a great many of the consumers in the Rockaways remain there only a few weeks or months in the summer time. On the other hand, if the City were to throw out the meters and put into effect the existing frontage rates, the charges would probably exceed somewhat the Company's existing minimum rates, but might not be any greater than the revenues derivable under City meter rates without a minimum charge. This latter point could not be definitely ascertained without a complete survey of the buildings in the Fifth Ward of the Borough of Queens, which has not been undertaken. It seems, therefore, that from the standpoint of purchase, if the City allowed a going value for the Company's business in the Rockaways, it would not represent so much a value to be acquired by the City as a value to be taken away from the Company. Nevertheless, there is a sense in which it could be said that the City would be acquiring a real value by the acquisition of the Company's mains under existing pavements and connected with the existing houses for service. That is to say, the mains so laid and the distribution system so connected would represent to the City less of a loss than would be incurred if modern pavements had to be cut through and new connections made.

(6) Working capital:

The Company pointed to its balance sheet and declared that it was necessary to carry a large amount of working capital to offset the accounts due and unpaid and to provide enough cash for the conduct of the current business. On May 31, 1914, the amount of cash on hand and in bank was $13,166.21, and the amount of water rates, hydrant rentals, etc., due and unpaid was $62,091.02. These two items together, making a total of about $75,000, were put forward by the Company as a rough measure of the amount of working capital required. On the other hand, it was pointed out that the minimum rates charged by the Company are payable in advance for the year. The amount of the minimum rates for the year ending May 31, 1914, was about $93,000. In the case of permanent consumers the minimum rates, though due in advance, are not all collected in advance, and in the case of new consumers the rates are payable at any time during the year when the service begins. It was also pointed out that the Company carries a large fund for meter deposits and for extension guarantees, which might be treated as working capital supplied by the consumers. The amount of the extension guarantees on May 31, 1914, was $38,215.65 and the amount of meter deposits on that date was $28,485, making a total of $66,700.65. On the extension guarantees the Company is not liable for interest. On the meter deposits, while it is nominally liable for interest, the amount of interest actually paid has thus far been a negligible quantity and has been treated as an offset to interest revenue.

After full consideration it seemed clear that on the basis of its present practices the Company is not entitled to an allowance for working capital, this capital being supplied in sufficient amount by the consumers themselves in the form of minimum rates paid in advance, extension guarantees and meter deposits. Moreover, if these sources of working capital should prove to be inadequate to supply the necessary cash for the conduct of the business and to carry the accounts due and unpaid, it seemed much more reasonable that the Company's rules should be modified so as to impose a penalty or an interest charge upon the consumers in arrears. The City imposes a penalty of 5% when the water rates are three months past due, and a further penalty of 10% when they are six months past due. A similar practice or the practice of adding interest at current rates on all past due accounts would make it unnecessary for the Company to claim a special provision for working capital on account of these unpaid bills. Such a practice would be reasonable and would tend to facilitate collections.

(7) Summary:

Taking into consideration all the elements of intangible values, it seemed clear that the Company was entitled to some general allowance to cover what might properly be described as going value. This case is one in which it has been extremely difficult to put the allowance for going value upon a scientific basis, either as to principle or as to amount. On the basis of 10% of the physical value, a percentage frequently used in purchase cases, this Company's going value would be about $156,000. On the theory that the reproduction of the business would cost the equivalent of six months gross revenues, the going value would be about $130,000. In the Omaha Water Works case, which was carried through the United States Supreme Court, the going value found was the equivalent of about $22.50 per tap, although it was not estimated on this basis. Using this figure, the Queens County Water Company's going value would be about $190,000. In the Staten Island purchase cases the commission of engineers allowed $10 per tap. They were not given access to the company's books and adopted the $10 per tap as a conservative figure. Applied to this case it would give $84,000. All things considered, it has seemed fair and reasonable to estimate the going value on the basis of the cost of reproduction at $150,000, including in it the value of the connections, the easements in private streets, the "happy outcome" of location, the testing of equipment and the establishment of the Company's watershed rights. It has seemed best to make the estimate of going value at this point on the basis of present value rather than on the basis of original cost. The matter of development cost can be taken up with greater propriety in connection with the determination of what the Company has actually invested in its plant and business.

(h) **Summary of present value of useful property on the basis of reproduction cost new less depreciation:**

Summarizing the preceding results I find that the present value of all the Company's property used and necessary for the public service, on the basis of reproduction cost new less depreciation, was, on June 30, 1914, $1,713,499, made up as follows:

Land	$122,000.00
Water supply sources and works	124,137.00
Buildings and mechanical equipment	214,794.00
Distribution system	1,052,170.00
Supplies, tools and miscellaneous equipment	50,398.00
Total physical property	$1,563,499.00
Add going value	150,000.00
Total tangible and intangible property necessary for water business	$1,713,499.00

XIII. PRESENT VALUE OF PROPERTY USED AND USEFUL FOR THE PUBLIC SERVICE BASED ON ACTUAL COST LESS DEPRECIATION.

It should be borne in mind that reproduction cost new less depreciation is only one of the elements to be considered in arriving at fair present value for rate fixing purposes. Engineers, courts and commissions have followed the reproduction cost method largely because it has often been difficult to ascertain the actual cost of the property. In more recent years, however, the reproduction cost method has been subjected to severe criticism and to several positive limitations. Public service commissions, which have to do constantly with the valuation of public utility properties and the fixing of rates, are coming more and more to the view that the original investment, if made honestly and with a fair degree of wisdom, is the most important criterion for the determination of the value upon which a public service corporation should be permitted to earn a fair return.

In the case of the Queens County Water Company it has not been possible to ascertain with complete accuracy the amount of the actual cost of the property, although the Company's books were thrown open to the Department and have been subjected to an exhaustive examination by Mr. Mark Wolff, our accountant. The Company has pursued the policy of never writing off anything from its capital account except for property sold. Property that has disappeared from the eye of the consumer may still be seen in the Company's balance sheet. Property that is still visible though no longer useful will also be found in the balance sheet. Replacements have been charged to capital account. Bond discounts and expenses, and certain deferred interest payments of the early days, are still there. Nevertheless, in spite of these difficulties and limitations, it may be possible to consider the Company's investment figures as one element in the determination of the present fair value of its property.

On May 31, 1914, the Company's books showed a total investment in fixed assets of $1,988,422.80, made up as follows:

Table 17—CLASSIFICATION AND DISTRIBUTION OF CAPITAL ACCOUNTS.

Description	In Queens	In Nassau	General	Total
Real estate..............	(Cr.) $4,971.84	$256,957.76	....	$251,985.92
Embankments, ditches, roads, etc............	....	13,968.92	....	13,968.92
Wells and suction........	27,573.60	60,196.87	....	87,770.47
Standpipe...............	30,365.36	....	....	30,365.36
Boilers and pumping machinery...............	35,499.52	145,764.30	....	181,263.82
Buildings and chimneys...	20,534.96	68,169.26	....	88,704.22
Mains, valves, hydrants, etc..................	463,443.77	468,380.74	....	931,824.51
Filters...................	38.00	53,298.13	....	53,336.13
Tools and implements....	....	....	$42,268.47	42,268.47
Meters..................	....	....	92,051.01	92,051.01
Intangible capital (unamortized debt discount and expense, etc.)................	....	....	214,883.97	214,883.97
Total............	$572,483.37	$1,066,735.98	$349,203.45	$1,988,422.80
To this should be added for "materials and supplies" included in inventory but not included in "fixed assets," the sum of..................				17,685.68
Total book investment in tangible and intangible property exclusive of cash and notes and accounts receivable....................				$2,006,108.48

We must now take up the distribution of the original investment and take into consideration the deductions to be made on account of property excluded as not necessary for water purposes, on account of superseded property, on account of depreciation of property still in use, and on account of intangibles which should have been amortized before now.

(a) Original Cost of Land:

The Company's real estate account is complicated by the fact that a portion of the plot in use at Rockaway Park was acquired many years ago with other property, so that the separate cost of the land itself cannot be fixed exactly, and by the fact that the original Valley Stream purchase in 1896 included large sums for pumping station, wells and other improvements, as well as an unknown amount to cover early losses, interest on advances, etc. The Valley Stream purchase was carried on the books at $361,413.31, but an analysis of certain old accounts showing the cost of the pumping station, wells, improvements, etc., included in the purchase enables us to exclude definitely the sum of $127,584.59. This leaves $233,828.72 as the price of the Valley Stream land including the various intangible elements referred to above. It is impossible to determine at this time what these intangibles amounted to, but it was no doubt a very considerable sum. It is to be noted also that in real estate are included any buildings or other improvements thereon acquired with the land except as they have been definitely excluded in the case of the Valley Stream purchase. These improvements amount to very little, however. Particular note should be made of the dwelling houses located on the land adjoining the Company's office at Far Rockaway. These were acquired in 1902 and 1904 because the former owners were being damaged by the occasional overflow of the standpipe. The standpipe has since been reconstructed and its height increased so that there is no longer any reason for the retention of this property by the water company.

As explained in a previous section of this report, the water company submitted to a voluntary loss of at least $127,000 in the sale of lands to the Norumbega Company, as the latter offered the water company $127,000 in cash in excess of the amount accepted by the water company. This is shown by the minutes of the water company's board of directors for the meetings of May 21, 1910. The water company maintains that it was justified in purchasing these extensive lands for the protection of its water supply, and that while these lands continued to be necessary for such protection, it was entitled to charge rates sufficient to yield a fair return upon their value. It seems clear, therefore, that when a portion of these lands was sold as no longer necessary, the Company should have obtained the highest price possible and should have credited its real estate account therewith. Indeed, there are indications that the water company regarded the land sold to the Norumbega Company as worth even more than the amount received for it plus the $127,000 additional offered but not accepted. Under these circumstances we can do no less than credit the real estate account with the extra $127,000 which the water company refused to take.

The present value of the real estate still held by the Company but not needed in its business should also be credited to the real estate account on the assumption that the Company could, if it chose, dispose of these surplus lands at the present time at their present value, and that if it did so, it would properly credit the account with the proceeds of these sales. The value of the real estate in Queens County, excluded as not being necessary for water purposes, has been arrived at on the basis of assessed valuation. The value of the land in Nassau County excluded as being now unnecessary for water purposes has been estimated by a process described in a preceding section of this report. This gives a figure of $140,000. It represents the estimated present value of approximately 225 acres, of which about 80 acres are salt meadow.

Without attempting at this point further to correct the Company's real estate account, we may show by the following table the purchases and sales in Queens and Nassau Counties from 1894 to 1914, inclusive, with the estimated adjustment for purchases prior to 1894 and deductions on account of the voluntary loss in the Norumbega sale and on account of real estate now held by the Company but not now deemed to be necessary for water purposes.

TABLE 18—REAL ESTATE INVESTMENT ACCOUNT

	PURCHASES		SALES	
	Queens	Nassau	Queens	Nassau
1894	$969.87	....	....	....
1895	....	....	....	....
1896	3,826.84	....	$300.00	....
1897	....	....	....	....
1898	....	$200.00	1,026.84	....
1899	....	....	....	....
1900	....	1,064.04	300.00	....
1901	....	13,512.98	450.00	....
1902	....	46,500.99	500.00	....
1903	2,150.00	78,194.32	400.00	....
1904	2,715.01	8,788.98	576.00	$3,605.40
1905	500.00	16,124.39	350.00	....
1906	2,500.00	62,606.23	18,888.28	....
1907	....	33,020.77	17,511.72	5,000.00
1908	5,485.28	1,382.19	....	....
1909	....	165.00	....	....
1910	....	171.57	....	29,617.40
1911	....	20.38	....	200,400.00
1912	....	....	....	....
1913	....	....	....	....
1914	....	....	....	....
Total	$18,147.00	$261,751.84	$40,302.84	$238,622.80
Total sales	40,302.84	238,622.80	....	....
Net investment 1894 to date	(Cr.) $22,155.84	$23,129.04	....	....
Purchases prior to 1894, estimated	17,184.00	233,828.72	....	....
Net total investment to date, estimated	(Cr.) $4,971.84	256,957.76	....	....

Net total investment to date (estimated) both counties		$251,985.92
Less voluntary loss on Norumbega sale	$127,000.00	
Less estimated value of real estate now held which is not needed:		
In Queens	17,700.00	
In Nassau	140,000.00	
		284,700.00
Net credit (estimated) in real estate investment May 31, 1914		$32,715.08

The figure of $32,715.08 just given represents the amount less than nothing that the real estate now adjudged to be useful in the water business has cost the stockholders of the Company. In other words, taking into consideration the terms of the Norumbega sale, and attributing a value of $17,700 and of $140.000 to the excluded real estate in Queens and Nassau Counties, respectively, the Company has obtained its land now used and useful in the water business for nothing, and has received a profit of $32,715.08 in the transaction.

If it were possible to analyze further the actual original cost to the Company's stockholders of the Valley Stream tract purchased about 1890 or 1891, the real estate account would doubtless show a still larger profit. With the deductions heretofore made, the real estate investment in the Valley Stream tract stands at $233,828.72. It is to be noted, however, that the Valley Stream property was leased to the Company on February 1, 1893, at a rental of $3,000 per month. It appears that the actual operation of the plant must have commenced some time in April, 1893, as the rental paid during the fiscal year ending May 31, 1893, was $4,750, which would seem to indicate April 13 as the actual date from which rent was figured. The Company continued to pay rent to the owners of the property until May 31, 1894, but from the latter date to April 15, 1896, no rent was paid. The rental for this period would have amounted to $60,000, but this was thrown off in the deal and, therefore, this amount should be deducted from the residual figure given as the investment in real estate at Valley Stream, leaving $173,828.72. Furthermore, the cost of the improvements made at Valley Stream from 1891 to 1893 appears to have been about $127,000. A fair allowance for interest during construction will be 6% on this amount, or $7,620. If this item also is deducted from the real estate investment, the cost of the Valley Stream land will be reduced to $166,208.72. There can be little doubt that this figure is greatly in excess of what the promoting stockholders actually paid for this land. The stockholders who purchased the land and constructed the pumping station on their own account had not received any dividends on the original stock of the Company issued in 1884 and subsequently. If we assume that 6% per annum upon the stock outstanding from the organization of the Company up to the date of the settlement in 1896 was included in the price at which the stockholders turned over the Valley Stream property to the Company, another deduction of $63,000 from the original investment attributed to real estate must be made. This reduces the figure still further to $103,208.72. If we assume that no other extraneous elements are to be found in this real estate account, it is nevertheless probable that the figure finally arrived at includes an allowance for interest upon the actual original purchase price of the land for the period extending from the date of the purchase to the completion of the Valley Stream plant and the actual commencement of operation. This period must have been at least two and a half years, which, at 6% per annum, would require an allowance of 15% for interest. On this basis the original purchase price of the land included in the Valley Stream development is reduced to $89,746. If we assume that this is the correct figure, the total profit to the Company in acquiring the lands now useful for water purposes is increased from the $32,715.08 from which we started to $176,797.80, or $19,097.80 more than the value attributed to the real estate now held by the Company but not considered useful for water purposes. In other words, on this basis the stockholders of the Company would appear to have made a profit on the land already sold of about $20,000 in excess of the entire original cost of the land retained, including both that which is useful and that which is not.

However, this conclusion can be defended only on the assumption that the items of loss to the Company now covered up in the Valley Stream purchase are to be taken care of separately in the Company's development costs. This will be done.

(b) **Original cost of depreciable tangible property:**

The books of the Company supplemented by certain records of original expenditure for the improvements at Valley Stream prior to the purchase of the Valley Stream property by the Company in 1896, show a total investment of $1,539,238.58 in depreciable property up to May 31, 1914, distributed as follows:

Embankments, ditches, roads, etc.	$13,968.92
Wells and suction lines	87,770.47
Filters	53,336.13
Buildings and chimneys	88,704.22
Boilers and pumping machinery	181,263.82
Mains, valves, hydrants, valve boxes, etc.	931,824.51
Standpipes	30,365.36
Meters	92,051.01
Tools, miscellaneous equipment and supplies	59,954.15
	$1,539,238.59

As already explained, these figures represent the gross investment as carried on the books in the several classes of property referred to, including replacements, as well as all property that has disappeared from the inventory without being replaced. In order to arrive at the present value on the basis of original cost it is proper to deduct from the figures given above the amount of the investment in property that has disappeared from the inventory and the amount of the depreciation that has accrued against the property still in use. In most cases it seems that the reproduction cost new, with the percentages allowed for overhead charges, will be considerably in excess of the actual original cost for the same units of property as shown by the Company's investment account. Therefore, the accrued depreciation, as shown in the reproduction cost new less depreciation estimate, cannot be used as the equivalent of the actual depreciation based on the original cost. This actual depreciation can be ascertained by applying the percentages of accrued depreciation found in the appraisal to the investment in the several classes of property as shown on the Company's books after the deduction of the original investment in disappeared property. It is not possible at this late day to make up a complete list of disappeared property with an accurate statement of its original cost. The Company supplied an approximate statement totalling $109,991, which does not include ditches and roads not appraised separately and charged on the books at $8,031.52. Distributing these items approximately among the various classes of property carried in the construction account and deducting them, we get the following figures for the original cost without allowance for depreciation of the property now in existence and included in the inventory.

TABLE 19—ELIMINATION OF SUPERSEDED PROPERTY FROM CAPITAL ACCOUNT.

CLASS OF PROPERTY	Original cost of all property	Original cost of property not in present inventory	Original cost of property in present inventory
Embankments, ditches, roads, etc.	$13,968.92	$8,031.52	$5,937.40
Wells and suction lines	87,770.47	25,000.00	62,770.47
Filters	53,336.13	....	53,336.13
Buildings and chimneys	88,704.22	5,437.00	83,267.22
Boilers and pumping machinery	181,263.82	16,950.00	164,313.82
Mains, valves, hydrants, etc	931,824.51	40,604.00	891,220.51
Standpipes	30,365.36	18,000.00	12,365.36
Meters	92,051.01	....	92,051.01
Tools, supplies and miscellaneous equipment	59,954.15	4,000.00	55,954.15
	$1,539,238.59	$118,022.52	$1,421,216.07

Applying now the percentages of accrued depreciation arrived at in the appraisal, we get the following results as representing the original cost less depreciation of the several classes of depreciable tangible property:

TABLE 20—ORIGINAL COST LESS DEPRECIATION OF TANGIBLE PROPERTY OTHER THAN LAND.

CLASS OF PROPERTY	Original cost	Accrued depreciation in per cent.	Original cost less depreciation
Embankments, ditches, roads, etc..	$5,937.40	87.4	$750.00
Wells and suction lines............	62,770.47	20.2	50,090.84
Filters..........................	53,336.13	13.9	45,922.41
Buildings and chimneys...........	83,267.22	21.4	65,448.03
Boilers and pumping machinery....	164,313.82	24.6	123,892.62
Mains, valves, hydrants, etc.......	891,220.51	20.0	712,976.41
Standpipes.......................	12,365.36	10.0	11,128.82
Meters..........................	92,051.01	18.0	75,481.83
Tools, supplies and miscellaneous equipment....................	55,954.15	22.1	43,588.83
Total.................	$1,421,216.07	20.5	$1,129,279.79

The figures given above are not to be considered as absolutely exact in relation to each particular class of property. For example, the extraordinary depreciation shown in the first item—embankments, ditches, roads, etc.—is due in part to the fact that the expenditure for roads has been segregated in the investment account, while in the present appraisal roads have been treated as having been absorbed in the land value. In other details, no doubt, comparisons by class might be criticised owing to the fact that the identification of particular items of property in the accounts of the Company is often difficult and the depreciation of the investment account may not correspond in all details with the distribution adopted in the present inventory. The general result, however, should be approximately correct.

(c) **Original cost of intangibles:**

The Company carries on its balance sheet as a part of its fixed assets intangibles representing a book investment of $214,883.97, made up as follows:

Organization and promotion of original company..................	$5,000.00
Engineering in connection with original plant.....................	10,775.78
Commission and contractor's profit in connection with original plant..	8,466.34
Taxes..	506.18
Legal services....................................	3,917.88
Interest on advances by the DuBois estate......................	47,909.72
Bond discounts....................................	70,230.00
Expenses of bond issues..............................	18,078.07
Premium on retirement of first mortgage bonds...................	50,000.00
	$214,883.97

To the items given above should be added the items of intangibles which we have already eliminated from the real estate account, where they lay concealed in the "Valley Stream purchase." These are the following:

Unpaid rentals, 1894–1896	$60,000.00
Interest during construction, 1891–1893	21,082.72
Unpaid dividends, 1884–1896	63,000.00
	$144,082.72

This makes a total of $358,966.69 of intangibles carried in the capital account.

If we assume that all these items were legitimate and necessary as a part of the gross original investment, we must nevertheless deduct certain of them as representing a depreciation of intangibles.

Of the items of intangibles carried on the Company's books, the $10,000 of bond discounts, the $5,000 for "organization and promotion," the $10,775.78 for "engineering" and the $8,466.34 "commission and contractor's profits," aggregating $34,242.12, represent an arbitrary distribution of a portion of the cost of construction at Far Rockaway prior to 1892 carried on the books in a lump sum. The amount distributed represents the excess of the book charge over any tangible assets which the Company can now trace to this original construction.

Of the remaining $60,230 charged to bond discounts, $5,230 represents discounts on first mortage 5% bonds issued from 1897 to 1902, and $55,000 represents discounts on second mortgage 4% bonds issued from 1904 to 1906.

The item $18,078.07 chargeable to expenses of bond issues is made up of $3,231.07 of expenses in connection with the issuance of the second mortgage bonds, and $14,847 of expenses in connection with the issuance of the general mortgage 5% bonds in 1912. This latter item appears to include $10,000 for legal services rendered by Lord, Day & Lord in connection with the Norumbega transaction, by which the water company rid itself of the excess land which had been purchased during the period of active competition with the City for the control of the watershed.

The item of $50,000 premium on the retirement of first mortgage bonds was an expense incurred when the first mortgage bonds issued in 1896 were called at 110 in 1911 and 1912 and general mortgage bonds issued in their place. This transaction was necessary on account of the disposal of the Norumbega property and because the first mortgage was limited to the $500,000 of bonds already outstanding. The new general mortgage made provision for the ultimate issuance of $1,500,000 of bonds, although only $667,000 have actually been issued thus far.

The item of taxes—$506.18—includes $500 paid in 1896 as a tax on the increase of capital stock, and an item of $6.18 paid in 1904 and charged to capital account without the reason therefor being shown.

The item of $3,917.88 for legal services relates to the cost of some of the earlier litigation for the protection of the Company's watershed rights. Subsequently in 1909 an item of $25,000 for additional legal services in connection with the protection of the Company's watershed was paid out of operating expenses, although it might more properly have been charged to capital account.

The item of interest on advances by the DuBois estate, amounting to $47,909.72, represents interest and costs included in certain judgments obtained against the Company in 1893, additional interest upon the amount of these judgments and upon certain additional moneys loaned up to January 1, 1896, and further additional interest on the sum of the judgments and moneys due, including back interest, from January 1, 1896, to April 15, 1896, the date of the Valley Stream purchase and the reorganization of the Company's finances.

The character of the original items which were taken out of the real estate account and charged here as intangibles was sufficiently explained in the section dealing with the original cost of the land.

In considering the value of the Company's property from the standpoint of original cost less depreciation we come to the question as to the extent to which these intangibles, representing an alleged original cost of $358,966.69, should be depreciated as of May 31, 1914.

The item charged to organization and promotion is not properly depreciable. The items charged to engineering and commission and contractor's profit should be depreciated with the plant to which they refer. These particular items relate to the construction of the original plant in 1884 and immediately thereafter. While it is impossible to determine from the present inventory and appraisal just what life might properly be assigned to the portion of the plant included in the original construction, it seems reasonable to attribute to it an average life of about fifty years and to assume an accrued depreciation of 60% in 1914. The small items for taxes and legal services represent principally expenses of an increase in capital stock and of certain litigation to establish the Company's watershed rights. Inasmuch as the Company charged only a small portion of expenses of watershed litigation to capital account, it would seem that no depreciation need be attributed to these items.

The item of interest on advances and the item of bond discounts represent costs which should have been paid out of operating expenses or completely amortized long before now. It seems best, therefore, to depreciate these items 100%.

The same rule will apply to a portion of the item of bond expense, amounting to $3,231.07. As to the balance of this item and the item of premium on retirement of first mortgage bonds, it appears that they constitute an expense incurred in connection with the issuance of the new mortgage, which is payable in 1940. The expense, or at least most of it, was incurred in 1912—two years after the date of the mortgage.

It would seem proper, therefore, to charge depreciation on these items on the theory that the bonds had 28 years to run. On the straight line basis, which is the basis we have adopted throughout in our calculations of depreciation, this would require us to deduct an accrued depreciation of 7.14% from these items. As to the items of unpaid rentals from 1894 to 1896 and unpaid dividends from 1884 to 1896, it is clear that they should have been taken care of out of current revenues and therefore we should now depreciate them 100%. As to the item of interest during construction, 1891 to 1893, it seems proper to depreciate the portion relating to the construction of depreciable property, namely, $7,620, to the same extent that the property itself is depreciated. The property in this case is the original pumping plant and well system at Valley Stream, and while it would be difficult to establish an exact percentage of accrued depreciation for this particular property, it would appear that 50% would be approximately correct or at least nearly enough correct for the purposes of this computation. The interest during construction attributable to the land need not be depreciated. Applying the percentages of depreciation suggested, the table of cost of intangibles may be revised to show the cost of intangibles less depreciation as follows:

TABLE 21—ORIGINAL COST OF INTANGIBLES LESS DEPRECIATION.

ITEM	Original cost	Accrued depreciation in percentage	Original cost less accrued depreciation
Organization and promotion.......	$5,000.00	....	$5,000.00
Engineering.....................	10,775.78	60.0	4,310.31
Commission and contractor's profit..........................	8,466.34	60.0	3,386.54
Taxes..........................	506.18	....	506.18
Legal services....................	3,917.88	....	3,917.88
Interest on advances..............	47,909.72	100.0	....
Bond discounts..................	70,230.00	100.0	....
Expenses of old bond issues.......	3,231.07	100.0	....
Expenses of general mortgage bond issue including premium on retirement of first mortgage bonds......................	64,847.00	7.14	60,216.93
Unpaid rentals...................	60,000.00	100.0	....
Interest during construction, land..	13,462.72	....	13,462.72
Interest during construction, pumping station and wells.........	7,620.00	50.0	3,810.00
Unpaid dividends................	63,000.00	100.0	....
Total..................	$358,966.69		$94,610.56

(d) **Development expenses:**

In a case like that of the Queens County Water Company where the earlier accounts are lost in the fog, and where the finances have been reorganized midway in the Company's history, it is impossible to approach exactness in the estimate of development costs. When the Valley Stream property was purchased in 1896 and the general reorganization effected by the issuance of stocks and bonds to cover all the claims of the stockholder promoters, the development costs which had accrued up to that time were capitalized. The Company suggests that the only practicable method of determining the existence and the amount of the accrued deficit in a fair return upon the investment is to take the stock at its par value from 1896 to date, estimate a fair rate of return thereon and offset this return with the amount of dividends actually paid. The Company points to the present value of its property as proof that it is not over-capitalized and is willing to estimate deficits in the fair return upon the assumption that the cost of borrowed money has been met in the actual interest paid upon the bonds, and that a fair rate of return upon the stock for the purpose of estimating deficits would be 6% per annum compounded at 6% when unpaid.

The appraisal of the physical property, including the real estate not considered necessary for water purposes, gives a present value substantially equal to the par value of the stocks and bonds outstanding, without taking into consideration going value. Assuming that the cost of the items of intangibles as set forth in the preceding section was necessary, and assuming that so far as the Company capitalized these items it was necessary and proper to do so, it would not be easy to show that the Company has been over-capitalized at any time since the reorganization in 1896. Under all the circumstances it seems reasonable to estimate development costs on the basis suggested by the Company with certain modifications which will now be discussed.

The item of $127,000 of voluntary loss incurred by the Company for the benefit of its stockholders in the sale of the Norumbega property in 1910 has already been deducted from the real estate account in our effort to arrive at the actual net cost or profit of the Company's real estate transactions. It is to be noted, however, that the Norumbega Company has never paid any cash for the land it acquired. Instead, it gave a note which bore no interest until March 27, 1913. Subsequent to that date it bore only 4% interest. It seems proper to assume that the Water Company should have received 6% on this money from the date of the Norumbega sale, May 21, 1910, and the difference between 6% and the amount of interest actually charged should be treated as an additional dividend to the stockholders to reduce the accumulated deficit in dividends paid. It seems, also, that 6% on the $127,000 lost in the Norumbega transaction should also be charged to the stockholders as an addition to dividends paid. With these corrections the cumulative deficiency in dividends below an annual rate of 6% on the par value of the stock outstanding from 1896 to 1914 would amount to $88,280.59 without compounding; to $280,320.11 if the deficiencies are compounded at 5% annual interest; and to $336,442.22 if the deficiencies are compounded at 6%. The way in which these results are reached is shown in the following table:

TABLE 22—CAPITAL STOCK OUTSTANDING, DIVIDENDS PAID, AND CUMULATIVE SURPLUS OR DEFICIENCY, JUNE 1, 1896, TO MAY 31, 1914.

YEAR ENDED MAY 31ST	Capital stock outstanding	Dividends	Return at 6 per cent.	WITHOUT INTEREST			WITH 5 PER CENT. COMPOUND INTEREST		WITH 6 PER CENT. COMPOUND INTEREST	
				Annual surplus	Annual deficiency	Cumulative deficiency without interest	Interest at 5 per cent. on cumulative deficiency	Cumulative deficiency with 5 per cent. interest added	Interest at 6 per cent. on cumulative deficiency	Cumulative deficiency with 6 per cent. interest added
1896	$500,000.00	....	*$6,000.00	....	$6,000.00	$6,000.00	....	$6,000.00	....	$6,000.00
1897	500,000.00	....	30,000.00	....	30,000.00	36,000.00	300.00	36,300.00	$360.00	36,360.00
1898	500,000.00	....	30,000.00	....	30,000.00	66,000.00	1,815.00	68,115.00	2,181.60	68,541.60
1899	500,000.00	....	30,000.00	....	30,000.00	96,000.00	3,405.75	101,520.75	4,112.50	102,654.10
1900	500,000.00	$10,000.00	30,000.00	....	20,000.00	116,000.00	5,076.04	126,596.79	6,159.25	128,813.35
1901	500,000.00	10,000.00	30,000.00	....	20,000.00	136,000.00	6,329.85	152,926.64	7,728.80	156,542.15
1902	500,000.00	15,000.00	30,000.00	....	15,000.00	151,000.00	7,646.33	175,572.97	9,392.53	180,934.68
1903	550,000.00	21,000.00	33,000.00	....	12,000.00	163,000.00	8,778.65	196,351.62	10,856.08	203,790.76
1904	550,000.00	22,000.00	33,000.00	....	11,000.00	174,000.00	9,817.58	217,169.20	12,227.45	227,018.21
1905	550,000.00	22,000.00	33,000.00	....	11,000.00	185,000.00	10,858.46	239,027.66	13,621.09	251,639.30
1906	550,000.00	22,000.00	33,000.00	....	11,000.00	196,000.00	11,951.38	261,979.04	15,098.36	277,737.66
1907	872,870.00	35,571.75	52,372.20	....	16,800.45	212,800.45	13,098.95	291,878.44	16,664.26	311,202.37
1908	1,028,000.00	48,051.75	61,680.00	....	13,628.25	226,428.70	14,593.92	320,100.61	18,672.14	343,502.76
1909	1,044,200.00	62,652.00	62,652.00	....	....	226,428.70	16,005.03	336,105.64	20,610.17	364,112.93
1910	1,050,000.00	62,826.00 †211.67 ‡270.42	63,000.00	308.09	....	226,120.61	16,805.28	352,602.83	21,846.78	385,651.61
1911	1,050,000.00	73,500.00 †7,620.00 ‡10,575.14	63,000.00	28,695.14	....	197,425.47	17,630.14	341,537.83	23,139.10	380,095.57
1912	1,050,000.00	84,000.00 †7,620.00 ‡10,575.14	63,000.00	39,195.14	....	158,230.33	17,076.89	319,419.58	22,805.73	363,706.16
1913	1,050,000.00	84,000.00 †7,620.00 **9,184.70	63,000.00	37,804.70	....	120,425.63	15,970.98	297,585.86	21,822.37	347,723.83
1914	1,050,000.00	84,000.00 †7,620.00 **3,525.04	63,000.00	32,145.04	....	88,280.59	14,879.29	280,320.11	20,863.43	336,442.22

* On $100,000.00 only.
† Interest at 6 per cent. on loss of $127,000 in sale to Norumbega.
‡ Interest on Norumbega note at 6 per cent.
** Interest on Norumbega note at 2 per cent. (4 per cent. charged against income).

In view of the fact that the investment, especially in its earlier years, was unremunerative, and that for a long time it seemed doubtful whether it would ever become profitable, especially while the Company's water supply was in more or less danger, it does not seem unreasonable on the whole to estimate the development costs on the basis of 6% compound interest. This rate is only slightly in excess of the actual rate paid upon the Company's bonds, when discounts are taken into consideration.

If it had been possible to ascertain the actual cash investment from year to year from the inception of the enterprise down to the present time, a more accurate method of estimating development expenses could have been used. By charging up each year the necessary operating expenses, the estimated current depreciation and an amount equivalent to a fair return upon the total investment, and by subtracting from the sum of these three items the actual gross earnings of the plant, we should have been able to ascertain the actual deficit in the year's operations, and on the basis of these annual deficits, followed in later years by annual surpluses, we could have built up a cumulative deficit which would properly represent the accrued development expenses as of May 31, 1914. In the absence of accurate data upon the basis of which to apply this method it seems reasonable to follow the method shown in the table, and to estimate the accrued development expenses as of May 31, 1914, at $336,442.22. This figure, therefore, will be taken for use in estimating the original cost less depreciation of the Company's plant and property.

It is to be noted that this estimate is reached without reference to any surplus or deficit shown on the balance sheet.

(e) **Surplus or deficit:**

In order to reach a final estimate of the original cost less depreciation of the Company's plant and property it is necessary to take into consideration the surplus or deficit which should be shown on the balance sheet. The balance sheet as made up shows a surplus of $172,565.23 as of May 31, 1914. This alleged surplus is shown as follows:

TABLE 23—BALANCE SHEET AS PER COMPANY'S BOOKS, MAY 31, 1914.

ASSETS:	
Fixed assets including land and materials and supplies	$2,006,108.48
Cash on hand and in bank	13,166.21
Notes receivable	177,825.25
Accounts receivable	107,311.75
Total	$2,304,411.69
LIABILITIES, CAPITAL STOCK, ETC.:	
Capital stock	$1,050,000.00
Funded debt	667,000.00
Notes payable and accrued interest on loans	45,123.75
Consumers deposit accounts	66,700.65
Prepayments	12,476.40
Accounts payable (audited vouchers and payrolls)	23,472.07
Dividend due and unpaid	42,000.00
Depreciation written off	225,073.59
Surplus	172,565.23
Total	$2,304,411.69

The item "accounts receivable" should be reduced by about $10,000 for uncollectable accounts. Thus revised, the total assets will be reduced to $2,294,411.69.

On the liability side an additional item should be set up for unpaid taxes. The face value of the taxes unpaid on June 30, 1914, with interest to that date, was $87,944.34, but on the basis of settlements effected in other tax cases by the Company's very efficient counsel it was expected that this liability would be about cut in half. After making an allowance for the cost of legal services in connection with these tax adjustments and certain other legal services rendered prior to May 31, 1914, but not yet paid for, it seems reasonable to set this item of liability for unpaid taxes and legal services at $60,000.

In view of the estimates already given it seems that the amount written off for depreciation is entirely inadequate. The amount that should have been written off is made up of the following items:

Superseded property and property excluded from the inventory as no longer useful, other than real estate	$118,022.52
Accrued depreciation of depreciable property included in the inventory	291,936.28
Accrued depreciation of intangibles	264,356.13
Total	$674,314.93

With these corrections the liabilities, capital stock, etc., will be increased by the amount of $509,241.34 to a total of $2,641,087.80. This transforms the surplus of $172,565.23, as shown on the balance sheet, into a deficit of $346,676.11, which should be added to the other items of cost shown in the following summary in order to get the total original cost of the Company's plant and property, less depreciation.

(f) **Summary of original cost less depreciation of useful property:**

Bringing together the results shown in the preceding sections, we have the following summary of original cost less depreciation:

Depreciable tangibles (exclusive of land)	$1,129,279.79
Depreciable intangibles	94,610.56
Development costs (deficit in dividends on a 6 per cent. basis)	336,442.22
Corrected balance sheet deficit (due to depreciation not written off)	346,676.11
	$1,907,008.68
Useful land (credit)	176,797.80
Total original cost less depreciation of useful property	$1,730,210.88

XIV. CAPITALIZATION—STOCKS AND BONDS ISSUED.

The total capitalization of the Queens County Water Company, including stocks and bonds, is $1,717,000, of which $1,050,000 is capital stock and $667,000 is general mortgage bonds.

The following table shows the time of issue and the consideration for the various blocks of stock going to make up the present total:

TABLE 24—CAPITAL STOCK ISSUED AND CONSIDERATION RECEIVED.

Year of Issue	Amount of stock	CONSIDERATION
1884	$40,000.00	Construction at Far Rockaway.
1885	10,000.00	Construction at Far Rockaway.
1888	50,000.00	Construction at Far Rockaway.
1896	361,413.31	Valley Stream purchase (Du Bois estate.)
1896	38,586.69	Accounts payable (Du Bois estate.)
1903	50,000.00	Cash.
1907	52,870.00	Cash.
1907	270,000.00	Retirement of second mortgage bonds.
1908	5,000.00	Retirement of second mortgage bonds.
1908	150,130.00	Cash.
1909	16,200.00	Cash.
1910	5,800.00	Cash.
Total	$1,050,000.00	

The $275,000 issued in exchange for second mortgage bonds includes the capitalization of $55,000 to cover the discount at which these bonds had been issued only a few years prior to their conversion into stock at par. As to the $100,000 sum issued for construction at Far Rockaway, it is impossible at this late day to determine whether it represented any inflation of capital, and if so, how much. All of the actual construction records of this early period are missing.

It is likewise impossible to tell to what extent the $400,000 of stock issued in 1896 on account of the Valley Stream purchase and the accounts payable to the DuBois estate represent inflation. As already shown, the purchase price of the Valley Stream property included the actual cost of the pumping plant, wells and other improvements at Valley Stream, an allowance for $60,000 unpaid rent, an allowance for interest during construction, the original cost of the land, possibly the deferred dividends on stock prior to 1896, and whatever other elements may have been persuasive in inducing the DuBois estate to accept the terms of the settlement.

The DuBois family retained a large, if not a controlling interest in the Company's stock until 1910 or 1911, when their shares were disposed of to other parties in connection with a scheme for refunding the Company's bonded debt.

Of the 10,500 shares of stock outstanding on May 31, 1914, the record shows 4,252 shares in the name of the F. B. Lord estate, 1,379 in the name of Franklin B. Lord, Jr., and 230 shares in the name of Silvie Lord. This gives the Lord family a clear majority of all the shares outstanding.

The amount of stock outstanding at the close of each fiscal year up to May 31, 1914, and the amount of dividends paid thereon is shown by the table below. It is to be noted that no dividends were paid prior to 1900. It is probable that unpaid dividends on stock outstanding prior to 1896 were included in the price of the Valley Stream property and thereby capitalized in the financial reorganization of 1896. At any rate, it is understood that the 1896 settlement was sufficiently favorable to the DuBois family, both as stockholders and as creditors, to cover all of their claims on account of previous investments and losses. Accordingly, the Company does not now lay claim to an allowance for development costs and early losses prior to 1896, admitting that if a fair return is allowed upon the capital stock outstanding from 1896 on, all the demands of justice to the investors will be satisfied.

TABLE 25—CAPITAL STOCK OUTSTANDING AND DIVIDENDS PAID.

YEAR	Stock	Dividends
1884	$40,000.00	....
1885	50,000.00	....
1886	50,000.00	....
1887	50,000.00	....
1888	100,000.00	....
1889	100,000.00	....
1890	100,000.00	....
1891	100,000.00	....
1892	100,000.00	....
1893	100,000.00	....
1894	100,000.00	....
1895	100,000.00	....
1896	500,000.00	....
1897	500,000.00	....
1898	500,000.00	....
1899	500,000.00	....
1900	500,000.00	$10,000.00
1901	500,000.00	10,000.00
1902	500,000.00	15,000.00
1903	550,000.00	21,000.00
1904	550,000.00	22,000.00
1905	550,000.00	22,000.00
1906	550,000.00	22,000.00
1907	872,870.00	35,571.75
1908	1,028,000.00	48,051.75
1909	1,044,200.00	62,652.00
1910	1,050,000.00	62,826.00
1911	1,050,000.00	73,500.00
1912	1,050,000.00	84,000.00
1913	1,050,000.00	84,000.00
1914	1,050,000.00	84,000.00
	$14,885,070.00	$656,601.50

This table shows the equivalent of $14,885,070 stock outstanding for one year, upon which dividends to the amount of $656,601.50 were paid, making an average dividend rate of 4.4% per annum.

At different times during the Company's history it has executed four mortgages as bases for bond issues. Under the original first mortgage $40,000 of 6% bonds were issued on June 3, 1884, for construction at Far Rockaway. The Company was unable to pay interest on these bonds and foreclosure proceedings were instituted. Subsequently, however, the creditors were satisfied through the reorganization effected in 1896 and the bonds were exchanged at par for first mortgage 5% bonds of a new issue.

In 1896 at the time of the purchase of the Valley Stream property and the settlement with the Company's creditors a new first mortgage was executed to secure an issue of 5% bonds. As a part of the settlement, bonds to the par value of $200,000 were immediately issued. Of these, $40,000 were issued in exchange for the original first mortgage bonds, and $160,000 were issued to the DuBoises as a part of the terms of settlement. It is difficult to estimate how much of this $160,000 represents early losses and other intangible elements.

No specific assignment of the classes of securities issued at this time for particular purposes was made, but the aggregate of $600,000, including $400,000 of stock and $200,000 of bonds, was made up as follows:

For retirement of old bond issue	$40,000.00
For satisfaction of judgment in action No. 1, dated February 21, 1893	66,890.80
For satisfaction of judgment in action No. 2, dated February 21, 1893	81,330.42
For cash loaned subsequent to February 21, 1893	19,350.00
For interest on judgment and on money loaned to April 15, 1896	31,015.47
For Valley Stream property	361,413.31
Total	$600,000.00

It appears from this distribution of the items that the price attributed to the Valley Stream property was merely the sum necessary to fill out the round figure of $600,000 after account had been taken of the original bond issue, the judgments, the loans and the interest thereon up to the date of settlement.

Subsequent to the financial reorganization in 1896 the Company issued from time to time, up to 1903, $300,000 additional first mortgage bonds as follows:

TABLE 26—BONDS ISSUED AND CASH RECEIVED THEREFOR.

FISCAL YEAR	Par value of issue	Cash received	Discount
1897	$65,500.00	$64,405.00	$1,095.00
1898	1,500.00	1,500.00	....
1899	2,000.00	1,960.00	40.00
1900	12,000.00	11,760.00	240.00
1901	63,500.00	60,805.00	2,695.00
1902	62,500.00	61,340.00	1,160.00
1903	74,000.00	74,000.00	....
1904	19,000.00	19,000.00	....
	$300,000.00	$294,770.00	$5,230.00

A second mortgage was executed in 1903 to secure the issuance of 4% convertible bonds. Bonds to a total value of $275,000 were issued under this mortgage as follows:

FISCAL YEAR	Par value of issue	Cash received	Discount
1904	$78,000.00	$62,400.00	$15,600.00
1905	88,200.00	71,200.00	17,000.00
1906	108,800.00	*86,400.00	22,400.00
	$275,000.00	$220,000.00	$55,000.00

* This includes $22,800 of accounts payable representing moneys previously advanced by F. B. Lord.

All of these second mortgage bonds were converted at par into capital stock in 1907 and 1908.

When the water company determined to dispose of a portion of its real estate in Nassau County to the Norumbega Company in 1910, a new general mortgage was prepared to secure the issuance of $1,500,000 of 30-year 5% bonds, and bonds to the amount of $667,000 were issued prior to March 31, 1912, as follows:

For cash	$39,000.00
In satisfaction of loans payable	178,000.00
In exchange for first mortgage bonds	450,000.00
	$667,000.00

It appears that in effecting the exchange of general mortgage bonds for outstanding first mortgage bonds a cash premium of 10% was paid for the latter, and in fact $50,000 par value of the first mortgage bonds were bought in for cash at 110, no general mortgage bonds being exchanged for them. Thus a cash premium of $45,000 on the first mortgage bonds exchanged, a cash premium of $5,000 on the first mortgage bonds bought in, and the face value, $50,000, of the latter, amounting in all to $100,000 in cash, were paid out of funds presumably secured by loans included in the $178,000 of loans payable for which new bonds were issued. It appears, therefore, that in this bond transaction at least the sum of $50,000 for premiums was permanently capitalized.

The following table shows the par value of the bonds outstanding at the close of each fiscal year up to May 31, 1914, and the amount of interest paid thereon. It will be noted that no interest was paid prior to 1896. It is understood that the interest due on the bonds outstanding during this early period was included in the judgments secured in 1893 and the interest allowances subsequently made in the financial reorganization in 1896. It appears, therefore, that the bond interest due up to 1896 was capitalized at that time.

TABLE 27—BONDS OUTSTANDING AND INTEREST PAID.

YEAR	Bonds	Interest
1885	$40,000.00	....
1886	40,000.00	....
1887	40,000.00	....
1888	40,000.00	....
1889	40,000.00	....
1890	40,000.00	....
1891	40,000.00	....
1892	40,000.00	....
1893	40,000.00	....
1894	40,000.00	....
1895	40,000.00	....
1896	200,000.00	$3,037.50
1897	265,500.00	12,654.61
1898	267,000.00	13,332.70
1899	269,000.00	13,426.38
1900	281,000.00	13,545.41
1901	344,500.00	15,128.45
1902	407,000.00	17,824.40
1903	481,000.00	21,432.52
1904	578,000.00	25,984.90
1905	666,200.00	29,554.51
1906	775,000.00	33,381.33
1907	505,000.00	30,500.00
1908	500,000.00	25,100.00
1909	500,000.00	25,000.00
1910	500,000.00	25,000.00
1911	667,500.00	25,013.55
1912	667,000.00	35,401.60
1913	667,000.00	33,350.00
1914	667,000.00	33,350.00
	$9,647,700.00	$432,017.86

This table shows the equivalent of $9,647,700 of bonds outstanding for one year, upon which a total of $432,017.86 interest was paid, making an average rate of about 4½% per annum. This should not be regarded as the full cost of the money borrowed, for in addition to the interest paid large sums of interest were capitalized directly or took the form of bond discounts or deferred interest charges.

On the whole, the Company gives a pretty good account of its capitalization, in view of the long period of probation it passed through before being able to pay dividends out of earnings. The present value of the physical assets checks up closely with the par value of the stocks and bonds outstanding. While there is no doubt that the capital stock covers in part early losses, bond discounts and various items which might properly have been treated as deficits in earnings, to be made up out of surplus earnings when the business became prosperous, yet the appreciations in several elements of the property have about made good these intangibles. The Company has not been subject to regulation by a public service commission and its method of keeping its books is not up to the best modern standards, but considering these conditions its practices with reference to capitalization have not been such as to merit opprobrium.

XV. FAIR PRESENT VALUE FOR RATE PURPOSES AND FAIR RATE OF RETURN ON INVESTMENT.

Thus far we have taken into consideration the reproduction cost new less depreciation of the useful property, the original cost less depreciation, and the amount of stocks and bonds outstanding. The results obtained furnish an interesting comparison shown by the following:

Reproduction cost new less depreciation	$1,713,499.00
Original cost less depreciation	1,730,210.88
Par value of stocks and bonds outstanding	1,717,000.00

It is to be remembered that real estate with an estimated value of $157,700 has been excluded from consideration, both in the reproduction cost and in the original cost figures.

While the general results from the two methods of valuation agree very closely, a large difference appears in the items of tangible property other than land. The reproduction cost less depreciation of this portion of the property is $1,441,499, while the original cost less depreciation of the same property is only $1,129,279.79. This shows a discrepancy of $312,219. At first blush, this large increase in the reproduction cost of the physical property as compared with the original cost would seem to indicate one or more of three things: (a) a liberal appraisal by the department's engineers; (b) unusual efficiency and economy in the Company's construction work; (c) a great appreciation in the cost of labor and materials since the works were built.

As to (a) the appraisal made by the engineers under my direction was very carefully done, and the rules followed and the prices and percentages adopted were accepted as the basis of a fair appraisal which could be defended in the courts if litigation were to ensue as the result of the fixing of rates by the Commissioner. The engineers were guided primarily by the experience of the Department in its own construction work. In the absence of any evidence that the contract prices paid by the City for pipe laying and other construction work have been excessive. it was not thought that the Department would be able to sustain an estimate of reproduction cost lower than the actual cost of similar work done by the City. The low unit prices given by the Company's engineer some years ago in connection with tax reports and tax litigation cannot be taken seriously. The unit prices adopted in this appraisal are somewhat lower than those adopted by the Commission of engineers in the appraisal of the Staten Island water companies, and in view of all the circumstances and conditions are believed to be fair both to the City and to the Company.

As to (b) it appears to be true that the Queens County Water Co. has carried on its construction with great economy and efficiency, and that the prices actually paid by the Company for labor and materials have been somewhat less than the prices paid by the City during the same period. Moreover, a large portion of the discrepancy is accounted for by the fact that interest during construction and contractor's profit, which are recognized as necessary elements of reproduction cost, do not appear on the Company's books as elements of original cost attributable to the physical property.

As to (c) there has doubtless been considerable increase in the cost of labor but very little, if any, in the cost of materials, particularly cast iron pipe.

In view of the fact that original cost less depreciation, taking into consideration the Company's profits on real estate on the one side and its development expenses and unpaid depreciation on the other, aggregates an amount somewhat in excess of the appraisal of the physical property, including going value, on the basis of reproduction cost new less depreciation, and in view of the fact that in this case it is necessary to distribute the property as between the Queens and Nassau services and also as between domestic service and fire protection, it seems best to use the reproduction cost new less depreciation figures as the fair present value of the physical property for rate purposes, these figures being available in accurate detail for the different classes and items of the property. The appraisal was made as of June 30, while the original cost figures were taken as of May 31, the close of the Company's fiscal year. For various practical reasons the latter date is more convenient for the estimate of basic values for rate fixing. The amount of construction work in June, 1914, was practically negligible. Accordingly, I have found the value of the property as of May 31, 1914, upon which the Company is entitled to earn a fair return, if this can be done without charging excessive rates, to be $1,713,499, which is the inventory value as of June 30.

Under the conditions of uncertainty which have heretofore surrounded this investment, it might be urged that a rate of return of only 6% per annum would not be fair and reasonable. On the other hand, if the City by contract protects the Company against competition, assumes the obligation to take over the Queens portion of the distribution system before additional capital expenditures will be required for the enlargement of the pumping plant and water supply works, insures to the Company a fair return for the cost of fire protection, and insures stability of rates with relation to the investment and the earnings while the Company continues to operate, then it would appear that the rate of return even under the conditions obtaining on the Rockaway peninsula might reasonably be reduced to 6%. A return of 7% upon the valuation found would enable the Company to continue to pay bond interest at the present rate and dividends of 8% on outstanding capital stock. It would appear, therefore, that we should first determine the cost of fire protection on a conservative basis and then fix the rates to domestic consumers so as to make up a 7% return to the Company, subject to a further reduction in domestic rates to put the investment on a 6% basis, in case the Board of Estimate and Apportionment, the Mayor and the Comptroller unite in approving a contract giving to the Company's undertaking the security which they alone can give.

XVI. ALLOCATION OF INVESTMENT AS BETWEEN QUEENS AND NASSAU SERVICES.

Applying the percentages worked out in subdivision VII to the valuations arrived at on the basis of cost of reproduction new less depreciation, we get a total of $1,148,896 of the investment properly attributable to the Queens service, and $564,603 properly attributable to the Nassau service. The following table shows the total valuations and the percentage and amount for each class of property attributable to the two areas respectively:

TABLE 28—APPORTIONMENT OF PROPERTY BETWEEN QUEENS AND NASSAU SERVICES.

	Total	Queens		Nassau	
		Per cent.	Amount	Per cent.	Amount
Land	$122,000	72.4	$88,328	27.6	$33,672
Water supply sources and works	124,137	72.4	89,875	27.6	34,262
Buildings and mechanical equipment	214,794	73.4	157,659	26.6	57,135
Tools, supplies and miscellaneous	50,398	73.4	36,992	26.6	13,406
Trunk mains in Nassau	194,312	76.8	149,231	23.2	45,081
Local distribution systems	857,858	61.4	526,811	38.6	331,047
Total physical property	$1,563,499	67.0	$1,048,896	33.0	$514,603
Add, going value	150,000	67.0	100,000	33.0	50,000
Total tangible and intangible property necessary in the water business	$1,713,499	67.0	$1,148,896	33.0	$564,603

XVII. ALLOCATION OF QUEENS INVESTMENT BETWEEN DOMESTIC SERVICE AND FIRE PROTECTION.

As shown in the preceding subdivision, the total investment attributable to the Queens service, on the basis of reproduction cost new less depreciation, was $1,148,896. It now becomes necessary, following the rule laid down in subdivision VIII, to distribute this investment between domestic and fire services.

Some classes of property are used exclusively for domestic service, or if used to any extent for fire protection such use is purely incidental and involves no increase in the investment over what would be necessary in a plant designed for domestic use alone. This classification includes, in the case of the Queens County Water Company, the following: Meters, corporation cocks, valve boxes and manholes other than hydrant valve boxes, filters, embankment used to exclude salt water, electrical equipment, coal storage, railroad switch tracks, railroad crossings, office and storage buildings, tools, supplies, miscellaneous equipment, land not used for wells or pumping plants, and going value. The entire investment in these classes of property has been assigned to domestic service.

Other classes of property are used both for domestic purposes and for fire protection and require a larger investment for both services than would be necessary for domestic uses alone. This classification includes the following: Trunk mains, distributing mains, pavement over mains, valves other than hydrant valves, standpipes, land used for water supply and pumping stations, wells and suction lines, buildings and chimneys at pumping stations, boilers, pumps and other mechanical equipment except as above noted. The investment in these classes of property has been distributed so that the portion necessary for a plant adequate for domestic uses only is attributable to domestic service and the excess to fire protection.

Still other classes of property are used exclusively for fire protection. These are fire hydrants and their connections, hydrant valves and hydrant valve boxes. The investment in this group has been attributed entirely to fire protection.

The following table gives for the several classes of property the reproduction cost new; the accrued depreciation in per cent. of reproduction cost new; the present value (reproduction cost new less accrued depreciation); the percentage and amount of present value attributable to domestic service; the additional investment, in percentage and amount, attributed to fire service; the total annual depreciation, and the distribution of such depreciation between domestic and fire services. The figures relate only to the investment attributable to the Queens service. The Nassau service and the $564,603 investment attributed thereto are left entirely out of consideration, as the City's power to fix rates and its obligation to pay for fire service are limited to the Queens area.

Table 29—ANALYSIS OF INVESTMENT ATTRIBUTABLE TO THE QUEENS' SERVICE.

	Reproduction cost new	Accrued depreciation %	Present value	Per cent. attributable to domestic service	Amount attributable to domestic service	Per cent. attributable to fire protection	Amount attributable to fire protection	Total annual depreciation	Annual Depreciation Charged to: Domestic service	Annual Depreciation Charged to: Fire protection
I. Property Attributed Exclusively to Domestic Service.										
Meters	$60,744.00	18.0	$49,810.00	100.0	$49,810.00	.....	....	$1,822.00	$1,822.00	....
Corporation cocks	2,985.00	.....	2,985.00	100.0	2,985.00	.....	....	....	....	....
Valve boxes and manholes in Queens other than hydrant valve boxes	3,343.00	10.0	3,008.00	100.0	3,008.00	.....	....	34.00	34.00	....
Railroad crossings in Queens	1,181.00	20.0	945.00	100.0	945.00	.....	....	20.00	20.00	....
Valve boxes, manholes and air valves on trunk mains in Nassau	542.00	10.0	487.00	100.0	487.00	.....	....	5.00	5.00	....
Railroad crossings over trunk mains in Nassau	168.00	20.0	135.00	100.0	135.00	.....	....	3.00	3.00	....
Filters and embankment	47,666.00	13.7	41,115.00	100.0	41,115.00	.....	....	585.00	585.00	....
Electrical equipment, coal storage and railroad tracks	9,441.00	41.5	5,529.00	100.0	5,529.00	.....	....	309.00	309.00	....
Buildings and chimney at Far Rockaway	18,774.00	25.4	13,998.00	100.0	13,998.00	.....	....	273.00	273.00	....
Useful land at Far Rockaway	21,670.00	.....	21,670.00	100.0	21,670.00	.....	....	....	....	....
Tools, supplies and miscellaneous equipment	47,483.00	22.1	36,992.00	100.0	36,992.00	.....	....	1,429.00	1,429.00	....
Going value	100,000.00	.....	100,000.00	100.0	100,000.00	....	....	....	....	....
II. Property Attributed in Part to Domestic Service and in Part to Fire Protection.										
Trunk mains in Nassau	167,630.00	12.7	146,405.00	78.3	114,635.00	21.7	$31,770.00	2,235.00	1,750.00	$485.00
Valves on trunk mains in Nassau	2,590.00	15.0	2,204.00	78.6	1,732.00	21.4	472.00	52.00	41.00	11.00
Land used for wells and pumping stations	66,658.00	.....	66,658.00	66.7	44,439.00	33.3	22,219.00	....	....	....
Wells and suction lines	61,065.00	20.2	48,760.00	66.7	32,507.00	33.3	16,253.00	1,627.00	1,085.00	542.00
Buildings and chimneys at pumping stations	47,801.00	19.8	38,313.00	75.0	28,735.00	25.0	9,578.00	710.00	532.00	178.00
Boilers, pumps and auxiliaries	132,430.00	24.6	99,819.00	50.0	49,910.00	50.0	49,909.00	3,586.00	1,793.00	1,793.00
Mains in Queens	469,520.00	21.7	367,474.00	78.0	286,630.00	22.0	80,844.00	8,528.00	6,652.00	1,876.00
Pavement over mains in Queens	41,536.00	20.0	33,227.00	70.0	23,259.00	30.0	9,968.00	692.00	484.00	208.00
Valves other than hydrant valves in Queens	17,611.00	25.5	13,112.00	81.3	10,660.00	18.7	2,452.00	425.00	346.00	79.00
Standpipes	29,250.00	10.0	26,325.00	50.0	13,162.00	50.0	13,163.00	731.00	365.00	366.00
III. Property Attributed Exclusively to Fire Protection.										
Hydrants and connections in Queens	32,355.00	30.0	22,648.00	.....	....	100.0	22,648.00	809.00	....	809.00
Hydrant valves in Queens	8,235.00	36.0	5,270.00	.....	....	100.0	5,270.00	248.00	....	248.00
Hydrant valve boxes in Queens	2,230.00	10.0	2,007.00	.....	....	100.0	2,007.00	22.00	....	22.00
Total	$1,392,908.00	17.5	$1,148,896.00	76.8	$882,343.00	23.2	$266,553.00	$24,145.00	$17,528.00	$6,617.00

As shown by the above table, the total investment attributable to domestic service in Queens is $882,343, and the total attributable to fire protection is $266,553, or 76.8% and 23.2% respectively. The amount of the investment in fire hydrants and their appurtenances is $29,925 on the basis of present value, and $42,820 on the basis of reproduction cost new. There are 632 of these hydrants, practically all of which have 4-inch outlets. About 400 of them were set with new mains and the others were cut in on old mains at considerably greater expense. The average investment per hydrant is found to be $67.76 cost new, or $47.35 present value. The total annual depreciation of the 632 existing hydrants and their appurtenances is estimated at $1,079 or $1.71 apiece. Of the classes of property used in part for fire service the aggregate investment attributable to this service is estimated at $236,628 and its annual depreciation at $5,538. The annual depreciation of the portion of the investment attributable to domestic service in Queens is estimated at $17,528.

To illustrate the method followed in determining the proportion of the investment properly chargeable to fire service the following table, showing the number of feet of each class of pipe in the local distribution system in Queens as existing, and the total number of feet of each class which would be sufficient for the same distribution system designed for domestic purposes only, will be interesting:

TABLE 30—COMPARISON OF DISTRIBUTION SYSTEM WITH SYSTEM REQUIRED FOR DOMESTIC CONSUMPTION ONLY.

DIAMETER AND KIND OF PIPE	Lineal feet in existing system	Lineal feet required in a system adequate for domestic service only
24″ C.I.	2,249	......
16″ C.I.	30,513	25,750
14″ C.I.	1,856	......
12″ C.I.	26,801	25,550
10″ C.I.	501	......
8″ C.I.	51,688	38,100
6″ C.I.	255,489	46,390
6″ S.R.	3,512	......
4″ C.I.	16,390	178,660
4″ S.R.	2,382	......
4″ W.I.	40	......
3″ C.I.	5,530	......
2½″ W.I.	700	......
2″ W.I.	42,831	128,615
1½″ W.I.	1,782	......
1¼″ W.I.	453	......
1″ W.I.	348	......
	443,065	443,065

The distribution of the investment in valves other than hydrant valves, pavement over mains and trunk mains in Nassau County was arrived at by similar methods.

In regard to water-bearing lands, wells and suction lines, it was estimated that the present developed capacity is about 12,000,000 gallons per day, and that the average peak load required for domestic service during the summer months is approximately 8,000,000 gallons per day. The actual peak load on certain days for brief periods exceeds the 8,000,000 rate, but this temporary peak could be readily taken care of without a well capacity of more than 8,000,000 gallons. It was therefore estimated that two-thirds of the developed well capacity and two-thirds of the investment in wells, suction lines and water-bearing lands was properly attributable to domestic service, leaving one-third of this investment to be reckoned as the extra investment made necessary on account of fire service.

In regard to the pumps, boilers and other mechanical equipment, except electrical equipment, coal storage and railroad switch tracks, it was estimated that the safe continuous capacity of the pumping plants is about 16,000,000 gallons per day. After taking account of the 8,000,000 gallons required for the average peak load of domestic consumption and leakage during the summer months, it appeared that an additional capacity of 8,000,000 gallons per day was reserved for fire emergencies. Accordingly, the investment in this class of property was distributed on the basis of 50% for domestic service and 50% for fire protection.

It is to be noted that the continuous developed capacity of the wells is only 12,000,000 gallons per day, while the safe daily capacity of the pumping plant is 16,000,000 gallons per day, and the requirements for domestic service plus fire reserve for a maximum possible demand in a most unfavorable time in both Queens and Nassau Counties is at the rate of about 18,000,000 gallons per day. It is believed that for the short period necessary to cover the domestic peak load and the peak demand for fire service the water storage in the filters and the speeding up of the pumps would furnish the extra supply of water and the pumping capacity required to meet all emergencies.

In regard to the buildings at the pumping stations, it was estimated that the cost of buildings adequate to house an equipment with 8,000,000 gallons daily capacity would be about 75% as much as the cost of existing buildings. Accordingly, the investment in these buildings was distributed in the ratio of 75% to domestic service and 25% to fire protection. The same division was made as to the chimneys at the Valley Stream station.

XVIII. OPERATING EXPENSES.

In the fixing of rates one of the major factors is the amount allowed as the necessary cost of operating the plant. The best guide to this cost is the actual experience of the operating company. In fact, in the absence of positive evidence to the contrary it is assumed that the actual operating expenses incurred by the Company are necessary and proper within the rather wide field of discretion which is left to the officials of a corporation in the management of a public utility under private ownership. This does not mean that salaries may be boosted with impunity or that materials may be bought at extravagant prices without let or hindrance, or that any other form of gross inefficiency or incompetence may be practiced ad libitum. It only means that the benefit of the doubt must be given to the actual experience of the Company in the management of its property.

The operating expenses of the Queens County Water Company, including taxes but excluding depreciation and replacements, amounted to $1,039,953.17 during the period from January 1, 1892, to May 31, 1914. During the same period the Company's gross earnings, including certain small items of non-operating revenue, amounted to $2,543,019.17. This gives an operating ratio over the entire period of 40.9%. For the four-year period ending May 31, 1914, taken by itself, the expenses were $334,981.15; the earnings, $946,864.51, and the operating ratio, 35.4%. The average annual expenses during this four-year period were $83,745.29.

It now becomes necessary to analyze the Company's operating expenses and consider them in detail.

(a) **Analysis of expenses:**

The Company's accounts of operating expenses are classified in considerable detail and have been kept in a relatively consistent manner for more than twenty years. As already explained, the replacements have been charged to capital account, not to operating expenses, but with this exception the accounts have been kept in sufficient detail and with sufficient accuracy to furnish a correct idea of the actual cost of the operation of the plant. The expenses are carried on the books under four general headings, as follows: Pumping Stations; Repairs; Miscellaneous; and General Expenses. The sub-classification of expenses under these general headings is in sufficient detail to enable us to reclassify the expenses in a more logical manner. As reclassified the expenses for each of the four fiscal years from June 1, 1910, to May 31, 1914, and for the entire four-year period, as well as the average annual expense for this period, are shown in the following table:

TABLE 31—ANALYSIS OF OPERATING EXPENSES, 1911 TO 1914, INCLUSIVE.

CLASSIFICATION	Year ending May 31, 1911	Year ending May 31, 1912	Year ending May 31, 1913	Year ending May 31, 1914	Total for the four years	Annual average for the four years
ADMINISTRATION						
Salaries	$8,379.09	$15,979.47	$14,928.52	$17,757.09	$57,044.17	$14,261.04
Stationery and office supplies	960.46	1,123.64	1,140.87	1,502.98	4,727.95	1,181.99
Office expenses	2,068.94	2,371.12	2,786.02	2,949.88	10,175.96	2,543.99
OPERATION						
Pumping Stations						
Wages	6,697.40	6,333.57	6,353.55	6,790.16	26,174.68	6,543.67
Coal	6,876.00	4,300.47	2,512.27	4,661.41	18,350.15	4,587.54
Oil, packing, waste, light	413.69	615.14	671.32	437.91	2,138.06	534.52
Minor equipment	183.30	317.74	204.06	208.53	913.63	228.41
Rockaway Park station	....	105.47	586.17	1,287.98	1,979.62	494.91
Reading meters	1,527.17	2,222.23	2,299.06	2,985.57	9,034.03	2,258.51
Bottling	163.02	216.03	210.02	190.04	779.11	194.78
Stable and garage expense	1,495.68	2,502.59	2,216.41	2,778.34	8,993.02	2,248.26
Filter	484.04	423.39	384.75	478.77	1,770.95	442.74
Brooks and streams	290.95	285.03	92.97	328.20	997.15	249.29
MAINTENANCE						
Mains	1,146.04	4,132.69	1,724.46	1,621.16	8,624.35	2,156.09
Boilers	259.85	145.02	487.40	571.69	1,463.96	365.99
Machinery	1,111.26	1,361.16	1,018.35	1,305.21	4,795.98	1,199.00
Buildings	1,394.02	1,140.83	1,546.94	2,067.04	6,148.83	1,537.21
Meters	3,858.55	6,029.09	4,399.77	4,603.17	18,890.58	4,722.65
Standpipe	....	....	....	153.68	153.68	38.42
Wells	839.99	391.12	402.12	151.03	1,784.26	446.07
Hydrants	1,177.31	1,439.83	1,261.78	1,580.66	5,459.58	1,364.90
Tools	325.77	275.49	240.43	202.62	1,044.31	261.08
Cleaning pipes	....	800.40	....	....	800.40	200.10
MISCELLANEOUS EXPENSES						
Permits and tapping	1,335.05	1,041.92	1,186.70	1,016.75	4,580.42	1,145.11
Inspection and collection	1,943.31	3,193.10	2,741.08	2,614.83	10,492.32	2,623.08
Insurance	531.41	307.00	275.46	992.42	2,106.29	526.57
Miscellaneous	2,107.55	2,155.98	2,707.68	4,748.38	11,719.59	2,929.90
GENERAL EXPENSES						
Legal expenses	15,573.92	6,833.71	....	24,192.05	46,599.68	11,649.92
Taxes	20,113.31	17,523.88	19,083.60	13,297.89	70,018.68	17,504.67
Farming (expense)	3,992.28	985.30	939.76	677.90	6,595.24	1,648.81
Total	$85,249.36	$84,552.41	$72,401.52	$102,153.34	$344,356.63	$86,089.22
Deduct						
Farming credits	3,181.48	1,325.68	2,520.78	2,147.50	9,175.44	2,293.86
Net total	$82,067.88	$83,226.73	$69,880.74	$100,005.84	$335,181.19	$83,795.36

(b) **Waste of water**

In considering the reasonableness of the Company's operating expenses it is necessary to inquire into the proportion of the water pumped that brings no revenue to the Company, either on account of its going to waste or because of its being furnished free for public or other uses. The total pumpage for the year ending May 31, 1914, was 1,070,285,000 gallons, of which only 664.762,200 gallons, or a little over 62%, passed through consumers' meters. Inasmuch as all the Company's domestic services are metered it becomes necessary to account for approximately 38% of the pumpage by various public and semi-public unmetered uses, by leakage and possibly by slippage in excess of the amount allowed for in the pumping records. Mr. Bettes, the chief engineer of the Company, in an effort to account for as much of the water pumped as possible, submitted the following estimates:

TABLE 32—SUBDIVISION OF PUMPAGE FOR YEAR ENDED MAY 31, 1914.

USE	Gallons	Percentage of total
Consumption by meter	664,762,200	62.1
City buildings, fire houses, etc., in part estimated	5,289,100	.5
Churches, in part estimated	1,000,000	.1
Fountains, estimated	200,000	....
Building purposes, estimated	8,500,000	.8
Flushing hydrants, estimated	4,350,000	.4
Wasted at creek crossings, estimated	1,700,000	.2
Used by water company, in part estimated	3,750,000	.3
Storm at Rockaway Beach, estimated	10,000,000	.9
Flushing sewers, estimated	30,000,000	2.8
Sprinkling, estimated	19,000,000	1.8
Used by Queens Borough Gas & Electric Co	7,171,100	.7
Unaccounted for	314,562,600	29.4
	1,070,285,000	100.0

It is to be presumed that with substantially equal pressures being maintained throughout the year the amount of leakage will be fairly constant. On the other hand, on account of the extraordinary increase in the demand during the summer months the amount of water actually consumed shows a very great increase. For example, during the three months, June, July and August, 1913, the total metered consumption was 328,280,400 gallons, or 49.4% of the consumption for the entire year. The pumpage for this three-months period was 424,690,000 gallons. This shows only 22.7% to be accounted for through miscellaneous uses and leakage during the summer months as compared with 37.9% for the entire year. In appears very probable that some of the estimates presented by Mr. Bettes, particularly those relating to the amount of water used for sprinkling and flushing sewers, are excessive, but after we make all due allowance for a reduction in his estimates of the amount of water consumed, the waste through leakage does not seem to be excessive as compared with that of other fully metered plants, where it is not unusual to find 25% or 30% of the total pumpage unaccounted for.

The unaccounted for waste of water from a distribution system that is fully metered takes place for the most part either through leaks in the mains or through leaks in the service pipes. Naturally, the greater the mileage of mains the more loss there is likely to be through leaks in the mains, and the greater the number of house connections the more loss there is likely to be through leaks in the service pipes. The Company operates about 179 miles of mains. This gives a loss of about 1,760,000 gallons per annum per mile of main, if we take Mr. Bettes' estimates of public and miscellaneous uses of water. On the basis of the excess of water pumped over metered consumption we should have 2,270,000 gallons per annum per mile of main to be accounted for through waste and public and miscellaneous uses. On the basis of the number of taps this shows a waste of 40,000 gallons per tap per annum, using Mr. Bettes' estimates, and of 51,000 gallons per tap per annum, using the difference between the total pumpage and the metered consumption.

(c) **Legal expenses**

The Company's books show no legal expenses prior to the fiscal year ending May 31, 1901. From 1901 to 1914, inclusive, the bills for legal expenses were $124,957.94, of which $5,185 represented taxes paid by counsel and $7,995.86 was charged to the real estate account and $16,808.95 to intangible capital. Of the $94,968.13 left, $4,000, though properly chargeable to operating expenses in connection with the negotiation of the Brooklyn contract, was used to offset revenue from this contract. This leaves $90,968.13 charged on the Company's books to operating expenses. Out of this total, an item of $25,000 represents legal expenses in connection with watershed litigation which, in the opinion of the expert accountants who reported to Commissioner Thompson in 1910, should have been charged to capital account. Leaving this item out and restoring the item of $4,000 above referred to, the legal expenses properly chargeable to operation and paid during the period of fourteen years amounted to $69,968.13 or $4,997.72 per annum. It should be noted that very nearly all of the payments for legal expenses were made to Lord, Day & Lord, a firm of which the late Franklin B. Lord, for many years president of the Company, was a member, and of which Henry deForest Baldwin, now president of the Company, is a member. The Company urges that there has been economy in operation, pointing to the fact that the general officers receive no salaries, except the secretary, whose salary is nominal. It should be noted in this connection, however, that the work of president and counsel has been in effect merged, and the compensation for both services included under legal expenses. Some bills for legal expenses chargeable to the period prior to

May 31, 1914, had not been presented up to that time. They are said to amount to about $5,000 plus an indefinite sum for services in connection with certain long-drawn-out tax proceedings, the amount of the latter charge being dependent in part upon the final terms of settlement with the tax authorities. The president and counsel of the Company in his dual capacity is unwilling to present and audit his own bills for services in connection with tax cases unless the bills come within the actual savings of the Company. In other words, counsel has at least to pay his way in disputing taxes. It is possible that if all unpaid and as yet unprepared bills for legal services prior to May 31, 1914, had been rendered and paid, the amount of legal expenses chargeable to operation during the 14-year period would have been increased by perhaps $20,000, which would have brought up the average to nearly $6,500 a year. The annual average of the legal expenses for the last four years has been $11,649.92, without taking account of the bills not yet rendered.

The absence of legal expenses prior to 1901 was probably due to the fact that the affairs of the Company were being managed by Mr. Franklin B. Lord, who received his compensation in the form of stock sold to him at a very large discount by the DuBoises. Most of the legal expenses of later years have been the result of tax litigation and quarrels with the City over watershed rights, rates and hydrant rental contracts. If the City and the Company succeed in adjusting their affairs on the basis of a contract equitable to both parties, the Company's legal expenses should be greatly reduced in the future.

(d) **Taxes**

The Company has made many loud complaints of excessive taxation and has paid its lawyers large fees to get its taxes reduced. As already stated, the taxes due and unpaid on June 30, 1914, with accrued interest, amounted to $87,944.34. Of this total, $2,195.29 was for corporate stock and gross earnings taxes, $79,476.43 was for special franchise taxes and $6,272.62 for other real estate taxes. The amount of taxes actually levied against the Company during the year ending June 30, 1914, was $16,049.36 of which all but $2,397.60 was paid during the year and this remainder was paid a few months later. The total amount of taxes actually paid by the Company from January 1, 1892, to May 31, 1914, was $142,204.97, or 5.6% of the Company's gross earnings during the same period. The total taxes paid during the four years, 1911 to 1914, inclusive, amounted to $70,018.68 or 7.2% of the gross earnings. The taxes levied during the year ending June 30, 1914, amounted to 6% of the gross earnings, and 8.6 mills on the dollar of the appraised value of the Company's property including the real estate not deemed necessary for the water business. It can hardly be maintained that this rate of taxation is excessive in comparison with the rates paid by other public service corporations exercising public franchises.

It is a matter of interest to note that as against $70,018.68 paid in taxes during the last four years, the Company received from the City of

New York and the several municipalities served in Nassau County only $55,181.71 for fire protection. For the single year ending May 31, 1914, the hydrant rentals amounted to $16,570.65, or $521.29 more than the taxes levied against the Company that year. The comparisons show a gradual increase in the revenue from hydrant rentals, and a gradual decrease in taxes due to the successful litigation carried on by the Company, especially for the reduction of special franchise assessments. The average amount of taxes paid during the past four years would seem to be somewhat high rather than low as a basis for estimating the amount of taxes to be paid in future years, relative to the amount of earnings that may be anticipated. Of course, it is to be expected that taxes will show some increase along with the increase in the value of the Company's property and the amount of its revenues.

(e) Allocation of operating expenses between Queens and Nassau services

The Company's accounts of operating expenses are not kept so as to make possible an exact distribution of expenses as between the Queens and Nassau services. The entire plant is operated as a unit and the accounts are kept accordingly. In regard to many of the classes of expenditure, the Company claims that the expense of operation in Queens is relatively greater than the expense of operation in Nassau. In some cases this claim seems to be justified by general considerations but cannot be supported by definite data that will enable us to measure the difference. For example, the Company asserts that the extreme peak load at certain hours of the day and on certain days of maximum use during the summer months is relatively much greater in Queens than in Nassau, but on account of the Company's inability to furnish a complete record of metered water consumed for a summer period shorter than three months it is impossible to prove this point. Moreover, it is to be noted that if the Company could prove the expenses of operation in Queens to be relatively excessive the conclusion would cut both ways. While it would tend, on the one hand, to increase the cost of service and therefore the rates to be allowed as reasonable in the Queens district, it would at the same time tend to diminish the value of the Queens business and thereby reduce the price which the City would have to pay for taking over the Queens distribution system and the service connected with it.

Great difficulty arises in attempting to apportion operating expenses between two districts, widely different in character, which are served as a unit. It would be possible to apportion such expenses on the basis of the allocation of capital, which, in the case of this Company, has already been made as between the Queens and the Nassau services. Such an apportionment would assign 67% of the expense of operation to Queens and 33% to Nassau. But this does not seem to be a just and accurate basis for the distribution of many classes of expenses, which, as a matter of fact, have very little relation to the capital investment.

It would also be possible to apportion the operating expenses on the basis of the gross earnings in the two districts. This would give 70% to Queens and 30% to Nassau. But many classes of operating expenses have no more direct relation to earnings than they have to capital investment. Another possible basis of distribution is the number of meters in the two districts. This basis would give 61.5% to Queens and 38.5% to Nassau, but it is obvious that operating expenses generally are not proportioned to the number of meters in use. After due consideration of the various bases that might be adopted it seemed necessary to take up the different classes of expenses in detail and to distribute each one of them upon the basis which seemed most appropriate for that particular expense.

It seemed proper, on the whole, to distribute administration expenses, including salaries, stationery and office supplies and office expenses, on the basis of gross revenues. The expenses of reading meters, of bottling and of inspection and collection, a portion of miscellaneous expenses and all of the legal expenses were also distributed on the basis of gross revenues. The expenses of operating the pumping station at Valley Stream were distributed on the basis of the total amount of water consumed in the two areas. The expenses of operating the filters, of maintaining brooks and streams, of maintaining boilers, machinery and wells, were also distributed on this basis. The expenses of the Rockaway Park auxiliary station were all assigned to Queens. The expense of maintaining the mains was distributed on the basis of the investment in mains attributed to services in the two areas respectively. The expense of fire insurance and of maintaining buildings was distributed according to investment in buildings. The expense of maintaining meters and hydrants was distributed according to the number of meters and of hydrants, respectively, in the two areas. The expense of maintaining the standpipes was distributed on the theory that the standpipe at Rockaway Beach is used exclusively for the Queens service, and that the standpipe at Far Rockaway is used equally for the Queens and the Nassau services. This made a division of 75% to Queens and 25% to Nassau. The expense of maintaining tools, a portion of miscellaneous expense and all of the taxes were distributed in proportion to the total investment attributed to the Queens and the Nassau services, respectively. The expense of permits and tapping was distributed according to the number of new taps placed during the past four years in the two areas, respectively, This gave 53% to Queens and 47% to Nassau. Stable and garage expenses were analyzed according to the particular use of labor and equipment and distributed on the basis of detailed percentages, which, put together, gave 71% to Queens and 29% to Nassau. Finally, the credit attributable to farming operations was distributed on the basis of the percentages of the total expense arrived at by the process already described, which were 69% for Queens and 31% for Nassau.

Applying the detailed percentages to the average annual expenses for the four-year period ending May 31, 1914, we reach the following result:

TABLE 33—DISTRIBUTION OF OPERATING EXPENSES BETWEEN QUEENS AND NASSAU SERVICES.

CLASS OF EXPENSE	Average expense for four years	Percentage attributable to Queens service	Amount attributable to Queens service	Percentage attributable to Nassau service	Amount attributable to Nassau service
Salaries	$14,261.04	70.0	$9,982.73	30.0	$4,278.31
Stationery and office supplies	1,181.99	70.0	827.39	30.0	354.60
Office expenses (including telephone)	2,543.99	70.0	1,780.79	30.0	763.20
Operation of pumping stations:					
Wages	6,543.67	72.0	4,711.44	28.0	1,832.23
Coal	4,587.54	72.0	3,303.03	28.0	1,284.51
Oil, packing, waste, light	534.52	72.0	384.85	28.0	149.67
Minor equipment	228.41	72.0	164.46	28.0	63.95
Rockaway Park station	494.91	100.0	494.91	....	....
Reading meters	2,258.51	70.0	1,580.96	30.0	677.55
Bottling	194.78	70.0	136.35	30.0	58.43
Stable and garage expenses	2,248.26	71.0	1,589.16	29.0	659.10
Operation of filter	442.74	72.0	318.77	28.0	123.97
Brooks and streams	249.29	72.0	179.49	28.0	69.80
Maintenance of mains	2,156.09	64.0	1,379.90	36.0	776.19
Maintenance of boilers	365.99	72.0	263.51	28.0	102.48
Maintenance of machinery (including pumps)	1,199.00	72.0	863.28	28.0	335.72
Maintenance of buildings	1,537.21	73.5	1,129.85	26.5	407.36
Maintenance of meters	4,722.65	61.5	2,904.43	38.5	1,818.22
Maintenance of standpipes	38.42	75.0	28.82	25.0	9.60
Maintenance of wells	446.07	72.0	321.17	28.0	124.90
Maintenance of hydrants	1,364.90	62.0	846.24	38.0	518.66
Maintenance of tools	261.08	67.0	174.92	33.0	86.16
Cleaning pipes	200.10	100.0	200.10	....	....
Permits and tapping	1,145.11	53.0	606.91	47.0	538.20
Inspection and collection	2,623.08	70.0	1,836.16	30.0	786.92
Fire insurance	526.57	73.5	387.03	26.5	139.54
Life insurance	600.00	70.0	420.00	30.0	180.00
Miscellaneous expenses	2,329.90	67.0	1,561.03	33.0	768.87
Legal expenses	11,649.92	70.0	8,154.94	30.0	3,494.98
Taxes	17,504.67	67.0	11,728.12	33.0	5,776.55
Total	$84,440.41	69.0	$58,260.74	31.0	$26,179.67
Less profits from "farming"	645.05	69.0	445.08	31.0	199.97
Net expenses	$83,795.36	69.0	$57,815.66	31.0	$25,979.70

The resultant assignment of 69 per cent. to Queens and 31 per cent. to Nassau differs very little from the division that would have been obtained by the use of gross earnings as the basis for distribution, namely, 70 per cent. and 30 per cent.; or by the use of the capital investment, namely, 67 per cent. and 33 per cent.

(f) Allocation of Queens operating expenses between fire protection and domestic service

Having determined the amount of the operating expenses attributable to the Queens service, it became necessary to ascertain what proportion of this amount is attributable to fire service and what proportion to domestic service. This distribution, as well as the distribution between the two areas, had to be made in detail, in accordance with the nature of the expense and in the light of any facts submitted by the Company which have a bearing upon particular items. After full consideration, it seemed proper to attribute to domestic service 100% of operating expenses of the following classes: stationery and office supplies; coal; oil, packing, waste and light; minor pumping station equipment; reading meters; bottling; filter; brooks and streams; maintenance of meters; maintenance of tools; permits and tapping; inspection and collection; miscellaneous expenses. The propriety of assigning the entire expense under these classifications to domestic service is in most cases obvious. In relation to coal and other pumping station supplies it appeared that the amount of water actually consumed for fire protection is so small as to make negligible the additional expense of these items on account of it.

The Company showed that it kept certain employees and certain extra telephone equipment solely as a protection in case of fire emergency. Accordingly, 6% of salaries, 40% of office expenses (mainly telephone), and 10% of pumping station wages were charged to fire protection. It was estimated that the expense of the Rockaway Park auxiliary station should be divided half and half between fire protection and domestic service. Of the cost of maintaining mains, 10% was attributed to fire protection and the cost of cleaning pipes was distributed between domestic service and fire protection on the same basis that the investment in mains had been distributed, namely, 74% for domestic service and 26% for fire protection. Of the cost of maintaining the boilers, pumping machinery and buildings, 25% was attributed to fire protection. The cost of maintaining standpipes was divided half and half. The cost of maintaining wells was divided in proportion to the distribution of the investment in wells, namely, 67% to domestic service, and 33% to fire protection. Taxes were distributed in proportion to the investment, that is to say, 74% to domestic service and 26% to fire protection. The cost of fire insurance was distributed on the same basis as the capital investment in buildings, boilers and pumps, namely, 62% for domestic service and 38% for fire protection. Stable and garage expenses were analyzed in detail with the result that 20% was attributed to fire protection and 80% to domestic service. A detailed examination of the bills of counsel led to the conclusion that about 20% of the legal expenses should be attributed to fire protection.

Applying these various percentages to the average annual amount of operating expenses under the various classifications attributed to the Queens service for the four-year period ending May 31, 1914, we reach the following result:

TABLE 34—DISTRIBUTION OF OPERATING EXPENSES ATTRIBUTABLE TO THE QUEENS AREA BETWEEN DOMESTIC SERVICE AND FIRE PROTECTION.

CLASS OF EXPENSE	Average annual expense for the 4-year period ending May 31, 1914	Percentage attributable to domestic service	Amount attributable to domestic service	Percentage attributable to fire protection	Amount attributable to fire protection
Salaries	$9,982.73	96.0	$9,383.77	6.0	$598.96
Stationery and office supplies	827.39	100.0	827.39	.....	....
Office expenses (including telephone)	1,780.79	60.0	1,068.47	40.0	712.32
Operation of pumping stations:					
Wages	4,711.44	90.0	4,240.30	10.0	471.14
Coal	3,303.03	100.0	3,303.03	....	....
Oil, packing, waste, light	384.85	100.0	384.85	....	....
Minor equipment	164.46	100.0	164.46	....	....
Rockaway Park station	494.91	50.0	247.46	50.0	247.45
Reading meters	1,580.96	100.0	1,580.96	....	....
Bottling	136.35	100.0	136.35	....	....
Stable and garage expenses	1,589.16	80.0	1,276.95	20.0	312.21
Operation of filter	318.77	100.0	318.77	....	....
Brooks and streams	179.49	100.0	179.49	....	....
Maintenance of mains	1,379.90	90.0	1,241.91	10.0	137.99
Maintenance of boilers	263.51	75.0	197.63	25.0	65.88
Maintenance of machinery (including pumps)	863.28	75.0	647.46	25.0	215.82
Maintenance of buildings	1,129.85	75.0	847.39	25.0	282.46
Maintenance of meters	2,904.43	100.0	2,904.43	....	....
Maintenance of standpipes	28.82	50.0	14.41	50.0	14.41
Maintenance of wells	321.17	67.0	215.18	33.0	105.99
Maintenance of hydrants	846.24	....	....	100.0	846.24
Maintenance of tools	174.92	100.0	174.92	....	....
Cleaning pipes	200.10	74.0	148.07	26.0	52.03
Permits and tapping	606.91	100.0	606.91	....	....
Inspection and collection	1,836.16	100.0	1,836.16	....	....
Fire insurance	387.03	62.0	239.96	38.0	147.07
Life insurance	420.00	100.0	420.00	....	....
Miscellaneous expenses	1,561.03	100.0	1,561.03	....	....
Legal expenses	8,154.94	80.0	6,523.95	20.0	1,630.99
Taxes	11,728.12	74.0	8,678.81	26.0	3,049.31
Total	$58,260.74	85.0	$49,370.47	15.0	$8,890.27
Less profits from "farming"	445.08	85.0	378.31	15.0	66.77
Net total expenses	$57,815.66	85.0	$48,992.16	15.0	$8,823.50

(g) Fair allowance for operating expenses

The amount of operating expenses charged on the books from year to year shows considerable fluctuations. This is largely due to the fact that the Company's counsel sometimes hold back their bills until they think that the Company is able to pay. For example, nothing was paid for legal expenses in the fiscal year 1912-1913, while in the next year the amount paid was $24,192.05. Moreover, this large payment only covered bills up to January 1, 1914, leaving five months' services valued by counsel at about $5,000 still unpaid. By making a readjustment of the legal expenses and taxes for the past four years, we get the following comparisons:

TABLE 35—OPERATING EXPENSES READJUSTED, 1911 TO 1914, INCLUSIVE.

YEAR	Legal expenses	Other expenses, including taxes	Total
1910–11	$8,189.60	$66,493.96	$74,683.56
1911–12	10,276.21	76,393.02	86,669.23
1912–13	11,600.83	69,880.74	81,481.57
1913–14	11,856.62	78,565.26	90,421.88
Total	$41,923.26	$291,332.98	$333,256.24
Average per annum	10,480.82	72,833.24	83,314.06

It has already been noted that the heavy legal expenses heretofore incurred by the Company in defending itself against the "perils" of "municipal persecution" ought to be considerably diminished in the future. At the same time the Company is entitled to pay a fair amount for the services of its president, and therefore if "legal expenses" are cut to the bone, it is possible that they may reappear in part in the form of salaries of general officers. Nevertheless, there should be considerable net decrease in these combined expenses. We have also noted that the amount of taxes levied during the fiscal year 1914 was only $16,049.36, while the average amount of taxes paid per annum during the three years just preceding 1914 was $18,906.93.

Giving these matters due consideration, and noting that the actual expenses of the year 1914, with all taxes and lawyers' bills paid, would have been approximately $90,421.88, I am of the opinion that $83,795.36 is a sufficient annual allowance for operating expenses, including taxes but excluding depreciation, on the basis of the amount of business done during the year ending May 31, 1914, but under the conditions of security which the City may properly give the Company in the future. This is the average actually paid during the four years 1911 to 1914, inclusive, and furnished the basis for the distribution between the Queens and Nassau services and between domestic service and fire protection. In the absence of a contract giving security to the Company's investment, the full allowance of $90,421.88 would probably have to be made.

Undoubtedly, operating expenses will increase with the increase of business, but whether or not in the same proportion is a matter to be considered at this point. We may first compare the rate of increase of operating expenses in the past with the rate of increase of gross revenues. We find, for example, that the operating expenses, exclusive of taxes, legal expenses and "farming" for the four years from 1901 to 1904, inclusive, amounted to 31% of the gross earnings. These same expenses ten years later, for the period 1911 to 1914, inclusive, amounted to only 22.8% of gross earnings. Or, put in another way, gross earnings increased 236%, while these operating expenses referred to increased only 147%. Taxes, legal expenses and farming are left out of consideration in this comparison because of their violent fluctuations. For example, the legal expenses paid shows an increase of 480% in ten years, but this cannot be regarded as a criterion for the future, under closer municipal supervision and less conflict between the Company and the public authorities. Another computation, leaving out the estimated expenses of pumping to Brooklyn on the one side and the revenues from the Brooklyn Contract on the other, and also leaving out legal expenses, taxes and farming, shows that on the average during the past fourteen years operating expenses have increased 64.3% as rapidly as gross earnings. On the basis of existing rates this would be a very useful figure in estimating the future increase in operating expenses in connection with the estimated increase of earnings. But, owing to the fact that rates are to be readjusted, it is necessary to make an estimate of the future increase in expenses on some other basis.

The increase in pumpage, exclusive of water pumped to Brooklyn, from 1900 to 1914 was 162.7%, while the increase in operating expenses exclusive of taxes, legal expenses, depreciation, Brooklyn Contract and farming was 188.6%. This gives a remarkable result, namely, operating expenses increasing more rapidly than amount of water pumped during the period when the Company was going from no-dividends to eight per cent. The comparison is practically worthless as a guide to the future. This seems to be due in part to the fact that the increase of pumpage has been held back by the general installation of meters and by a probable relative decrease in leakage.

The increase in the number of live taps from 1900 to 1914 was 342.7% as compared with 188.6% for operating expenses exclusive of the items mentioned above.

The following table will show for the past fourteen years (1) operating expenses, exclusive of taxes, depreciation, legal expenses, farming and Brooklyn Contract; (2) gross revenues, exclusive of Brooklyn Contract; (3) taps in use; (4) total pumpage, exclusive of Brooklyn Contract.

Table 36—COMPARISON OF RATES OF INCREASE IN EXPENSES, REVENUES, TAPS AND PUMPAGE.

Year	Expenses, exclusive of legal, taxes, farming, and Brooklyn Contract	Revenues, exclusive of Brooklyn Contract	Active taps (number)	Pumpage (gallons)
1901	$19,879.14	$57,533.42	2,081	455,068,621
1902	20,631.30	68,306.19	2,450	497,742,534
1903	20,636.66	78,520.14	2,693	596,665,324
1904	28,365.96	84,296.32	2,947	694,275,878
1905	33,087.54	93,534.29	3,196	774,058,171
1906	35,005.61	103,886.45	3,604	871,514,654
1907	39,448.66	121,828.92	4,116	926,586,296
1908	38,925.62	135,637.50	4,585	932,031,422
1909	40,920.70	153,037.74	5,130	935,081,000
1910	44,267.06	176,645.36	5,865	1,022,355,320
1911	40,869.85	194,112.21	6,408	1,077,966,000
1912	57,799.52	211,778.69	6,857	1,108,378,780
1913	51,024.16	222,222.42	7,476	993,716,120
1914	63,235.50	258,637.10	8,022	1,070,285,000
1900 deduct from 1914	21,911.07	51,404.88	1,812	407,369,110
Amount of increase, 1900 to 1914	$41,324.43	$207,232.22	6,210	662,915,890
Per cent. of increase, 1900 to 1914	188.6	403.1	342.7	162.7
Average per cent. of annual increase	7.86	12.23	11.21	7.14

Ratios of increase

Expenses to revenues 64.27%
Expenses to active taps 70.12%
Expenses to pumpage 110.08%

This table shows for the period from 1900 to 1914 an average annual rate of increase in operating expenses, exclusive of legal expenses, taxes, farming and Brooklyn Contract, 70.12% as great as the rate of increase in live taps. But for the last four years of this period, taken by themselves, these expenses increased 118% as fast as taps. This difference is rather bewildering.

If we take the period from 1897 to 1914, inclusive, and include all expenses except those incident to the Brooklyn Contract, we get a more significant result. Reducing expenses to the tap-year basis for this entire period, we get $12.02 as the average annual expense per tap. This figure is remarkably constant. Taking the eleven year period, from 1904 to 1914, inclusive, we get the same average figure. Taking the five year period from 1910 to 1914, inclusive, we get $12.09, an increase of seven cents per tap-year. The fluctuations in the annual expense per tap are shown by the following:

TABLE 37—RELATION OF TAPS TO EXPENSES.

YEAR	Number of active taps	Gross expenses, exclusive of Brooklyn Contract, depreciation and interest	Expenses per tap
1897	1,423	$19,945.00	$14.01
1898	1,526	21,486.00	14.09
1899	1,633	17,669.00	10.82
1900	1,812	26,863.00	14.82
1901	2,081	23,905.00	11.49
1902	2,450	25,161.00	10.27
1903	2,693	28,053.00	10.43
1904	2,947	40,380.00	13.70
1905	3,196	43,608.00	13.64
1906	3,604	45,331.00	12.58
1907	4,116	49,535.00	12.03
1908	4,585	51,855.00	11.31
1909	5,130	50,381.00	9.82
1910	5,865	91,756.00	15.64
1911	6,408	77,368.00	12.07
1912	6,857	81,817.00	11.93
1913	7,476	68,627.00	9.18
1914	8,022	99,256.00	12.37
Total	71,824	$862,996.00	.....
Average expense per tap year			$12.02

This table does not give the facts quite complete, for as already noted in a previous section of this report, back taxes for certain years were still in part unpaid. Allowing for the years back of 1910, the additional sum of $57,249 on this account, we should have the average expense per tap during these years (1897 to 1909, inclusive) $13.48, instead of $11.94, as shown by the figures in the table; and counting in $2,751, the amount of unpaid taxes for 1914, the average annual expense per tap for the years 1910 to 1914, inclusive, would be $12.17 instead of $12.09. But if we take the expenses already allowed as reasonable for the 1914 business under the more favorable conditions to be expected under the proposed contract, and deduct the expense incident to the Brooklyn Contract, we get the average of the operating expenses and taxes per active tap reduced to about $10.33 in 1914.

All these figures seem to show pretty conclusively that this Company's expenses may be expected to increase at a somewhat lower rate than the taps. On the whole, it seems reasonable to make allowance for operating expenses and taxes in a forecast of the future upon the basis of $10.33 per tap per year, including both domestic service and fire protection, or excluding the latter, $8.78.

XIX. ANNUAL DEPRECIATION OF PROPERTY ATTRIBUTABLE TO THE QUEENS SERVICE.

Depreciation has been figured on the straight-line basis on the theory that this particular plant has reached the stage in its development where the replacements required from year to year will constitute a relatively constant item of expenditure which should be met out of an annual allowance taken from earnings rather than be charged to capital account, as has been done heretofore.

The controlling considerations in adopting the straight-line rather than the sinking fund method in this case are, in the first place, simplicity of accounting, and, in the second, the fact that the plant will never have to be renewed as a whole and can never be brought much above, and need never be permitted to fall much below, the standard of practical efficiency now maintained. In other words, there is no call for the extremely complex and futile computations which would be necessary if we were to assume that a fund must be set aside for each individual unit of the plant sufficient to replace the particular unit when worn out or obsolete. Replacements will have to be made from time to time, and although they will doubtless fluctuate considerably, perhaps even sharply, from year to year, the general average will be maintained. This makes the use of the straight-line method of charging depreciation as appropriate as it is easy.

The equal-annual-payment method of charging depreciation, which has recently received considerable theoretical support, is altogether too complex to be applied to an old plant like that of the Queens County Water Company, with an irregular past development and great uncertainty in regard to investment details.

The accrued depreciation found in the entire property attributable to the Queens service is 17.5% of reproduction cost new, or, eliminating land and going value from consideration, 20.3%. This fact would lend support to the belief that the depreciable property as a whole in a growing plant like this one can be kept up substantially to a standard of 80% of cost new. This would put the investment into a moving equilibrium 20% below cost new, and would mean under normal conditions that the investors could properly withdraw as no longer needed in the business 20% of the original investment. Unfortunately, it generally seems easier to put more capital into a utility than to withdraw any already there, and whenever the withdrawal becomes practically possible, the desire of the investor is to leave his money in the enterprise. Moreover, the appreciations in land and other parts of the plant, on the one hand, and early losses from operation and the cost of developing the business on the other hand, enter in to modify or upset the theoretically correct adjustment of the capital account. Under the decisions of the courts, when the regulation of rates is undertaken for the first time it is necessary to assume that the accrued depreciation of the property has either been withdrawn or been offset by appreciation.

The annual depreciation attributed to the parts of the plant used for the Queens service exclusively, plus the proper proportion chargeable to Queens of the depreciation attributed to parts of the plant used in common for the Queens and Nassau services, amounts to $24,145, as already shown in detail in Table 29 given under subdivision XVII. This is on the basis of the investment as of June 30, 1914. Additional depreciation will have to be allowed for construction subsequent to that date.

Doubtless actual depreciation and the necessity for replacements may occur in a manner and to an extent quite different from the detailed estimates of the engineers. But it is believed that $24,145 per annum is a proper, fair and adequate allowance for depreciation of the property in use for the Queens service on June 30, 1914. Out of this allowance the company should be required to pay for all replacements by whatever cause made necessary. After a proper system of accounting has been installed for a few years, if it is shown that the depreciation allowance is too small or too large for the Company's necessities, including a reasonable reserve fund for replacements of an unusual character made necessary by unforeseen events, the annual amount allowed for depreciation can be changed.

The Company may enjoy certain incidental advantages in having a depreceiation allowance that can be used at times to round out other sources of working capital, but these advantages, if they accrue, may properly be considered as a sort of lubricant for efficiency.

XX. NET EARNINGS REQUIRED TO AFFORD A FAIR RETURN ON CAPITAL ATTRIBUTABLE TO THE QUEENS SERVICE.

The total investment attributable to the Queens service has been found to be $1,148,896. The fair annual rate of return upon this investment necessary to enable the Company to pay interest to its bondholders and profits to its stockholders, has no direct relation to rates of interest and dividends actually paid. If the investment is entitled to earn 6%, the Company can pay out in dividends whatever it can save in interest. If the rate of return is 7%, the difference between the interest rate and the dividend rate will be considerable. The higher the rate of return allowed the greater will this difference be, not only because the stockholders do not share profits with the bondholders, but also because the larger the profits are, the safer and therefore the more attractive are the bonds, with the result that interest rates will be somewhat lower or bond discounts less. In other words, the greater the margin of security for the investment the cheaper will money be.

On a 6% basis the Company would be entitled to net earnings from the Queens business over and above depreciation and operating expenses and taxes to the amount of $68,934 per annum on the investment as of June 30, 1914. On a 7% basis the net earnings should be $80,423, and on an 8% basis, $91,912.

An adjustment on account of capital expenditures subsequent to the date of the inventory can be made on the same bases.

XXI. FAIR COST OF FIRE SERVICE IN QUEENS.

The basis upon which the cost of fire service is estimated has already been explained in detail. The method pursued was the most conservative for which any scientific basis could be found. A larger estimate of cost could have been supported by high authority. As determined, the annual cost of fire service is made up of three elements: (1) return upon that portion of the investment necessary to provide fire protection; (2) depreciation of the property representing such investment; (3) portion of operating expenses incidental to the rendering of fire service. On the basis of a 6% return upon the investment, the annual cost of the fire service being rendered to the Fifth Ward of Queens as of June 30, 1914, is estimated to be $31,434, made up as follows:

Return on investment of $266,553.00 at 6 per cent.	$15,993.00
Depreciation on investment of $266,553.00	6,617.00
Fifteen per cent. of operating expenses and taxes	8,824.00
	$31,434.00

As already explained, this cost should be separated into two parts: (1) a lump sum, and (2) a rental per hydrant in use. Such a division will enable the city to require the installation of additional hydrants whenever needed without obligating itself to pay several times the cost of each new hydrant.

We have found the average reproduction cost of the hydrants, including valves, valve boxes and connections to be $67.76, with a present value of $47.35, the difference being due to accrued depreciation. In estimating the return on investment to get a proper hydrant rental rate to take care of that portion of the cost of fire service which increases wih an increase in the number of hydrants it seems proper to use the reproduction cost new figure, as all new hydrants will represent when set an additional investment measured by cost new. The special annual cost attributable to each hydrant is estimated as follows:

Interest on investment, 6 per cent. on $67.76	$4.07
Depreciation, $1,079 on 632 hydrants	1.71
Maintenance, $1,147 on 632 hydrants	1.82
Taxes, 8.6 mills on present value, $47.35	.41
Total	$8.01

It would appear, therefore, that a proper hydrant rental in the case of this Company, with its investment made secure, would be $8 per annum. At this rate the total annual hydrant rentals payable by the city for the Queens service would be $5,056 on the basis of the number of hydrants in service at the date of the inventory. This would leave $26,378 to be paid as a lump sum representing the remainder of the annual cost of the fire service being rendered on that date.

The increase in cost for hydrants will be in accordance with the number of new hydrants set less the number of old hydrants discontinued subsequent to the date of the appraisal. The increase in the lump sum will depend upon the amount and character of the additional investment made for fire protection. Upon this investment depreciation and interest should be figured in accordance with the rules followed in the inquiry into the property included in the appraisal.

On the basis of a 7% return, without the security that would reduce legal expenses, the total annual cost of the fire service in Queens would be $34,786, of which $29,288 would be payable in a lump sum and the balance, $5,498, would be payable in the form of hydrant rentals at the rate of $8.70 per hydrant.

If we allowed an 8% return, with the same absence of security, the total cost would be $37,452, the lump sum payment $31,511, and the hydrant rentals $5,941, at the rate of $9.40 per hydrant.

The Company maintains that a larger allowance per hydrant should be made for maintenance and taxes, on the theory that these maintenance charges will not be reduced along with other operating expenses by the greater security expected under the proposed contract, and that each hydrant, being separately listed in the tax reports, will be assessed at approximately its full value. With these modifications, the company estimates the annual rental on the 6% at approximately the same figure as we have given on the 7% basis. All these estimates relate to four-inch hydrants, the type heretofore installed in practically all cases by this Company.

XXII. FAIR COST OF DOMESTIC AND MISCELLANEOUS SERVICES IN QUEENS, WITH SCHEDULE OF RATES

To get a 7% return on the investment the Company needs gross earnings in Queens from all sources, on the basis of 1914 conditions as to investment and business, amounting to $166,959 per annum, as follows:

Return on investment, 7 per cent. on $1,148,896	$80,423.00
Depreciation	24,145.00
Operating expenses	62,391.00
	$166,959.00

On the basis of a 6% return and a secured investment the amount required would be reduced by $16,064 to $150,895, and on the basis of an 8% return the total would be increased by $11,489 to $178,448.

The gross earnings from the Queens area during the fiscal year 1914 from hydrant rentals and from the sale of water, amounted to $172,367, to which should be added miscellaneous operating revenues estimated at $2,260, making a total of $174,627. This total should be decreased by a certain amount for uncollectable accounts. Judged by the experience of the past, these amount to about seven-eighths of 1% of gross earnings. This would make about $1,526 on the revenues from the Queens business in 1914, leaving the total available earnings for that year $173,101. This would indicate that on the 7% basis the company earned $6,142 more than a fair return during 1914. The readjustment of the fire service charges on the plan already outlined, on the 7% basis, will increase the Company's revenue from that source by $23,778.

Moreover, under the general plan recommended in this report the City ought to pay at regular meter rates for water furnished to public buildings or for other uses properly classed as domestic or business contion. For fire protection the City pays only the actual cost of maintaining the additional equipment necessary for that purpose. The cost of the water itself used in extinguishing fires is nominal. It seems reasonable that all proper public uses of water, where the water is taken from the hydrants, such as sprinkling, flushing streets and flushing sewers, should be treated as incidental to the cost of fire protection. The Company should permit the City to use as much water as is necessary for these purposes, subject to reasonable restrictions to prevent waste and unnecessary interference with domestic service at the hours of peak load. Under such restrictions the additional cost of pumping this water would so small and so difficult of calculation as to be properly negligible as an expense separate from the cost of fire service. On the other hand, water for schoolhouses, hospitals, police stations, fire houses, sewage disposal plant, flush tanks and other public uses, requiring separate taps and a constant flow or readiness to flow, cannot be regarded as incidental to fire protection, but should be measured and paid for the same as water used by domestic consumers. Just how much this will amount to is not definitely known, but the Company's estimate of the amount used for these purposes in 1914 is more than 5,000,000 gallons, which at the lowest rate to domestic consumers would bring in $1,000 or more.

As the Company does not demand a net increase of rates, the total additional amount assumed by the City, estimated at $24,778 per annum, can, without dispute, be taken off the domestic rates.

As shown above, the earnings in 1914 gave approximatly a 7½% return upon the entire investment. The valuation and the fixing of rates by public authority constitute in themselves a considerable element of security for the future. Under all the circumstances, it seems entirely just to reduce the Company's earnings to a 7% basis, irrespective of the approval of the proposed contract. This will allow a further reduction in domestic rates of $6,142 per annum. With the increase in burdens assumed by the City, this will give us a margin of $30,920 for reduction in domestic rates.

During 1914 the Company sold in the Queens area 205,940,000 gallons of water at the 40-cent rate. This accounts for a revenue of $82,376, but by reason of minimum charges on premises using 11,625,000 gallons less water than they were entitled to, this revenue for 40-cent water was increased $4,650 to a net total of $87,026. The elminination of the 40-cent charge as the primary rate would reduce the Company's Queens revenues by 10 cents per 1,000 gallons on 205,940,000 gallons now sold at the 40-cent rate, or $20,594, less the additional salvage that would accrue to the Company from the minimum rates. This salvage, based upon a careful estimate of the total amount of water used by consumers who take less than 33,333 gallons each (the amount that would be allowed under the $10 minimum charge at the 30-cent rate), would aggregate about $1,484. This indicates that the Company would lose only about $19,110 a year in the Queens area by reason of the elimination of the 40-cent rate.

The amount of water sold in the Queens area at the 30-cent rate in 1914 was 188,315,900 gallons, which, added to the 40-cent water, makes 394,255,900 gallons that would be affected by a reduction below the 30-cent rate, except as the effect would be limited by the minimum rates. Five cents per 1,000 gallons taken off this total would cause a further reduction of $19,713, less the additional salvage from the minimum rates. But the margin we have left for reduction is only $11,810. It appears from a careful computation that a reduction of about $11,400 would be effected if the 30-cent rate were kept, but limited to the first 40,000 gallons of water consumed. The charge for water used in excess of 40,000 gallons up to 450,000 would be 25 cents, and for all above 450,-

000 gallons, 20 cents, as at present. This additional reduction, therefore, can be made without cutting the Company's net earnings below 7% on the total investment.

In case the City and the Company enter into a contract by which additional security is given to the Company's investment, a further reduction of about $13,100 can properly be made.

The entire elimination of the 30-cent rate would make a net additional reduction in revenues of about $7,017, leaving $6,083 to be cut elsewhere. The limitation of the 25-cent rate to the first 100,000 gallons consumed would further reduce the revenues about $6,533, and a little more than meets the requirements.

In connection with these proposed rate schedules, it is proper to call attention to the fact that the City itself on metered premises charges 10 cents per 100 cubic feet of water consumed, which is about equivalent to 13 cents per 1,000 gallons. The City has no minimum charge, but on the other hand, requires the consumer to furnish and maintain the meter. We do not know exactly how much on the average this meter burden is. Most of the meters in use on the City service are on business premises and therefore would average of a somewhat larger size than the meters in use on the Queens County service, where all premises are metered. It has been estimated that meters on the City service represent an average investment of about $27 apiece, including the cost of setting, and that the average annual cost of repairs is about $2.40 for each meter. If the investment be reduced to $16 apiece and the repairs to $1.50, the average meter burden which the Queens County consumers would have to pay under City rates and of which they are relieved by the Company would be about $2.50 per annum. This consideration reduces considerably the actual difference between City rates and the schedule rates herein proposed. Taking into consideration the physical difficulties of supplying water to the Rockaway peninsula, I am of the opinion that the proposed rates cannot be regarded as unfair to the consumer or higher than the service is reasonably worth at the present time.

If the City takes over the business of supplying water in this area, uniform City rates will be put into effect automatically here, as elsewhere on the City service, even though this particular portion of the business may be done at a loss. But so long as the service is rendered by a private Company, all that the City can reasonably do for the relief of the people is to pay the cost of fire service and other public uses, and permit the Company to collect from private consumers whatever additional sum may be necessary to pay the reasonable cost of the service rendered.

For reasons already given in a preceding section of this report, I see no good reason for eliminating or changing the minimum rates now charged by this Company. I deem the following schedules to be fair, just and reasonable on the basis of the business done in 1914:

1. Fire protection and hydrant service.

For each fire hydrant set and maintained at the request of the City of New York.

A. Under existing conditions ....$8.70 per annum

B. If proposed contract is approved by the City...........$8.00 per annum

For general fire protection, including readiness to serve and water used for extinguishment of fires, and for water reasonably necessary for sprinkling streets and for flushing streets and sewers where such water is taken from the fire hydrants—

A. Under existing conditions ....$29,288 per annum

B. If proposed contract is approved by the city ....$26.378 per annum

All charges under this heading to be payable in four quarterly installments by the City of New York after the service has been rendered.

2. Minimum rates for metered service:

On all services supplied from taps in the mains except services connected with City buildings or used exclusively for City purposes, the following minimum rates payable in advance:

Through ½-inch or ⅝-inch meter..........................	$10.00 per annum
Through ¾-inch meter....................................	15.00 per annum
Through 1-inch meter....................................	20.00 per annum
Through 1½-inch meter...................................	30.00 per annum
Through 2-inch meter....................................	40.00 per annum
Through 3-inch meter....................................	80.00 per annum
Through 4-inch meter....................................	160.00 per annum
Through 6-inch meter....................................	300.00 per annum

3. Metered consumption.

A. Meter rates under existing conditions:

For the first 40,000 gallons consumed during the fiscal year, 30 cents per 1000 gallons;

For the next 410,000 gallons consumed during the fiscal year, 25 cents per 1,000 gallons.

For all water in excess of 450,000 gallons consumed during the fiscal year, 20 cents per 1,000 gallons.

B. Meter rates if proposed contract is approved by the City:

For the first 100,000 gallons consumed during the fiscal year, 25 cents per 1,000 gallons.

For all water in excess of 100,000 gallons consumed during the fiscal year, 20 cents per 1,000 gallons.

Each consumer, other than the City of New York, to be entitled under the minimum rates to use the quantity of water which, at meter rates would cost the minimum rate; payment for water used in excess of the minimum allowance to be made after the water is consumed. Water for all City services not taken from the hydrants to be metered and paid for at the regular meter rates. On all water bills remaining unpaid thirty days after they become due a penalty of 5% to be added, and on bills still unpaid six months after they become due a further penalty of 10% upon the original amount of the bill to be added; but this not to curtail the right of the Company to discontinue its service because of non-payment of charges.

The Company, in its discretion, to require a meter deposit of $10 for each meter put in service, but the Company to return the amount of such deposit to the consumer when the service is discontinued and all bills paid. The Company to pay interest at 6% per annum on all meter deposits. Interest to be paid once a year and whenever the service is discontinued.

XXIII. EXTENSIONS AND IMPROVEMENTS IMMEDIATELY REQUIRED.

As a result of the rapid extension of building down the Rockaway peninsula, the consumption of water during the summer months has overtaxed the Company's facilities for conveying the water to the Rockaway Beach section. The result has been inadequate pressure, so that in some cases the water would not flow on the second floor, and an inadequate supply of water in case of fire emergency. This condition became acute several years ago, but the uncertain relations existing between the Company and the City and the inadequate payment made by the City for fire protection in the shape of hydrant rentals resulted in the Company being dilatory in making the improvements that would have been necessary to give complete and adequate service, both for domestic purposes and for fire protection, throughout the Queens area served by it. As a temporary expedient to avoid the necessity of the immediate investment of a large amount of capital in strengthening its distribution system, particularly in laying an additional trunk main between Far Rockaway and Belle Harbor, the Company in the summer of 1911 started up an auxiliary station at Rockaway Park, pumping raw water from deep wells into the mains, in order to increase the supply and furnish the pressure required in that district. The water derived from the Rockaway Park wells has a very high content of iron and in its raw state is very unsatisfactory for domestic uses. The use of this water during a portion of each summer season since 1911 has resulted in very serious and widespread complaints by the residents whose service has been affected by it. Filters are now being installed, which, it is believed, will improve the water so as to make it fit for use during the summer emergency, but the maintenace of an auxiliary station and filter plant for this emergency supply is, under the circumstances, too expensive and unsatisfactory to be regarded as a permanent solution of the service problem.

About three years ago the City made a careful survey of the Company's system in Queens with a view to determining the additional requirements for fire protection. As a result of that investigation a form of contract between the City and the Company was prepared, in accordance with which the Company was to make improvements in its Queens distribution system within a period of two years at an estimated expense of $228,000. The City was to authorize a large increase in the number of hydrants and was to increase the hydrant rental from $20 to $25 per annum. This contract was transmitted by Commissioner Thompson to the Board of Estimate and Apportionment under date of May 19, 1913, but never received the approval of the Board. Subsequent to the institution of the present investigation the contract was withdrawn by Commissioner Williams, under date of February 19, 1915.

Some of the improvements that were to have been made under the proposed 1913 contract have been made since that time. The Company has been gradually working toward the strengthening of its distribution system, as recommended by the Department, and the work already done and now under way has been done with the approval of the Department. Briefly, the improvements deemed necessary by the Department included a large increase in the number of fire hydrants, the replacement of a considerable amount of small mains by 6-inch and 8-inch mains and the laying of an additional trunk main most of the way from the Far Rockaway standpipe to Belle Harbor near the westerly limit of the area of service. The specific requirements of the 1913 proposed contract were as follows:

> "Within eighteen months from the execution and delivery of this contract the Company shall at its own expense replace existing small mains with 6-inch and 8-inch mains, as indicated on the map hereinafter referred to, dated March, 1912; but the work on such replacements shall be commenced immediately after the execution and delivery of this contract and the order in which this work is done may be determined by the Commissioner.
>
> "Before the expiration of one year from the execution and delivery of this contract, the Company shall at its own expense lay an additional main of at least 16-inches inside diameter (unless it is impracticable so to do and in case it is impracticable to lay such 16-inch main the Company shall replace an existing 12-inch main with a main of at least 20 inches inside diameter) from its existing Rockaway Park standpipe to Carlton Avenue and lay an additional main of at least 16 inches inside diameter from Cronin's Crossing to Grand View Avenue and an additional main of not less than 12 inches inside diameter from said Rockaway Park standpipe through Belle Harbor to Park Avenue.
>
> "Within two years from the execution and delivery of this contract the company shall at its own expense lay an additional main of not less than 16 inches inside diameter from Grand View Avenue to its Far Rockaway standpipe and lay the new 6 inch and 8 inch laterals indicated on said map dated March, 1912."

Including work already done and now under way, the Company will have completed by June 30 of this year the laying of the additional 16-inch main from the Far Rockaway standpipe southward and westward to Cronin's Crossing. It has also laid a section of the additional 16-inch main required from the Rockaway Park standpipe to Carlton Avenue. The section already laid extends from Neptune Avenue, (three blocks from the standpipe), eastwardly to the junction of Henry Street and the Boulevard. The Company has also laid a portion of the new 12-inch main extending westwardly from the Rockaway Park standpipe. The section laid goes to Fifth Avenue.

The Company has also relaid some of its small mains upon which fire hydrants are located, and has installed about 200 additional hydrants

The construction of the section of the new 16-inch line between Henry Street and Carlton Avenue has been delayed, in part, by the difficulty of securing a proper route for the main. The Boulevard is already crowded with sub-surface structures. A new Boulevard, north of the Long Island Railroad, has been laid out on the City map and is open for part of the way between the points referred to. The Company declares its intention to proceed with the completion of this link of the 16-inch line as soon as the proper right of way for it can be secured.

The following table will show, roughly, the progress being made in carrying out the improvements agreed upon in the negotiations of three years ago, and the approximate cost of the work still to be done.

TABLE 38—IMPROVEMENTS TO DISTRIBUTION SYSTEM IN QUEENS AREA.

DESCRIPTION	Estimated cost	Part chargeable to fire protection	Part completed prior to June 30, 1914	Part completed since June 30, 1914, or now under way	Balance to be done
16″ main from Far Rockaway standpipe to Cronin's Crossing, 14,600 ft.	$55,480.00	$41,890.00	$17,000.00	$30,000.00	$8,480.00
16″ main from Carlton Ave. to Rockaway Park standpipe, 10,000 ft.....	46,100.00	11,525.00	7,000.00	....	39,100.00
12″ main from Rockaway Park to Park Ave., 8,600 ft......	19,350.00	4,860.00	....	....	19,350.00
Mains smaller than 6″ upon which hydrants are set to be replaced by 6″ and 8″ mains; 5,900 ft. 8″ mains, 21,500 ft. 6″ mains..........	31,325.00	31,325.00	1,700.00	....	29,625.00
New 6″ and 8″ mains in streets where hydrants are required and 10,000 ft. of 2″ mains to be replaced; 4,050 ft. 8″ mains, 28,300 ft. 6″ mains.............	41,855.00	8,370.00	3,300.00	2,000.00	36,555.00
423 hydrants to be added............	33,840.00	33,840.00	16,000.00	160.00	17,680.00
Total.........	$227,950.00	$131,810.00	$45,000.00	$32,160.00	$150,790.00

In connection with the contract now proposed the following specific requirements are recommended on the advice of the Department's engineers:

Within three months after the execution and delivery of the contract, the completion of the new 16-inch main now under construction, from the Far Rockaway standpipe to Cronin's Crossing.

Within six months after the legal opening of Far Rockaway Boulevard and Beach Channel Drive from Lincoln Avenue (Beach 77th Street) to Henry Street (Beach 102nd Street) or other suitable route, the laying of a new 16-inch main from the intersection of Lincoln Avenue and Far Rockaway Boulevard to the intersection of Henry Street and Rockaway Beach Boulevard.

Within one year after the execution and delivery of the contract, the extension of a new 12-inch main from the intersection of Rockaway Beach Boulevard and Fifth Avenue (Beach 116th Street) through Fifth Avenue to Newport Avenue to Park Avenue (Bay 141st Street), thence through Park Avenue to Washington Avenue (Rockaway Beach Boulevard).

Within two years after the execution and delivery of the contract, the laying of new 6-inch and 8-inch mains in place of existing smaller mains and as new extensions and cross connections where better fire protection is needed, on the following streets:

SCHEDULE 1.

STREETS IN WHICH NEW 6″ AND 8″ MAINS ARE TO BE LAID TO REPLACE SMALLER MAINS ON WHICH HYDRANTS ARE NOW PLACED, AND CROSS-CONNECTIONS TO ELIMINATE DEAD ENDS.

Street	Size of main to be laid
Greenwood Ave., Far Rockaway, Lincoln Ave. to Broadway	6″
Grove St., Far Rockaway, Clark Ave. to Cornaga Ave.	6″
Briar Ave., Far Rockaway, Brinckerhoff Ave. to Collier Ave	6″
Healy Ave., Far Rockaway, Bayview Ave. to Ocean Ave	6″
Prospect Ave., Far Rockaway, Cornell Ave. to Bayswater Ave	6″
Rockaway Turnpike, Far Rockaway, Lockwood Ave. to Clark Ave	8″
Sprayview Ave., Edgemere, Beach Ave. to Grandview Ave	6″
Atlantic Ave., Arverne, Boulevard to Atlantic Ocean	8″
Kieley Ave., Arverne, Boulevard to Atlantic Ocean	8″
Bayside Pl., Rockaway Beach, L.I.R.R. to Jamaica Bay	6″
Ocean Ave., Rockaway Beach, Dodge Ave. to Pleasant Ave	6″
Hammel Ave., Rockaway Beach, L.I.R.R. to Jamaica Bay	6″
Fairview Ave., Rockaway Beach, Boulevard to Atlantic Ocean	8″
Grove Ave., Rockaway Beach, Boulevard to Atlantic Ocean	8″
Grove Ave., Rockaway Beach, Boulevard to Jamaica Bay	6″
Holland Ave., Rockaway Beach, Railroad Ave. to Grove Ave	6″
Remsen Ave., Rockaway Beach, Boulevard to Washington Ave	6″
Remsen Ave., Rockaway Beach, L.I.R.R. to Jamaica Bay	6″
1st Ave., Rockaway Park, Washington Ave. to Ocean Parkway	6″
3d Ave., Rockaway Park, Washington Ave. to Ocean Parkway	6″
4th Ave., Rockaway Park, Washington Ave. to Ocean Parkway	6″
6th Ave., Rockaway Park, Washington Ave. to Ocean Parkway	6″
7th Ave., Rockaway Park, Washington Ave. to Ocean Parkway	6″
8th Ave., Rockaway Park, Washington Ave. to Ocean Parkway	6″
9th Ave., Rockaway Park, Washington Ave. to Ocean Parkway	6″

SCHEDULE 2.

STREETS IN WHICH NEW 6″ AND 8″ MAINS ARE TO BE LAID WHERE NO HYDRANTS EXIST AND REPLACING ABOUT 10,000 FT. OF 2″ PIPE.

Street	Size of pipe to be laid
Broadway, Far Rockaway, Oak Ave. to Jarvis Ave	6″
Rue de St. Felix, Far Rockaway, Grandview Ave. to St. Felix Pl	6″
Cornell Ave., Far Rockaway, The Strand to Waterview Pl	6″
Forrest Ave., Far Rockaway, Cornaga Ave. to Bayswater Ave	6″
Lockwood Ave., Far Rockaway, Rockaway Turnpike to Grandview Ave	8″
Brinckerhoff Ave., Far Rockaway, Briar Ave. to Grove Ave	6″
Brinckerhoff Ave., Far Rockaway, Wavecrest Ave. to Sea View Ave	6″
Loretto Pl., Far Rockaway, L.I.R.R. to Sea View Ave	6″
Brookhaven Ave., Far Rockaway, Briar Ave. to Grove Ave	6″
Smith St., Far Rockaway, L.I.R.R. to Atlantic Ave	6″
Sea Girt Ave., Far Rockaway, Seneca Ave. to Jarvis Lane	6″
John St., Far Rockaway, Place Ave. to Seneca St	6″
Butler St., Far Rockaway, Leland Ave. to Scott St	3″
Sylvan St., Far Rockaway, Oak Ave. to Merrall Road	6″
New St., Far Rockaway, Merrall Ave. to 250 feet south	6″
Seneca St., Far Rockaway, Central Ave. to Crescent Ave	6″
Pinson Pl., Far Rockaway, Althouse St. to Horton St	6″
Althouse St., Far Rockaway, Pinson Pl. to Sheridan Bld	6″
Clinton St., Far Rockaway, Mott Ave. to 800 feet north	6″
Kensington Gardens, Far Rockaway, Westbourne Bld. to Bay View Terrace.	6″
Summit Drive, Far Rockaway, Mott Ave. to Bay View Terrace	6″
Bay View Terrace, Far Rockaway, Summit Drive to Kensington Gardens	6″
Storm Ave., Arverne, L.I.R.R. to Jamaica Bay	6″
Meredith Ave., Arverne, L.I.R.R. to Anstel Boul'd	6″
Gaston Ave., Arverne, Boulevard to Anstel Boul'd	6″
Wavecrest Ave., Arverne, Morris Ave. to Alemeda Ave	8″
Alemeda Ave., Arverne, Germain Ave. to Wavecrest Ave	6″
Germain Ave., Arverne, Alemeda Ave. to 250 feet north	6″
Division Ave., Rockaway Beach, Ocean Ave. to Atlantic Ocean	6″
Eldert Ave., Rockaway Beach, L.I.R.R. to Jamaica Bay	6″
Thomas Ave., Rockaway Beach, L.I.R.R. to Boulevard	6″
Bruce Pl., Rockaway Beach, Eldert Ave., westerly	6″
Rider Pl., Rockaway Beach, Railroad Ave. to Atlantic Ocean	6″
Waverly Ave., Rockaway Beach, Boulevard to L.I.R.R	6″
Thompson Ave., Rockaway Beach, Boulevard to L.I.R.R	6″
Stubing Pl., Rockaway Beach, Centre St. to Waverly	6″
Wainwright Court, Rockaway Park, Centre St. to Waverly	6″
Monmouth Ave., Rockaway Park, Bayside Ave. to dead end	6″
Pelham Ave., Rockaway Park, Bayside Ave. to Jamaica Bay	6″
Orienta Ave., Belle Harbor, dead end to Jamaica Bay	6″
Orienta Ave., Belle Harbor, dead end to Atlantic Ocean	6″
Winthrop Ave., Belle Harbor, dead end to Atlantic Ocean	6″
Chester Ave., Belle Harbor, dead end to Atlantic Ocean	6″
Montauk Ave., Belle Harbor, dead end to Atlantic Ocean	6″
Montauk Ave., Belle Harbor, dead end to Jamaica Bay	6″
Suffolk Ave., Belle Harbor, dead end to Atlantic Ocean	6″
Henley Ave., Belle Harbor, dead end to Atlantic Ocean	6″
Henley Ave., Belle Harbor, dead end to Jamaica Bay	6″
Brighton Ave., Belle Harbor, dead end to Newport Ave	6″

XXIV. POSSIBLE ACQUISITION OF PLANT BY THE CITY

In pursuance of the program outlined in the Department's letter of February 18, 1915, it is necessary to consider in detail the possibility of the City purchasing a portion of the Company's plant.

The situation of the Queens County Water Company's plant with reference to the City is peculiar. The portion of the area served by this Company within the City limits is a long strip of ocean front separated from the rest of New York City by Jamaica Bay and approachable for water mains only by a detour through Nassau County or else by submarine construction across the Bay. No important part of the Company's property except its local distribution system lies within the City limits.

The water supply and main pumping station, which are used in common for the Queens and Nassau services, are not within the City limits and in fact are situated near the center of the Nassau County area supplied by the Company. It would be impracticable to divide the pumping station and source of supply so as to permit the City to acquire a portion of it with which to continue to meet the demands of the water consumers of the Fifth Ward, leaving the other portion to continue to meet the demands of the Nassau County consumers. The pumping station and water supply were developed as a unit and cannot well be separated into two parts for independent service.

Under existing laws, the City has no authority to distribute water to domestic consumers outside of its corporate limits. Therefore, it would be impracticable for the City to purchase the entire plant, including the distributing mains in the incorporated villages and other communities of Nassau County. If it should purchase them, it would be unable to make use of them in supplying water to these communities and it would, at the same time, deprive the communities of the service to which they are entitled.

The Company has suggested that the City buy its pumping plant and such portion of its water supply lands as the City might desire. The Company urged that this pumping plant, which had for a number of years been used advantageously in pumping water to Brooklyn at times when the demands of the Company's own consumers were insufficient to keep the plant busy to its full capacity, was so designed and so situated that it could be advantageously used by the City especially in case the City should take over the Jamaica Water Supply Company's business. Mr. Baldwin stated that if the City did this the Company would be willing to construct a new pumping plant and develop a new water supply on certain of its lands which it had reserved and which would be adequate to supply the needs of the Nassau

County consumers. In case the pumping plant and developed water supply were to be taken over with the distribution system in Queens,, it would be necessary also to take over one or more of the trunk mains connecting the plant with the Queens system. It seemed inadvisable for the City to consider this proposition, as the advent of Catskill water is expected to result immediately in putting all of the existing Brooklyn pumping stations out of commission, at least temporarily. It seems undesirable, therefore, for the City to acquire at this time any additional water lands or pumping stations on Long Island. Moreover, it is to be noted that while not accepting the position taken by the Department's engineers to the effect that certain of the lands now held by the Company are not necessary for the water business, Mr. Baldwin, in the proposition made by him, frankly maintained that after selling the pumping plant and developed supply to the City, the Company would still be able to develop additional sources on lands already owned by it or by the Norumbega Company sufficient to meet the demands of the Nassau consumers. Moreover, the Company has strongly resisted the City's claim of the right to pump water from this watershed, maintaining that to do so would be to endanger and limit the Company's own supply. If the Company was right in this contention, then it would be injurious to the City's interests to have a portion of the available supply taken for Nassau County after a pumping station adequate to pump all the water available had been sold to the City.

Accordingly, partly because the City at the present time is not in of purchasing additional pumping stations and water lands on Long Island, and partly to avoid this other complication—which might involve a determination of the value of water in the ground and of the amount of water in the ground which the Company would deliver—it has seemed best not to consider seriously the possibility of acquiring, with the Queens distribution system, the Company's pumping plant and water supply in Nassau County and leaving the Company to build a new station and develop a new well system to supply Nassau's local needs.

In contemplating the possibility of acquiring the plant or a portion of it by condemnation proceedings, it appeared that the City would be able to condemn the Queens distribution system but would not be able to condemn the local distributing mains in Nassau County or any part of the pumping plant or water supply necessary for the service of the Nassau County consumers under the Company's franchise requiring it to supply them. It is to be noted especially that the Company is operating under a single franchise originally granted by the old town of Hempstead, covering both what is now the Fifth Ward of Queens and the present town of Hempstead. It appeared that in case the City should condemn the Queens distribution system only, it would probably be compelled to pay very heavy damages by reason of the fact that it would be taking away 70% of the Company's revenues without taking more than about 40% of its physical property.

It seemed, therefore, that in pursuance of the policy of ultimately extending the municipal water service to all districts within the corporate limits, the City would do well to negotiate with the Company a voluntary agreement providing for the eventual transfer of the Queens distribution system at a time when the economic loss resulting from the disruption of the Company's business and the severance of its plant would be reduced to a minimum. Eventually, the Nassau County area, if it continues to increase in population, will need the entire water supply controlled by the company. If the transfer of the Queens distribution system and business to the City should be postponed until the Nassau County demand for water has grown up to the capacity of the Company's water supply plant and pumping station,—or even until it has grown to a point where the combined demands of the two areas would require further capital expenditures for the installation of new pumps or the development of additional supplies,—the taking over of the Queens business might well be in the nature of relief rather than of loss to the Company. It has seemed best, therefore, to negotiate with the Company for the ultimate purchase of those portions of the Company's plant which the City will be able to use and which the Company will not need in its Nassau County business. As the basis for such a contract, it was necessary to make additional computations from the appraisal figures already determined.

(a) **Portion of plant required**

Because of the impossibility of making an actual physical distribution and separation of the plant into the parts attributable to the Queens and Nassau services respectively, it seemed proper to separate for purchase those portions only of the plant which can be segregated and which also, after purchase, would continue to be of use to the City. The local distribution system of the Queens area includes not only the mains, valves, hydrants, etc., in the streets, but also the meters installed on the consumer's premises, and the stand-pipes. Assuming that the water to be delivered into this distribution system under municipal ownership would be supplied by gravity rather than by pumping, the stand-pipes would be of little use to the City. If the City continues to serve water to the consumers through meters, those now owned by the Company could properly be retained in use. It is to be noted, however, that under existing laws and ordinances the Department would have no authority to require the continued use of the meters, except on business premises, and even there would have no right to furnish and maintain meters at its own expense. It would be possible, by mutual consent of the Department and the property owner, to continue the use of meters on residential premises, but this policy would be disadvantageous to the City, from the revenue standpoint; for the meter rates, without a minimum charge, would under Rockaway conditions, certainly amount to less than the frontage rates. The City would naturally desire to reduce as much as possible the prospective loss in supplying this isolated district with water at the regular City rates, and yet the plans of the Department, looking to the ultimate adoption of the policy of universal metering, would probably make it worth while to acquire the Queens County meters and continue them in service as long as the consumers would consent to it.

Besides the distribution system, the Company has certain lands, buildings, wells, filters and mechanical equipment situated within the City limits. One small parcel of land, with a width of 20 feet on the north side of Crescent Avenue and extending to the Long Island Railroad right of way, with a depth of about 102 feet, is held by the Company as a right of way for a 16-inch main which is an integal part of the local distribution system. This plot of land the City might well acquire for the continuation of its present use. The other parcels of land situated in Queens County, with the buildings at Far Rockaway and the wells and pumping machinery at Rockaway Park, could not be used advantageously by the City. While the City would need a supply and repair yard, no one of the parcels of land owned by the Company is both large enough and well enough situated to serve this purpose for the Fifth Ward, under conditions of operation that would prevail in case of City ownership. It appears, therefore, that of the Company's property located in Queens County, all of the land except the Crescent Avenue parcel and all of the standpipes, buildings, wells, filters and mechanical equipment, as well as the office furniture, tools and miscellaneous supplies, would be of little or no use to the City, and should therefore be excluded from the valuation of the useful property to be acquired.

Of the property situated in Nassau County, the only portion that could properly be acquired by the City would be one or more of the trunk mains extending from the City limits to the pumping station at Fenhurst. There are three of these mains; one is a 24-inch main throughout, another is a 16-inch main throughout, and the third is a 16-inch and 20-inch main combined. In order to get water to the Rockaways, the City will need one or more trunk mains. It appears that the City's 72-inch steel pressure pipe line extends from Brooklyn out through Nassau County, running through Valley Stream, about one mile north of the Company's pumping station. It would be possible, therefore, for the City to make use of the Company's 24-inch trunk main by extending it about one mile northerly from the pumping station to a connection with the 72-inch main. The Company itself could well dispense with this 24-inch line. If the City did not purchase, it, but left it on the Company's hands, together with the pumping plant and other property in Nassau County, the damages payable by the City for the severance of the Company's plant would no doubt be increased almost, if not quite, to the extent of the value of this main. It would seem desirable, therefore, for the City to acquire this main along with the Queens distribution system, if proper arrangements can be made as to the purchase price and the right of way for its future maintenance and extension.

As an incident to the contract under which the Company for several years pumped water into the Brooklyn Aqueduct for the Brooklyn supply, a 20-inch pipe line was laid from the Company's pumping station to connection with the Aqueduct, along substantially the same route that might be followed in the extension of the 24-inch main. For the 20-inch pipe line, the City furnished the pipe and the Company did the work of laying it. The status of this main is a little uncertain. The Department has assumed that the main was the property of the City, but it appears that it was laid for the most part, not on public streets, but outside of public streets on property formerly owned by the water company but now held by its real estate off-shoot, the Norumbega Company. There is also some doubt as to whether this main was laid with sufficient care to withstand the high pressures that would be necessary if it were to be used as a link for the delivery of Catskill water to the Rockaways.

At first it seemed advisable that the City should acquire not only the Company's 24-inch trunk main, but also its 16-inch line. It was thought that the 16-inch line could be connected with the 20-inch main just referred to, and in conjunction with the 24-inch line extended, thus give a double service to the Rockaway district. Upon further consideration, however, it appeared that the Company itself would probably need both the 16-inch main and the 16-inch and 20-inch main, before the end of ten years as means of supplying the local needs of the portion of its Nassau territory lying between the pumping station and Far Rockaway. Moreover, it seemed that a 16-inch line would not be adequate as a duplicate means of delivering water to the Rockaway peninsula in case of a break in the 24-inch line. It has therefore seemed best to include in the negotiations only one of the trunk mains, namely, the 24-inch line. In case the City takes over the Queens distribution system, this single pipe line for delivering water will have to be supplemented either by a submarine line across Jamaica Bay or by another trunk main skirting the head of the bay by way of Rockaway Road or other available route.

It appears, therefore, that the portion of the Company's plant which the City might advantageously acquire includes the following:

1—24 inch trunk main extending from the pumping station to the City line at Far Rockaway.

2—All the local distributing mains, valves, hydrants and other appurtenances in use within the limits of the Fifth Ward of the Borough of Queens.

3—The meters actually in service in the Queens area.

4—A small parcel of land on the north side of Crescent Avenue,

Far Rockaway, described as Lot 31 of Block 26, Volume 4, Ward 5, Borough of Queens.

(b) **Present value of property to be acquired**

As shown by the appraisal, the present value of the several portions of the Company's plant which the City might properly acquire is $599,665, as follows:

24″ main and appurtenances in Nassau County	$98,179.00
Distributing mains, valves, corporation cocks, etc., in Queens County	420,751.00
Hydrants, hydrant valves and connections in Queens County	29,925.00
Land, lot on Crescent Ave	1,000.00
Meters in use in Queens County	49,810.00
Total	$599,665.00

The physical property included in this estimate is subject to depreciation, which should be taken into account in determining the price finally paid, in case purchase by the City is deferred for a number of years. According to the estimates of the Department engineers, the total annual depreciation of this portion of the plant is $13,970, and this sum, less the cost of replacements, should be deducted from the value above given for each year that the purchase is deferred from May 31, 1914.

For additions and improvements made by and at the Company's expense in Queens County to the extent that such additions and improvements become a part of the useful property to be acquired, the purchase price should be increased by their actual cost to the Company, less such depreciation as may accrue from year to year, over and above the cost of replacements.

Going value is attributable to the plant as a whole, and as time goes on will be absorbed more and more by the Nassau County end of the business. Moreover, the business acquired by the City, even if the purchase is postponed for the full period of ten years, will hardly be profitable at City rates under the necessary conditions of operation in this territory and supply thereto. Accordingly, the City should pay nothing on account of going value as such.

(c) **Provision for new capital as needed**

When once the City has definitely adopted a policy looking to the ultimate acquisition of a private water company's distribution plant, certain considerations point to the desirability of the immediate assumption by the City of the obligation to furnish whatever additional capital may be required for future extensions in the district affected. In the first place, the Company would be relieved of the necessity of putting additional capital into the system, which, in any case, would be added to the purchase price when the City came to take over the mains. In the second place, if the City furnishes the capital, it will have a closer supervision of the construction work and a freer hand in developing the system to meet the ultimate requirements of the municipal plant than it would have if the additional funds were furnished by the Company.

Arrangements should be made on a just basis for the payment of a fair rental by the Company so long as it continues to operate the extensions built at the expense of the City. Such rentals would be treated as a part of operating expenses. On the portion of the additional investment attributable to fire protection, it would be unnecessary for the Company to pay a rental, and conversely it would be unnecessary for the City to increase its payment to the Company for fire service on account of such investment, except by an amount sufficient to cover the cost of maintenance. So far as the new investment would be properly attributable to domestic service, the rental payable by the Company, in case the revenues would warrant it, should be sufficient to cover the interest and sinking fund charges on the investment and the depreciation of the physical property. In case the City should pursue the policy of extending the mains for domestic service on streets where there was insufficient business to make the investment profitable, the rental paid by the Company should be less. Under the theory of such an arrangement the City would have control of the extensions and would be required to take the risk of loss if it chose to construct them without guaranty of an adequate demand for water for domestic purposes.

In the case of the Queens County Water Company, where an expenditure of approximately $180,000 subsequent to June 30, 1914, is necessary in order to bring the distributing system in the Fifth Ward up to a standard fully adequate for the present demands of domestic service and fire protection, it seems reasonable that these specific improvements, already described in a preceding subdivision of this report, should be made within a limited time and up to a limited amount at the Company's own expense. Such an arrangement would be just and convenient in this particular case because the Company has means available for raising the necessary capital to complete these improvements, without increasing its capital stock or selling any more of its bonds. It still holds the Norumbega note representing the purchase price of the land sold off in 1910. This note has been held partly for the very purpose of keeping funds available for these improvements in the Queens district. It would seem advantageous, therefore, that in case the City enters into a contract for the ultimate purchase of the distribution system in Queens, the Company should be required to put in new capital up to the sum of $180,000 in the specific improvements immediately necessary, or such additional extensions and improvements as may be required from time to time up to this limit. The City should undertake to furnish all the capital necessary over and above the sum of $180,000.

It might be thought that in the Rockaway district the Queens County Water Company's experience in construction and its knowledge of its own distribution system and of the street conditions under which new extensions would have to be made would enable it to perform the work of construction more conveniently and at less cost than the City would do the same work. While possibly this is true, the incentive to economy in construction work would be largely removed if the City was under obligation to pay the bills, and the Company would probably claim an additional allowance as contractor's profit for doing the work. Everything considered, it would seem best that as soon as the improvements for which the Company is to furnish the capital have been completed, all additional construction work should be done either by the Department's own forces, or under regular City contracts.

(d) **Business loss to the Company from the severence of its plant**

As already pointed out, the immediate acquisition by the City of the portions of the Company's plant that would be useful to it at a price representing their present physical value would result in taking from the Company about 70% of its revenues and leaving it with a disproportionate part of its investment to be maintained on the earnings of its Nassau County business. The severance of the plant and the disruption of the business at the present time would involve a large loss to the Company which, in justice, the City would have to assume if it carried through the purchase suggested. It seems, on the other hand, that if the Company should be permitted to continue operation in Queens up to the time when the increase of its entire business would be such as to require the enlargement of its water supply and pumping plant, and if at such time before the additional investment was made the City should take over the Queens distribution system and business, the severance of the plant might be a positive advantage to the Company; at least, the possible loss would be greatly reduced.

In order to arrive at a figure which would represent the estimated business loss to the Company resulting from the acquisition by the City of the physical property useful to it as of May 31, 1914, it is necessary to consider, in the first place, the difference between the total investment attributable to the Queens service and the portion of the investment which the City would take over. We have found that the investment attributable to the Queens service amounted to $1,148,896, while the present value of the portion of the plant and property which the City would acquire in case of purchase amounted to $599,665. This means that as a result of the purchase the Company would be left with an investment of $549,231 properly attributable to the Queens service and upon which it could not at the present time properly earn a return from its Nassau County business. In other words, the purchase would leave an investment of $549,231 temporarily idle. Only a small part of the property represented by this investment, that part being chiefly certain lands in Queens County, could be immediately disposed of by the Company for other purposes.

Assuming that the Company would continue to use its lands and buildings at Far Rockaway in connection with its Nassau County business, the only property included in the appraisal which it could properly dispose of immediately after the purchase would be the land at Rockaway Park, which represents an appraised value for selling purposes of $15,467. The balance of the investment made idle by the purchase, amounting to $533,764, would be made up of property now attributable to the Queens service, which would become valueless, and other property representing an undivided interest in pumping plant, well system, filters, land and trunk mains in Nassau County, and tools and miscellaneous equipment, all attributable to the Queens service but which would gradually come into use again along with the future increase of the Nassau County business. The portion of this property that would have to be scrapped immediately includes two standpipes, the wells at Rockaway Park and the mechanical equipment at Rockaway Park and at Arverne. The appraised present value of this property, less its estimated scrap value, is $41,042.53, as follows:

Standpipes	$26,325.00
Mechanical equipment	7,752.60
Wells	6,665.27
Suction mains	299.66
	$41,042.53

This would leave a value of $492, 721.47 for the portion of the property now attributable to the Queens service which would be made idle by the purchase, but which would gradually be restored to use with the increase of the Nassau County business.

Thus the $549,231 of investment cut loose from its moorings by the purchase would be distributed as follows :

Land at Rockaway Park available for immediate sale	$15,467.00
Standpipes, wells, mechanical equipment, etc., which would become an immediate total loss	41,042.53
Undivided portion attributable to Queens of property that would remain in use	492,721.47
	$549,231.00

If the City by a co-operative contract should relieve the Company of the necessity of making further large investments for the joint service of the two districts, the Nassau business will ultimately be sufficient to absorb the portion of the joint investment now attributable to the Queens service and not to be taken over by the City. The element of business loss here under consideration, in case the severance had been effected on May 31, 1914, would be the value of the property immediately to be scrapped, namely $41,043, plus the present worth of the carrying charges and depreciation allowances on the portion of the investment in joint use left idle by the severance, commencing with

$492,231, as of May 31, 1914, and diminishing by equal annual instalments to nothing at the period when this investment will have been completely absorbed.

At this point it is necessary to make a forecast of the prospective growth of the Company's business in the two districts. Any contract which the City might be willing to make could not, under the law, run for a longer period than ten years. (See Sec. 81, Transportation Corporations Law). The Company's fiscal year ends on May 31, and the peculiar character of the water business in the Rockaways and weighty accounting considerations make it practically necessary that the City should take over the Queens portion of the business, if at all, as of June 1, in the year of acquisition. Therefore, all estimates of future revenues, expenses, number of taps, etc. are based on the continuation of the present fiscal period beginning June 1 and closing May 31 of the following year.

It has been difficult to make a reasonable estimate of the future development of the Company's business, and especially to distribute the probable increase between the two districts. The character of the business in Queens is not the same as it is in Nassau. The number of taps is increasing at a different rate. The amount of revenues per tap is decidedly different, and the actual expense per tap is different. The increase of population is not at the same rate, and the conditions affecting future increases are different. Assistant Engineer B. M. Wagner, before he left the Department, made some careful computations under my direction as to the probable increase of summer and winter population in the Queens area, and as to the ultimate population capacity of this area. He also made some estimates for Nassau County, but stated that the construction of a high speed trolley line, already talked of, through the Nassau territory would make these estimates entirely useless. After full consideration of the difficulties inherent in the problem and after applying various tests from the Company's actual experience, Mr. Wolff and I have been able to work out an estimate that we consider reasonably satisfactory. It is based upon the assumption that the number of active taps in the two districts respectively will increase during the next ten years at approximately the same rate at which they increased during the five years from 1909 to 1914. If we had gone back further than 1909 the rate of increase would have been larger, as the past few years have been a period of comparative stagnation in Nassau realty development. The expenses per tap are considerably less in Nassau than in Queens, and although their natural tendency in the Nassau area, which is conveniently situated about the pumping station as a center, would be to decrease, we have assumed them constant for the future. The expenses per tap in Queens are not only absolutely greater than in Nassau, but they will tend to increase rather than diminish as the service is pushed farther and farther down the peninsula away from the pumping plant and the center of gravity of the Company's operations. We have assumed that the average expense per tap on the entire system will remain constant. Assuming the more favorable conditions expected under the proposed contract, and deducting the 15% of operating expenses and taxes attributable to fire protection and to be taken care of in the rates paid by the City, we get $8.78 per tap as the probable annual expense chargeable to domestic service after 1915. We assume that while an increasing proportion of taps will be found in Nassau County involving an annual expense of $6.60 each, which is based upon the estimated Nassau average for the last four years, with the deductions just referred to, a decreasing proportion of the taps will be found in Queens involving an average annual expense per tap, increasing from $10.35 in 1916 to $11.03 in 1924.

The gross revenues, exclusive of hydrant rentals and miscellaneous receipts, which means the gross revenues derived from the sale of water to private consumers, amounted in 1914 to $33.07 per active tap in the Queens area and $21.48 in the Nassau area. The revenues per tap have been slowly increasing in both areas, but the increase in Nassau has been at a somewhat higher rate than the increase in Queens. On the basis of the old rates, it is possible to make an estimate of the future increase in revenues from the sale of water in the two districts respectively. Combining this estimate with the estimated increase in number of taps, we get as the average revenues per tap, figures which check closely with the actual increase in revenues per tap shown by past experience. Combining with these estimates the estimated expense per tap, we finally get the estimated net revenues from the sale of water to domestic consumers on the basis of the old rates. The following table gives the results and shows that by May 31, 1922, the Nassau business, both as to taps and as to net revenues, will have increased so as to be substnatially the same as the combined business on May 31, 1914, the same rates being assumed for both years.

TABLE 39—ESTIMATE OF FUTURE DEVELOPMENT OF WATER BUSINESS IN QUEENS AND NASSAU AREAS, RESPECTIVELY (BASED ON PAST RECORDS AND OLD RATES).

Year	Active Taps			Gross Revenue From Sale of Water to Private Consumers			Gross Revenue Per Tap From Sale of Water to Private Consumers		
	Queens	Nassau	Both Counties	Queens	Nassau	Both Counties	Queens	Nassau	Both Counties
1908-9	3,366	1,764	5,130	$103,114.00	$34,167.00	$137,281.00	$30.63	$19.37	$26.76
1909-10	3,725	2,140	5,865	116,955.00	42,772.00	159,727.00	32.20	19.99	27.23
1910-11	3,966	2,442	6,408	122,557.00	53,537.00	176,094.00	30.90	21.92	27.48
1911-12	4,190	2,667	6,857	134,840.00	57,470.00	192,310.00	32.18	21.55	28.05
1912-13	4,543	2,933	7,476	143,310.00	59,998.00	203,308.00	31.55	20.46	27.19
1913-14	4,837	3,185	8,022	159,949.00	68,402.00	228,351.00	33.07	21.48	28.47
1914-15	5,191	3,577	8,768	174,506.00	78,507.00	253,013.00	33.61	21.95	28.86
1915-16	5,568	4,015	9,583	190,307.00	90,031.00	280,338.00	34.18	22.42	29.25
1916-17	5,970	4,504	10,474	207,437.00	103,177.00	310,614.00	34.75	22.91	29.65
1917-18	6,399	5,049	11,448	225,999.00	118,161.00	344,160.00	35.32	23.40	30.06
1918-19	6,854	5,659	12,513	246,109.00	135,220.00	381,329.00	35.90	23.89	30.47
1919-20	7,340	6,337	13,677	267,855.00	154,657.00	422,512.00	36.49	24.41	30.89
1920-21	7,857	7,092	14,949	291,442.00	176,701.00	468,143.00	37.09	24.92	31.32
1921-22	8,401	7,938	16,339	316,903.00	201,800.00	518,703.00	37.72	25.42	31.75
1922-23	8,978	8,881	17,859	344,417.00	230,295.00	574,712.00	38.36	25.93	32.18
1923-24	9,599	9,921	19,520	374,127.00	262,649.00	636,776.00	39.00	26.47	32.62

TABLE 39—Continued.

Year	Expenses Per Tap for Domestic Service Including Taxes			Net Revenue Per Tap From Sale of Water to Private Consumers			Total Net Revenue From Sale of Water to Private Consumers		
	Queens	Nassau	Both Counties	Queens	Nassau	Both Counties	Queens	Nassau	Both Counties
1908-9	......	......	......	......	......	......	....	....	....
1909-10	......	......	......	......	......	......	....	....	....
1910-11	$11.44	$8.35	$10.26	$19.46	$13.57	$17.22	$77,178.00	$33,138.00	$110,316.00
1911-12	11.45	8.08	10.14	20.73	13.47	17.91	86,859.00	35,924.00	122,783.00
1912-13	8.86	6.12	7.80	22.69	14.34	19.39	103,091.00	42,059.00	145,150.00
1913-14	12.04	8.21	10.51	21.03	13.27	17.96	101,722.00	42,265.00	143,987.00
1914-15	11.94	7.67	10.20	21.67	14.28	18.66	112,489.00	52,080.00	164,569.00
1915-16	10.35	6.60	8.78	23.83	15.82	20.47	132,685.00	63,517.00	196,202.00
1916-17	10.42	6.60	8.78	24.33	16.31	20.87	145,250.00	73,460.00	218,710.00
1917-18	10.49	6.60	8.78	24.83	16.80	21.28	158,887.00	84,823.00	243,710.00
1918-19	10.57	6.60	8.78	25.33	17.29	21.69	173,612.00	97,844.00	271,456.00
1919-20	10.66	6.60	8.78	25.83	17.81	22.11	189,592.00	112,862.00	302,454.00
1920-21	10.74	6.60	8.78	26.35	18.32	22.54	207,032.00	130,025.00	337,057.00
1921-22	10.84	6.60	8.78	26.88	18.82	22.97	225,819.00	149,393.00	375,212.00
1922-23	10.93	6.60	8.78	27.43	19.33	23.40	246,267.00	171,670.00	417,937.00
1923-24	11.03	6.60	8.78	27.97	19.87	23.84	268,484.00	197,130.00	465,614.00

These estimates point to 1922 as the period when the Nassau business will be able to absorb all of that portion of the investment jointly used, now attributable to the Queens service but not to be taken over by the City at the time of purchase. The estimates are based on the old rates, but that will not effect this result, as it is not proposed to reduce the Company's net revenues below what would have been a fair return upon the entire investment for the year 1914. If the City makes a readjustment by which payments for fire service are increased and domestic rates reduced in the Queens area, it is to be presumed that the Company will secure a similar readjustment for the Nassau area. If it does not, it will probably continue to charge rates that in the aggregate are compensatory. At least we must assume that the increase in the Nassau business will bring with it the ability to support an increasing investment.

Assuming, therefore, that the investment made idle by the severance will have been absorbed in the Nassau service by May 31, 1922, the loss incurred by the Company on account of this idle investment, if the purchase had taken place on May 31, 1914, would have been $129,-717, as follows:

TABLE 40—ESTIMATED LOSS IN INTEREST AND DEPRECIATION ON INVESTMENT OF $492,231 MADE IDLE BY CITY'S PURCHASE OF QUEENS DISTRIBUTION SYSTEM AS OF MAY 31, 1914.

Year ending May 31	Average amount of investment idle during year	Interest on idle investment at 6%	Current depreciation on idle investment	Combined loss; interest plus depreciation	Time for which loss is deferred	Present worth as of May 31, 1914 of deferred loss, discounted at 6% per annum
1915......	$461,467.00	$27,688.00	$7,964.00	$35,652.00	½ yr.	$34,615.00
1916......	399,938.00	23,997.00	6,902.00	30,899.00	1½ yrs.	28,170.00
1917......	338,409.00	20,305.00	5,840.00	26,145.00	2½ yrs.	22,408.00
1918......	276,880.00	16,612.00	4,778.00	21,390.00	3½ yrs.	17,231.00
1919......	215,351.00	12,921.00	3,716.00	16,637.00	4½ yrs.	12,595.00
1920......	153,822.00	9,229.00	2,654.00	11,883.00	5½ yrs.	8,451.00
1921......	92,293.00	5,538.00	1,592.00	7,120.00	6½ yrs.	4,757.00
1922......	30,764.00	1,846.00	530.00	2,376.00	7½ yrs.	1,490.00
Present worth on May 31, 1914, of future losses..................						$129,717.00

The Company will also lose a certain amount on account of taxes to be paid for the years during which the investment remains idle. On the basis of the taxes levied in 1914 in relation to the entire investment, the Company's loss on this score, if the severance had taken place on May 31, 1914, would have been approximately $14,443.

It is to be presumed also that operating expenses, exclusive of taxes, would be relatively higher in proportion to earnings if the Company's business in Queens were taken away and it had to maintain a complete organization and staff for Nassau business alone. It is not easy to make a satisfactory estimate of the Company's loss from this point of view, but clearly this loss would be diminished by the fact that operation tends to become more expensive in Queens and less expensive in Nassau. Perhaps the best available test of the effect of severance would be to get an operating ratio for a number of years when the Company's entire business was relatively small, and apply this ratio to the Nassau business alone for a period of years when the latter was substantially equivalent to the former. The Company's gross revenues from both districts during the years 1900 to 1903 inclusive averaged $63,941. The gross revenues from the Nassau County business alone for the years 1911 to 1914 inclusive averaged approximately $66,115. The ratio of operating expenses, exclusive of taxes, to gross revenues for the eariler period was 37%. Applying this ratio to the average Nassau revenues for the later period we get $24,462 as the normal annual operating expenses of a separate plant doing the equivalent of the present Nassau County business. The average amount of operating expenses attributed to the Nassau service for the four years 1911 to 1914 inclusive, and assumed to be a fair allowance on the basis of the 1914 business under the new conditions established by the proposed contract, was $20,203. This would indicate an annual loss on account of severance of $4,259 due to a relative increase of 21% in the cost of operation. Perhaps some concession should be made to the increased cost of labor as between the 1900-1903 period and the 1911-1914 period. With this in view, we may allow a relative increase of 25% instead of 21% and a loss on the 1914 operations of $5,000. This annual loss, like the other losses we have considered, would be gradually absorbed in the growing Nassau County business and would disappear entirely by 1922 if our estimates are correct. The present worth of these yearly diminishing losses in operating expenses as of May 31, 1914, would be $14,647.

The property in Queens that would have to be scrapped immediately, representing an appraised value of $41,043, would be a dead loss to the Company. But this would diminish from year to year by the allowance for annual depreciation not expended on replacements. As these standpipes, wells, etc. would hardly need replacement during the period of the contract, the full amount of the normal annual depreciation, namely $1,680, should be deducted year by year from the loss.

The general mortgage covering all the Company's property gives security to $667,000 of bonds now outstanding. If the City took over a portion of this property, this mortgage would have to be retired unless a way were found for the City to assume the bonds. The bonds are subject to call at 105, and if called would require the payment of an aggregate premium of $33,350, if no more bonds are issued. The bonds will be due in 1940. If the City defers the purchase until 1924 and can then borrow money at 4½%, the saving of one-half of 1% per annum for the remaining life of the bonds would about offset the premium to be paid if the bonds are called. If the purchase were to be effected earlier, the saving from the lower rate of interest would be still greater. It seems likely, therefore, that the cost of calling the bonds at the time of severance will have to be faced as a dead and undiminishing loss to the Company. Indeed, if additional bonds should be issued under the mortgage before the severance takes place, the ultimate loss would be greater rather than less.

Taking all these elements of loss together and estimating their amounts as of May 31 of each year until 1924, we get the following results:

TABLE 41—COMPANY'S ESTIMATED LOSSES FROM SEVERANCE OF ITS SYSTEM.

DATE OF SEVERANCE	Loss from interest depreciation and taxes on idle investment	Loss from scrapped investment	Loss from increase in operating ratio	Loss from calling of bonds	Total loss at end of each year
May 31, 1914........	$144,160.00	$41,043.00	$14,647.00	$33,350.00	$233,200.00
May 31, 1915........	108,997.00	39,363.00	11,206.00	33,350.00	192,916.00
May 31, 1916........	81,616.00	37,683.00	8,171.00	33,350.00	160,820.00
May 31, 1917........	57,771.00	36,003.00	5,568.00	33,350.00	132,692.00
May 31, 1918........	37,687.00	34,323.00	3,423.00	33,350.00	108,783.00
May 31, 1919........	21,604.00	32,643.00	1,728.00	33,350.00	89,325.00
May 31, 1920........	9,773.00	30,963.00	521.00	33,350.00	74,607.00
May 31, 1921........	2,483.00	29,283.00	....	33,350.00	65,116.00
May 31, 1922........	....	27,603.00	....	33,350.00	60,953.00
May 31, 1923........	....	25,923.00	....	33,350.00	59,273.00
May 31, 1924........	....	24,243.00	....	33,350.00	57,593.00

The losses which the Company would sustain from the severance of the plant as of a particular date should be offset by any profits in excess of 6% on the investment from the time the contract goes into effect till the date of purchase. In order to estimate these profits it is necessary to estimate not only the number of taps, the revenues per tap under the new rates, and the expenses per tap, but also the investment per tap and the interest and depreciation thereon. The appraisal of the Company's property is of one date only. We have no complete appraisal of the property as of 1913 or any earlier year. We have, however, the book investment, representing the gross original cost of the plant. Taking the figures for a series of six years, going back to 1909, and reducing the book investment by a percentage that will bring it down in 1914 to the inventory value, and taking the total number of taps in active service each year, we get the average investment per tap for the entire system. This is $213.60 for the year 1914. Again, taking the apportionment of the investment between the Queens and the Nassau services, and comparing this with the number of active taps in the two districts respectively, we find an average investment per tap in 1914 of $237.35 in Queens and $177.54 in Nassau. The investment per tap is decreasing in both areas, but more rapidly in Queens. Projecting these rates of decrease into the future we find the estimated investment per tap in Queens reduced to $177 in 1924, and in Nassau to $141. With the number of taps assumed, it is an easy matter to reckon the estimated total investment attributable to the service in the two districts respectively at the end of any year. The results are shown in the following table:

Table 42—ESTIMATED INVESTMENT PER TAP.

Year	Total Investment			Number of Active Taps			Investment Per Tap		
	Queens County	Nassau County	Both Counties	Queens County	Nassau County	Both Counties	Queens County	Nassau County	Both Counties
1909	$942,973.00	$357,680.00	$1,300,653.00	3,366	1,764	5,130	$280.00	$203.00	$254.00
1910	968,328.00	403,242.00	1,371,570.00	3,725	2,140	5,865	260.00	188.00	234.00
1911	998,825.00	500,912.00	1,499,737.00	3,966	2,442	6,408	252.00	205.00	224.00
1912	1,073,224.00	528,603.00	1,601,827.00	4,190	2,667	6,857	256.00	198.00	234.00
1913	1,126,690.00	537,552.00	1,664,242.00	4,543	2,933	7,476	248.00	183.00	223.00
1914	1,148,044.00	565,455.00	1,713,499.00	4,837	3,185	8,022	237.00	178.00	214.00
1915	1,195,413.00	619,563.00	1,814,976.00	5,191	3,577	8,768	230.00	173.00	207.00
1916	1,245,251.00	680,932.00	1,926,183.00	5,568	4,015	9,583	223.00	169.00	201.00
1917	1,295,718.00	746,712.00	2,042,430.00	5,970	4,504	10,474	216.00	165.00	195.00
1918	1,348,119.00	815,553.00	2,163,672.00	6,399	5,049	11,448	210.00	161.00	189.00
1919	1,400,296.00	889,583.00	2,289,879.00	6,854	5,659	12,513	204.00	157.00	183.00
1920	1,466,695.00	967,811.00	2,434,506.00	7,340	6,337	13,677	198.00	153.00	178.00
1921	1,523,987.00	1,062,190.00	2,586,177.00	7,857	7,092	14,949	193.00	150.00	173.00
1922	1,578,595.00	1,166,357.00	2,744,952.00	8,401	7,938	16,339	188.00	147.00	168.00
1923	1,636,906.00	1,274,111.00	2,911,017.00	8,978	8,881	17,859	182.00	144.00	163.00
1924	1,692,502.00	1,391,658.00	3,084,160.00	9,599	9,921	19,520	177.00	141.00	158.00

This table is very interesting. It shows an increase in the Nassau investment of $601,000 from 1914 to 1922, the period already fixed upon as the time required for the Nassau business to absorb $492,231 of the capital attributed to the Queens service in 1914. This estimate allows for $109,000 increase in the exclusively local investment in Nassau. But we find that, if necessary, Nassau could carry a further investment of $350,000 without bringing the per tap investment above that of 1914. This would allow Nassau about $450,000 for local mains in addition to the complete absorption within eight years of the joint investment attributable to Queens in 1914. The figures also point to an additional capital expenditure of over $400,000 on the local Queens system by 1922. Under the terms of the proposed contract, all but $180,000 of this amount would be furnished by the City, but the Company, if it continued to operate in Queens, would have to pay the carrying charges on the City's investment.

The investment per tap found in this way is the total investment, while the revenues per tap (Table 39) are only the revenues from the sale of water to private consumers. It is estimated that 23.2% of the entire investment is attributable to fire protection, and it is assumed that under the proposed contract the City will pay the actual cost of this service. The total investment per tap should be reduced accordingly to get the investment per tap for domestic service. Interest on the investment so found should be charged at 6%. Depreciation should be charged at 2.1%. Thus 8.1% on the investment should be set aside for carrying charges. The operating expenses and taxes per tap should be added to the carrying charges.

The gross revenues per tap from the sale of water to private consumers on the basis of the 1914 rates have already been estimated. The schedule of rates proposed, in case security is given to the investment, would result in a reduction of about 27% in these revenues. The estimated earnings per tap in future years should be reduced accordingly.

Putting these figures together we have the net profit per tap from the sale of water to private consumers in excess of 6% per annum, or the deficiency below 6%. Multiplying these figures into the estimated number of taps, we get the aggregate variance each year either above or below the 6% line. The total profits should be increased or the losses diminished by the amount of the miscellaneous operating revenues to be expected each year. The largest single item of miscellaneous revenues is from new taps, and during the last five years these revenues have amounted to $4.80 for the net increase in the number of taps. We may properly assume that miscellaneous operating revenues, which under the conditions assumed in these computations will be clear profit, will amount to $4.80 per new tap in future years as they have in the past. The following table shows the results of all these estimates in the shape of the net profit above or the net deficiency below 6% for each year till 1924 in each district:

TABLE 43—ESTIMATE OF FUTURE PROFITS FROM OPERATION.

	1 Gross Revenue Per Tap from sale of water to private consumers—old rates			2 Gross Revenue Per Tap from sale of water to private consumers—new rates			3 Expenses Per Tap (including taxes) for domestic service			4 Net Revenue Per Tap from sale of water to private consumers—new rates after 1915		
	Queens	Nassau	Both Counties	Queens	Nassau	Both Counties	Queens	Nassau	Both Counties	Queens	Nassau	Both Counties
1914–1915...	$33.61	$21.95	$28.86	......	......	......	$11.94	$7.67	$10.20	$21.67	$14.28	$18.66
1915–1916...	34.18	22.42	29.25	$24.95	$16.36	$21.35	10.35	6.60	8.78	14.60	9.76	12.57
1916–1917...	34.75	22.91	29.65	25.37	16.72	21.64	10.42	6.60	8.78	14.95	10.12	12.86
1917–1918...	35.32	23.40	30.06	25.78	17.09	21.94	10.49	6.60	8.78	15.29	10.49	13.16
1918–1919...	35.90	23.89	30.47	26.21	17.44	22.24	10.57	6.60	8.78	15.64	10.84	13.46
1919–1920...	36.49	24.41	30.89	26.64	17.82	22.55	10.66	6.60	8.78	15.98	11.22	13.77
1920–1921...	37.09	24.92	31.32	27.08	18.19	22.86	10.74	6.60	8.78	16.34	11.59	14.08
1921–1922...	37.72	25.42	31.75	27.54	18.56	23.18	10.84	6.60	8.78	16.70	11.96	14.40
1922–1923...	38.36	25.93	32.18	28.00	18.93	23.49	10.93	6.60	8.78	17.07	12.33	14.71
1923–1924...	39.00	26.47	32.62	28.47	19.32	23.81	11.03	6.60	8.78	17.44	12.72	15.03

	5 Total Investment Per Tap			6 Investment Per Tap exclusive of property attributable to fire protection			7 Interest and Depreciation on Investment Per Tap exclusive of property attributable to fire protection at 8.1 per cent.			8 Net Profit Per Tap after allowing 6 per cent. on investment		
	Queens	Nassau	Both Counties	Queens	Nassau	Both Counties	Queens	Nassau	Both Counties	Queens	Nassau	Both Counties
1914–1915...	$230.00	$173.00	$207.00	$177.00	$133.00	$159.00	$14.34	$10.77	$12.88	$7.33	$3.51	$5.78
1915–1916...	223.00	169.00	201.00	171.00	130.00	154.00	13.85	10.53	12.47	.75	.77	.10
1916–1917...	216.00	165.00	195.00	166.00	127.00	150.00	13.45	10.29	12.15	1.50	*.17*	.71
1917–1918...	210.00	161.00	189.00	161.00	124.00	145.00	13.04	10.04	11.74	2.25	.45	1.42
1918–1919...	204.00	157.00	183.00	157.00	121.00	140.00	12.72	9.80	11.34	2.92	1.04	2.12
1919–1920...	198.00	153.00	178.00	152.00	118.00	137.00	12.31	9.56	11.10	3.67	1.66	2.67
1920–1921...	193.00	150.00	173.00	148.00	115.00	133.00	11.99	9.31	10.77	4.35	2.28	3.31
1921–1922...	188.00	147.00	168.00	144.00	113.00	129.00	11.66	9.15	10.45	5.04	2.81	3.95
1922–1923...	182.00	144.00	163.00	140.00	111.00	125.00	11.34	8.99	10.12	5.73	3.34	4.59
1923–1924...	177.00	141.00	158.00	136.00	108.00	121.00	11.01	8.75	9.80	6.43	3.97	5.23

	9 Number of Taps			10 Total Net Profit or Loss from sale of water to private consumers after allowing 6 per cent. return on investment			11 Miscellaneous Operating Revenue			12 Total Net Profit or Loss from operation after allowing 6 per cent. return on investment		
	Queens	Nassau	Both Counties	Queens	Nassau	Both Counties	Queens	Nassau	Both Counties	Queens	Nassau	Both Counties
1914–1915...	5,191	3,577	8,768	$38,050.00	$12,555.00	$50,605.00	$1,700.00	$1,882.00	$3,582.00	$39,750.00	$14,437.00	$54,187.00
1915–1916...	5,568	4,015	9,583	4,170.00	*3,092.00*	1,078.00	1,810.00	2,102.00	3,912.00	5,980.00	*990.00*	4,990.00
1916–1917...	5,970	4,504	10,474	8,955.00	*766.00*	8,189.00	1,930.00	2,347.00	4,277.00	10,885.00	1,581.00	12,466.00
1917–1918...	6,399	5,049	11,448	14,398.00	2,272.00	16,670.00	2,059.00	2,616.00	4,675.00	16,457.00	4,888.00	21,345.00
1918–1919...	6,854	5,659	12,513	20,014.00	5,885.00	25,899.00	2,184.00	2,928.00	5,112.00	22,198.00	8,813.00	31,011.00
1919–1920...	7,340	6,337	13,677	26,938.00	10,519.00	37,457.00	2,333.00	3,254.00	5,587.00	29,271.00	13,773.00	43,044.00
1920–1921...	7,857	7,092	14,949	34,178.00	16,170.00	50,348.00	2,482.00	3,624.00	6,106.00	36,660.00	19,794.00	56,454.00
1921–1922...	8,401	7,938	16,339	42,340.00	22,306.00	64,646.00	2,611.00	4,061.00	6,672.00	44,951.00	26,367.00	71,318.00
1922–1923...	8,978	8,881	17,859	51,444.00	29,663.00	81,107.00	2,770.00	4,526.00	7,296.00	54,214.00	34,289.00	88,403.00
1923–1924...	9,599	9,921	19,520	61,722.00	39,386.00	101,108.00	2,981.00	4,992.00	7,973.00	64,703.00	44,378.00	109,081.00

In Table 43 the expenses and profits for the year ending May 31, 1915, are estimated on the basis of the old rates and the old operating conditions. For 1916 and subsequent years the estimates are as nearly as possible on the basis of the operating conditions and rates that would prevail under a secure investment earning a net return of 6% with the amount of the investment and of the business done the same as in 1914. These estimates show a prospective profit from the Queens business in excess of a 6% return, beginning with $5,980 in the year ending May 31, 1916, and increasing to $64,703 in the year ending May 31, 1924. If the Company were to be limited to a 6% return with no additional reward for efficiency and economy other than what it could save from the operating expenses and increased investment allowed in these estimates, the loss resulting from the severance of the plant at any given date should be diminished by the cumulative excess profit earned subsequent to the execution of the proposed contract giving security to the investment and subsequent to the installation of the new schedule of rates based upon the terms of such contract. The profits for the year ending May 31, 1915, cannot be considered, as they have already accrued under the old rates and the old operating conditions. If we assume that the new contract will be made effective as of June 1, 1915, the net status of the Company with reference to the severance of its plant on May 31, 1916, and each year thereafter until 1924, according to these estimates, will be as shown by the following table:

TABLE 44—ESTIMATED LOSSES FROM SEVERANCE OFFSET BY PROFITS IN EXCESS OF 6% PRIOR TO SEVERANCE.

DATE OF SEVERANCE	Losses from severance	Profits from Queens operation up to time of severance in excess of 6% on investment cumulated at 6% per annum	Excess of losses from severance over surplus profits prior to severance	Excess of surplus profits prior to severance over losses from severance
May 31, 1916	$160,820.00	$5,980.00	$154,840.00	....
May 31, 1917	132,692.00	17,224.00	115,468.00	....
May 31, 1918	108,783.00	34,714.00	74,069.00	....
May 31, 1919	89,325.00	58,995.00	30,330.00	....
May 31, 1920	74,607.00	91,806.00	....	$17,199.00
May 31, 1921	65,116.00	183,974.00	....	118,858.00
May 31, 1922	60,953.00	239,963.00	....	179,010.00
May 31, 1923	59,273.00	308,575.00	....	249,302.00
May 31, 1924	57,593.00	391,792.00	....	334,199.00

If the estimates shown in this table are correct the Company will have made enough by 1920 in the shape of surplus profits over a six per cent. return to offset the loss from severance, and if permitted to operate in Queens until 1924 without further reduction of rates will be $334,000 to the good. This would indicate that the indemnity payable by the City on account of the disruption of the Company's business in case of purchase of the Queens distribution system ought to be eliminated within about five years. The City ought then to be able to acquire the property at its physical value. Whenever the City takes over the business, the general City rates then established will naturally be put into force in this district. If purchase by the City should be deferred beyond 1920, the consumers would be entitled to a further reduction in the rates charged by the Company. Of course it should not be forgotten that these results are based on estimates only, and could not be safely guaranteed at the present time either by the City or by the Company.

(e) Sources of Supply open to the City.

In case the City takes over the distribution system and water business in the Fifth Ward it will have to get the water there in some way. The Company's experience proves that it would be impracticable to develop a good supply from deep wells on the Rockaway peninsula itself. The City might buy water of the Company so long as the Company had an extra supply over and above the needs of the Nassau County consumers. This course would be feasible for a few years, but it does not seem likely that the Company would have a sufficient surplus to meet the peak load of domestic consumption and also maintain a sufficient fire reserve beyond the year 1924 at the furthest. After that the Company's supply would have to be supplemented from other sources. Ultimately the city must be prepared to bring in a supply from its own sources. This could be done by means of a submarine main or pair of mains across Jamaica Bay in the extension of Flatbush Avenue. To run a 30-24 inch main from Clarkson Avenue, Brooklyn, as far as the Rockaway Park standpipe by this route would probably cost nearly $500,000, and in case of a break in the submarine portion the main might be out of commission for several weeks for repairs. This way of bringing in the water would be very unsatisfactory unless the City had laid a duplicate submarine main or had an adequate land connection around the head of Jamaica Bay. While the direct submarine route to a point near the western end of the Rockaway peninsula, especially if supplemented by the land connection mentioned, would make an ideal distribution for a district difficult of access, the heavy original cost and the difficulty of maintenance unite to make the submarine route of doubtful expediency. It is much more likely that the 24-inch main to be purchased of the Company would be extended northward to connect with the City's 72-inch pressure pipe line, and that a duplicate main would be laid by a new route from Far Rockaway around the head of the bay by Rockaway Road to connect with the City's system south of Jamaica. A 24-inch main could be laid along this route and the extension of the existing 24-inch main effected for a total cost of from $160,00 to $175,000. Water for the Rockaway service could be taken from the Catskill supply or pumped from the near-by stations of the Brooklyn watershed.

(f). Courses open to the City in case it does not purchase:

It is well to canvass the possibilities open to the City in case it should not acquire the Company's distribution system in Queens. The Queens County Water Company is in a position where it can supply the Fifth Ward advantageously for a number of years if properly compensated for the expenditures necessary to maintain and extend its service. This would mean the continuance of high rates for domestic consumers and large annual payments by the City for fire protection. There is little hope that the consumers of this district can ever be supplied by the Company at existing City rates, unless the City pays not only the actual minimum cost of fire protection as now proposed, but a large additional sum by way of subsidy. Therefore, the first possibility that presents itself in case the City does not take over the business, is the perpetuation of high rates for both private and public uses, unless the Company is enabled to lower its domestic rates below cost by reason of subsidies from the City.

Since the City has the right to lay its own water mains in the public streets of the Fifth Ward, it may be urged that competition with the Queens County Water Company is an eligible alternative to the purchase of its distribution system. The adoption of this alternative is legally and physically possible, but exceedingly improbable. In the first place, it would cost much more than the appraised value of the Company's mains to parallel them. Mr. Edward Wegmann, former consulting engineer of the Department, appraised the cost of repaving over mains as of January 1, 1913, at about $145,000, including overhead charges. This appraisal was not apportioned between the two counties, but most of the modern pavements are in Queens. Mr. Wegmann's appraisal antedated the Court of Appeals decision in the Kings County lighting case. Our appraisal excludes pavement laid after the mains were in and allows only about $33,000. Moreover, Rockaway Beach Boulevard, the main thoroughfare of the peninsula, is already crowded with subsurface structures, and the cost of putting in a duplicate set of mains would be almost prohibitive. Also the City would have to invest several hundred thousand dollars in trunk mains to get an adequate water supply into the district. After this was done the City would have to fight for a share of the business where the entire business at City rates would hardly be adequate to carry the investment. The Company's mains are already connected with the houses, and it would cost the consumers a pretty penny to transfer their taps to the City mains. The Company would undoubtedly have to lower its rates to save a portion of the value of its property, but if it did so the consumers would be slow to change over to the City system, especially as the Company furnishes excellent water save for the small auxiliary supply that is taken from the Rockaway Park wells in the summer months. From every point of view competition by the City with the Queens County Water Company would be expensive and profitless. The location and contour of the Rockaway peninsula give monopoly in water service exceptional advantages in that district.

XXV. SUMMARY AND RECOMMENDATIONS.

The principal findings of this investigation may be summarized as follows:

Fair present value as of May 31, 1914, of company's entire plant useful for water purposes		$1,713,499.00
Portion of this investment attributable to the Queens service		$1,148,896.00
Portion of the Queens investment attributable to domestic service, 76.8 per cent		$882,343.00
Portion of the Queens investment attributable to fire protection, 23.2 per cent		$266,553.00
Fair rate of return to be allowed upon investment:		
If security is given by proposed purchase contract		6 per cent.
Under present conditions		7 per cent.
Gross earnings required on the basis of 1914 business to yield 7 per cent. net return on investment:		
Operating expenses and taxes	$62,391.00	
Depreciation	24,145.00	
Return on investment	80,423.00	
		$166,959.00
Gross earnings on the Queens business for the year ending May 31, 1914		$173,101.00
Net reduction possible on the 7 per cent. basis and old operating conditions		$6,142.00
Gross earnings required on the basis of 1914 business to yield 6 per cent. net return on investment under security given by proposed purchase contract:		
Operating expenses and taxes	$57,816.00	
Depreciation	24,145.00	
Interest on investment	68,934.00	
		$150,895.00
Net reduction possible on the 6 per cent. basis and with new operating conditions		$22,206.00
Net cost of fire protection in the Queens area on the basis of 1914 investment:		
Allowing 7 per cent. return on investment		$34,786.00
Allowing 6 per cent. return on investment, with security		31,434.00
Net cost of domestic and miscellaneous services in the Queens area on the basis of the 1914 investment and business:		
Allowing 7 per cent. return on investment		$132,173.00
Allowing 6 per cent. return on investment, with security		$119,461.00

Present rates for metered consumption:

For first 50,000 gallons consumed	40 cents per 1,000
For next 200,000 gallons consumed	30 cents per 1,000
For next 200,000 gallons consumed	25 cents per 1,000
For all consumption over 450,000 gallons	20 cents per 1,000

Rates for metered consumption required on the basis of a 7 per cent. return on investment:

For first 40,000 gallons consumed................................30 cents per 1,000
For next 410,000 gallons consumed..............................25 cents per 1,000
For all consumption over 450,000 gallons........................20 cents per 1,000

Rates for metered consumption required on the basis of a 6 per cent. return on investment with security:

For first 100,000 gallons consumed..............................25 cents per 1,000
For all consumption over 100,000 gallons........................20 cents per 1,000

Existing minimum rates are fair and reasonable under the peculiar conditions of operation on the Rockaway peninsula.

Cost per hydrant of hydrant service:

Allowing 7 per cent. return upon investment......................$8.70 per annum
Allowing 6 per cent. return upon investment...................... 8.00 per annum

Cost of general fire protection exclusive of hydrant service and without reference to the number of hydrants:

Allowing 7 per cent. return upon investment..................$29,288.00 per annum
Allowing 6 per cent. return upon investment.................. 26,378.00 per annum

Present value as of May 31, 1914, of the portion of the company's plant which, if acquired by the city, would be useful as a part of the municipal water system:

Mains, valves, corporation cocks, etc., in Queens.......	$420,751.00	
Hydrants, hydrant valves and hydrant connections in Queens..	29,925.00	
Meters in Queens..................................	49,810.00	
Land in Queens....................................	1,000.00	
24-inch trunk main in Nassau........................	98,179.00	
		$599,665.00
Amount of annual depreciation on portion of plant above described......		$13,970.00

Estimated loss to the company from the severance of its plant by the acquisition of portions above described by the city:

Severance as of May 31, 1914..................................	$233,200.00
Severance as of May 31, 1915..................................	192,916.00
Severance as of May 31, 1916..................................	160,820.00
Severance as of May 31, 1917..................................	132,692.00
Severance as of May 31, 1918..................................	108,783.00
Severance as of May 31, 1919..................................	89,325.00
Severance as of May 31, 1920..................................	74,607.00
Severance as of May 31, 1921..................................	65,116.00
Severance as of May 31, 1922..................................	60,953.00
Severance as of May 31, 1923..................................	59,273.00
Severance as of May 31, 1924..................................	57,593.00

Estimated profit to the company in excess of six per cent. from Queens business on basis of schedule of rates recommended under proposed contract:

Year ending May 31, 1916	$5,980.00
Year ending May 31, 1917	10,885.00
Year ending May 31, 1918	16,457.00
Year ending May 31, 1919	22,129.00
Year ending May 31, 1920	29,271.00
Year ending May 31, 1921	36,660.00
Year ending May 31, 1922	44,951.00
Year ending May 31, 1923	54,214.00
Year ending May 31, 1924	64,703.00

Year when accumulated surplus profits under proposed rate schedule will entirely offset loss from severance, if estimates are correct..... 1920

The results from actual operation will undoubtedly differ from the estimates given in this report for particular years. Probably, when the figures for the year ended May 31, 1915, are all in, it will be found that the business for the year has not quite come up to the estimate. But the past year has been one of great depression in the City and it could not be expected to show the normal increase in taps and earnings. Yet I am satisfied that the general estimates are fair and reasonably conservative, and that, barring some unlooked for local disaster, they mark out pretty closely the lines and rates of development to be expected during the next ten years.

In view of the foregoing I respectfully recommend that a new schedule of rates calculated to yield the Company a net revenue of seven per cent. per annum be put into effect as of June 1, 1914. In this schedule the City should be charged with the actual cost of fire protection, and the rates to private consumers should be reduced.

I further recommend that the negotiations for a contract along the lines of your letter to the Company dated February 18, 1915, be concluded as speedily as possible, and that when the Department and the Company have reached a final agreement on all the details, a draft of the proposed contract be submitted to the Board of Estimate and Apportionment, the Mayor and the Comptroller for their separate approval, in order that the rates charged by the Company may be further reduced, the long-standing friction between the City and the Company brought to an end and a definite plan for the ultimate extension of the municipal water service to the Fifth Ward of the Borough of Queens adopted.

Respectfully submitted,

(Signed) DELOS F. WILCOX,
Deputy Commissioner.

New York, June 1, 1915.

COMMISSIONER'S ORDER FIXING RATES

THE CITY OF NEW YORK

Department of Water Supply, Gas and Electricity

Office of the Commissioner

Municipal Building

New York City

June 1, 1915.

Queens County Water Company,
Far Rockaway, L. I.

Sirs:—In the case of Jacob Lauchheimer, et al, vs. the Queens County Water Company, brought to test the correctness of the rates charged by you for water furnished to consumers in the Fifth Ward of the Borough of Queens, and pending since May 1, 1914, I report to you herewith my conclusions.

I have caused to be made an appraisal of your property necessary and useful in the supply of water for domestic and public purposes in said Fifth Ward of Queens and an inquiry as to proper allowances for current depreciation, operating expenses and taxes. The result of such appraisal and inquiry is contained in the report of Deputy Commissioner Wilcox bearing even date herewith, which I have approved. It will be printed and made available for general inspection as soon as practicable.

I find that for the year ending May 31, 1914, after account has been taken of the allowances above referred to, you received a net return of less than eight per cent. on the fair present value of your property deemed by me to be useful and necessary for your water business. I have excluded from consideration certain large assets which you contend are useful and necessary, and if these were included the return on your investment would be less than seven per cent. Negotiations are pending with you for a contract which, if approved by the competent authorities, will obligate the City to take over a portion of your distribution system within the City limits within a prescribed period and which will give you security against competition and other perils to your property. These things will have the effect of reducing the rate of return which you can properly demand.

As your fiscal year commences on June 1, it is important that a decision be rendered forthwith in said case, notwithstanding the pending negotiations, in order that your new rates may become effective today. I find that your rates to private consumers have been too high. I find, also, that the compensation paid you by the City in return for fire protection and for water used for other public purposes has been wholly inadequate to reimburse you even for the actual cost thereof. I have so readjusted the rates as to correct these matters.

The new rates will result in a certain reduction in your total earnings, but, in return, it is of substantial value to you that the amount payable to you by the City for fire protection shall have been authoritatively determined; also, the reduction of rates to your private consumers will through improved relations result ultimately in benefit to you.

Under the authority conferred upon me by Section 472 of the Greater New York Charter, I hereby establish, beginning June 1, 1915, the following schedule of rates, which rates I find to be just and reasonable:

1. *For hydrant service and fire protection.*

For each fire hydrant, set and miantained at therequest of the City of New York, as a proper return on the special investment devoted exclusively to public purposes, and to cover maintenance thereof and depreciation and taxes thereon............... $8.70 per annum

As a proper return on that portion of the general investment made necessary by the need for fire protection, and to cover maintenance thereof and depreciation and taxes thereon, and for water used for the extinguishment of fires, and for water reasonably necessary for sprinkling streets and for flushing streets and sewers, where such water is taken from the fire hydrants...............$30,000.00 per annum

All charges under this heading shall be payable in four quarterly installments by the City of New York after the service has been rendered, the first installment being due September 1, 1915.

2. *Minimum rates for metered service.*

On all services supplied from taps in the mains except services connected with City buildings or used exclusively for City purposes the following minimum rates shall be payable in advance:

Through ½-inch or ⅝-inch meter..................................$10.00 per annum
Through ¾-inch meter.. 15.00 per annum
Through 1-inch meter.. 20.00 per annum
Through 1½-inch meter... 30.00 per annum
Through 2-inch meter.. 40.00 per annum
Through 3-inch meter.. 80.00 per annum
Through 4-inch meter..160.00 per annum

3. *Metered Consumption.*

Meter rates shall be as follows:

For the first 40,000 gallons consumed during the year.........30 cents per 1,000 gallons.
For the next 410,000 gallons consumed during the year........25 cents per 1,000 gallons.
For all water in excess of 450,000 gallons consumed during the year...20 cents per 1,000 gallons.

Each consumer, other than the City of New York, shall be entitled under the minimum rates to use the quantity of water which, at meter rates, would cost the minimum rate; payment for water used in excess of the minimum allowance to be made after the water is consumed. Water for all City services not taken from the hydrants shall be metered and paid for at the regular meter rates.

On all water bills except City bills remaining unpaid thirty days after they become due, a penalty of five per cent. shall be added, and on all such bills still unpaid six months after they become due, a further penalty of ten per cent. upon the original amount of the bill shall be added, but this shall not curtail the right of the Company to discontinue its service because of non-payment of charges.

In case said proposed contract, after approval by the Board of Estimate and Apportionment, the Mayor and the Comptroller, as required by Section 471 of the Charter, is finally executed, this order will be modified to conform to the terms thereof.

Please notify me not later than June 10, 1915, whether or not you accept and will comply with the terms of this order.

Respectfully,

(Signed) WILLIAM WILLIAMS,
Commissioner.

COMPANY'S LETTER ACCEPTING COMMISSIONER'S ORDER

LORD, DAY & LORD

49 Wall Street, New York

June 7, 1915.

Hon. William Williams,
Commissioner of Water Supply, Gas and Electricity,
Municipal Building, New York City.

Sir: I have to acknowledge the receipt of your communication, dated June 1, in the case of Jacob Lauchheimer et al. v. The Queens County Water Company, brought to test the correctness of the rates charged by the Company in the Fifth Ward of the Borough of Queens.

I presented this communication to the Board of Directors of the Company, and at the same time reported to them that you had exhibited to me an opinion by the Corporation Counsel to the effect that you had authority, under Section 472 of the Greater New York Charter, to fix rates for hydrant service and fire protection, as well as for private consumers, without the concurrence of any other City board or officer. Thereupon I was instructed by the Board of Directors to notify you that the Company accepts and will comply with your order dated June 1.

Respectfully,

(Signed) H. DE F. BALDWIN,
President, Queens County Water Company.

www.ingramcontent.com/pod-product-compliance
Lightning Source LLC
LaVergne TN
LVHW010605110826
845149LV00003B/784

* 9 7 8 1 4 1 8 1 8 7 4 0 8 *